# Computation
# Recreations
# in *Mathemat*

D0732430

# Computational Recreations in *Mathematica*®

Ilan Vardi

**ADDISON-WESLEY PUBLISHING COMPANY**
*The Advanced Book Program*
Redwood City, California • Menlo Park, California
Reading, Massachusetts • New York • Don Mills, Ontario
Workingham, United Kingdom • Amsterdam • Bonn
Sydney • Singapore • Tokyo • Madrid • San Juan

Publisher: *Allan M. Wylde*
Marketing Manager: *Laura Likely*
Production Manager: *Jan V. Benes*
Production Assistant: *Karl Matsumoto*
Cover Design: *Iva Frank*

The following are trademarks used in this book:
Chicken McNuggets is a trademark of McDonald's.
UNIX is a trademark of AT&T.

**Library of Congress Cataloging-in-Publication Data**

Vardi, Ilan.
    Mathematica recreations/Ilan Vardi.
        p.   cm.
    Includes bibliographical references (p.) and index.
    1. Mathematica (Computer Program) 2. Mathematics--Data Processing
    I. Title.
    QA76.95.V36  1991                510'.285'536--dc20                91-14410
    ISBN 0-201-52989-0

1 2 3 4 5 6 7 8 9 10-MA-95 94 93 92 91

# Preface

"There's a world where I can go and tell my secrets to"

*In My Room*, Brian Wilson and Gary Usher.

There is a close, though somewhat uneasy, relationship in mathematics between theory and computation. Theoretical results consist of discovering patterns and a good way of trying to discover a pattern is to look at many specific examples. On the other hand, one can often facilitate computation by using the patterns of theoretical mathematics. The aim of this book is to illustrate this relationship with some simple examples in discrete mathematics and number theory. In computer terminology, these examples show how to do computational "hacks".

Most of the mathematics in the book uses only so called "elementary" methods, in other words, there is limited use of theorems relying on a large technical body of knowledge. I have written the book in two modes, the first one being aimed at computer scientists, the other for mathematicians—professional or amateur. The mathematical prerequisites will therefore vary from chapter to chapter between a general level as expected of scientific publications such as "Scientific American" or "Science" to a more specialized level as would be expected from readers of the American Mathematical Monthly.

The *Mathematica* language is used to implement the algorithms presented in the text, and there is emphasis on the actual code used. The intention is to show that *Mathematica* is a useful tool for doing nontrivial computations. It is my hope that these chapters will be of interest even to those with no *Mathematica* interests (one can give examples of books with a mix of code and theory where the analogous statement is true).

Ultimately, my reason for writing this book is, to quote Beeler, Gosper, and Schroeppel in *HAKMEM*: "Compiled with the hope that a record of the random things people do around here can save some duplication of effort—except for fun."

## *Mathematica*, recreations and beyond

The *Mathematica* language is used to implement the algorithms presented in the text. The obvious reason for using *Mathematica* is its built-in mathematical functions and combining these with its high level of abstraction can allow for a clearer transition from algorithmic ideas to implementation.

The capabilities of *Mathematica* can be roughly divided into three categories

*(i)* Mathematical computation such as arbitrary precision arithmetic, number theory functions, and evaluation of special functions.

*(ii)* Symbolic manipulation such as symbolic integration or polynomial arithmetic.

*(iii)* Graphics.

Most *Mathematica* related material has been devoted to (ii) and (iii), so I felt it would be interesting to write a book that dealt almost exclusively with applications using (i)—the point being that *Mathematica* is in fact an adequate tool for such computation. Though *Mathematica* is not ideally suited for record breaking computation, this book does contain a number of new world records done exclusively in *Mathematica*, some of these improving results appearing recently in *Mathematics of Computation* (Section 2.2).

I believe that there are two reasons for this. First, writing and debugging programs is often easier in *Mathematica* due to its high level of abstraction and the fact that it is an interpreted language. Obviously, the fact that it has built-in mathematical functions allows one to avoid writing messy subroutines to implement them so these computations can be done more quickly (for example any use of integers bigger than $10^9$ disqualifies plain versions of C and Pascal) and an argument can be made that computation time as presented in the final results should also include the time taken to actually write the program! Another reason is that *Mathematica* becomes competitive in problems where most of the computation is done by built-in functions, for instance when there are a few operations on very large numbers, for example in Chapter 7. This means that one should try to pick problems that emphasize such computations.

Since I often emphasize specific *Mathematica* implementations, the reader is assumed to be familiar with the *Mathematica* language, as described in the *Mathematica* book of Stephen Wolfram, and especially with *Mathematica* programming. On the other hand, a number of chapters and sections are in fact independent of *Mathematica*, namely, Sections 2.3, 3.4, 4.2, 6.2, 7.1, 7.2, 8.1, and Chapters 9 and 10.

The notation of *Mathematica* approximates mathematical notation, but is somewhat different, so I will sometimes use slightly different notations for the mathematical analysis of a function and its implementation. For example, the mathematical function $f(n)$ will be written as f[n], while the *Mathematica* function PrimePi[x] will be denoted by the usual $\pi(x)$ in the mathematical discussion. Note that the *Mathematica* notation {a,b} refers to an *ordered* pair $(a, b)$, as opposed to the unordered pair $\{a, b\}$.

The programs stress elegance, *Mathematica*-style, in other words, minimizing the number of temporary variables, commands, or other structures that are not intrinsic to the algorithm. The programs are not always optimally fast, though there is an effort to attain the correct *order* of efficiency. Since *Mathematica* is an interpreted language, there is a lot of overhead in doing fairly routine operations, so a more complicated program that is theoretically faster (e.g., has fewer multiplications at the cost of more additions) will often not run faster. As a general principle I do not try to complicate a *Mathematica* program unless I believe that it will result in at least a factor of two speedup.

Because of the structure of *Mathematica* using *functional programming* will in general reduce the amount of interpretation overhead and so is usually preferable to the procedural programming of Pascal or C,

Figure 0.1: Functional programming

or to recursive programming as in Lisp (see [135, Section 4.1]). An important exception is memory intensive computation since iteration or recursion are much more memory efficient than the parallel constructs of functional programs. In Chapter 7, I switch from functional to recursive programs as the computational load increases.

Functional programming takes some getting used to (see Exercise I.1–2, Figure 0.1). I have observed that typically a person's *Mathematica* programming style starts with procedural programming, then moves to recursive programming, and finally to functional programming. Obviously, the choice of style is ultimately a question of personal preference.

Finally, due to interpretation and other overhead, *Mathematica* usually be slower at doing equivalent programs than compiled languages such as C and Lisp (certain automotive analogies come to mind but are left to the reader). Moreover, since *Mathematica* is a general purpose symbolic computation language it can hardly compete with other languages at doing very simple operations. For example, the simple operation

$$2 + 2 = 4$$

requires *Mathematica* to decide if 2 is a multiple precision number (*bignum*). Once it does this it has to allocate memory for these numbers and keep reference counts. This means a great deal lost over the same operation in C, though the time requirement is comparable to Lisp (actually, this operation could take much longer in some dialects of Lisp due to an impromptu garbage collection). In any case, it is clear that using lower level languages can be worth the extra coding effort, and that this is often indispensable when trying to beat a world record computation. Chapter 5 (How not to use *Mathematica*) shows how this can be done and I have included the C and Lisp programs used for these cases.

## Mathematics versus *Mathematica*

In general the chapters will alternate between emphasis on *Mathematica* and emphasis on mathematical theory, though there will obviously be some overlap. The chapters dealing mostly with *Mathematica* are 1, 3, and 5, while chapters 9, and 10 are essentially independent of *Mathematica*. Chapters 2, 4, 6, 8, 9, and 10 require some mathematical sophistication.

The main references to the mathematical topics in the book are *Concrete Mathematics* by Graham, Knuth, and Patashnik [49], *An Introduction to the Theory of Numbers* by Hardy and Wright [57], *Seminumerical Algorithms* by D.E. Knuth [66], and *Solved and Unsolved Problems in Number Theory* by Shanks [114]. A good reference for many of the algorithms and their implementations is *Combinatorial Algorithms* by Nijenhuis and Wilf [91]. Obviously, the programming reference is the *Mathematica* book by S. Wolfram [135].

## About the Exercises

As well as challenging the reader, the exercises are meant to complement the material in the text. I have often included as exercises results that can be found in references.

The exercises will either be of a mathematical nature in which case they will be denoted by an **M**, or will ask for a program and be denoted

by a **P**. The notation **HM** will mean that the exercise requires specialized mathematical knowledge not covered in the text. The exercises
range in difficulty and exercises whose answer I do not know will be
denoted by a *. This does not necessarily imply that these are open
problems! Finally, let me note that I have not provided answers to all
the exercises.

Some of the topics in the book are the classical homework assign-
ments of a first year programming class, so the exercises could be used
as programming exercises if such a class were taught in *Mathematica*.

# About the illustrations

## by Scott Kim

Since this book uses *Mathematica*, I decided to produce the illustra-
tions using *Mathematica* itself. The three-dimensional elements were
produced in *Mathematica*, then combined with two- dimensional elements in Adobe Illustrator on an Apple Macintosh computer.

Each chapter opening illustrates a specific mathematical idea. To
understand the illustration, you may have to read the chapter. Here
are some of the ideas I had in mind:

**Chapter 1.** *Mathematica* combines the formal power of mathematics
with the algorithmic ability of computer programming.

**Chapter 2.** This is a three-dimensional fantasy based on a diagram
in the chapter.

**Chapter 3.** Each odometer shows a date in one of the calendars. The
roads show the genealogy of the different calendars.

**Chapter 4.** We don't know if there is a next number in some of these
sequence.

**Chapter 5.** This picture has many interpretations. The original idea
was to show a problem being split into many subproblems and
translated into C, in order to make it run faster and get over a
computational hill.

**Chapter 6.** I produced the queen by tracing the outline of a queen onto graph paper. I typed in the coordinates, then wrote a *Mathematica* function to convert a series of points into a surface of revolution. Most of the three-dimensional graphics I did in *Mathematica* used surfaces of revolution.

**Chapter 7.** This is one way of visualizing the problem. All positive integers appear somewhere in this matrix. The odd numbers appear along the bottom edge. Moving upward multiplies the number by two. The arrows show the operation of multiplying an odd number by 3, adding 1, then dividing by 2.

**Chapter 8.** This illustration compares the Riemann zeta function with its absolute value as in one of the chapter diagrams.

**Chapter 9.** The Running Time of TAK. The stairs are based on a diagram in the chapter. The doors show how the lattice path may wrap around from the $y$-axis back to the line $x = y$.

**Chapter 10.** The Condom Problem. This is a three-dimensional rendition of one of the diagrams.

### Acknowledgements

Blue Sky Research provided PostScript versions of the Computer Modern typefaces. Jan Benes of Addison Wesley was the art director. Art Ogawa helped with *Mathematica*, Illustrator and Computer Modern. Ilan Vardi invented many of the ideas for the chapter openings.

# Different versions of *Mathematica*

The programs in the book have been written for Version 2.0 of *Mathematica*, but most will also run in Version 1.2. The only global difference is the use of `Fold` and `FoldList` which can be implemented in Version 1.2 as

```
Fold[function_, x_, list_]:=
Last[Accumulate[function, Prepend[list, x]]]
```

```
FoldList[function_, x_, list_]:=
Accumulate[function, Prepend[list, x]]
```

All other uses of V2.0 functions will include a note at the end of the chapter with V1.2 source code whenever possible. These functions are `LogGamma,N[Pi, n]`, `NSum`, `PollardRho`, `PrimePi`, `RiemannSiegelTheta`, `RiemannSiegelZ`, and `SumOfTwoSquares`. Note that `PollardRho` and `SumOfTwoSquares` are implemented as part of `FactorInteger` in V2.0.

A list of all the *Mathematica* functions written in the text is given in Appendix B. These will be available on a separate diskette.

# Acknowledgments

First, I would like to thank the people who have made major contributions to the book: P. Flajolet, J. Keiper, S. Kim, D.E. Knuth, and I. Rivin.

I would also like to thank T. Alper, A.O.L. Atkin, D. Bump, H. Cejtin, V. Chvátal, P.J. Cohen, J.H. Conway, H. Cunningham, W. Duke, J. Friedman, R.W. Gosper, D. Hickerson, J. Justeson, S. Levy, F. Morain, A. Odlyzko, A. Ogawa, Y. Peres, Z. Rudnick, P. Sarnak, R. Schroeppel, J. Shallit, D.B. Shapiro, H. Wilf, A. Wolf, and S. Wolfram.

I thank readers of the newsgroups `rec.puzzles` and `sci.math` (some of the exercises and their answers are based on messages posted there and I have tried to attribute everything correctly).

Finally I would to thank the people at Addison-Wesley: J. Benes, L. Likely, K. Matsumoto, and A. Wylde.

Ilan Vardi

Palo Alto, 9 Brumaire, an CXCIX

# Exercises

**Exercise 0.1.** [P] Rewrite the package `ContinuedFraction.m` in functional form. This package consists of

```
ContinuedFraction[x_Real, n_Integer?Positive] :=
   Block[{xi, xp = x, r={}},
         Do[   xi = Floor[xp] ;
               AppendTo[r, xi] ;
               xp = 1 / (xp - xi) ,
            {n} ] ;
         r
      ]

FromContinuedFraction[a_List] :=
Block[{x, ar = Reverse[a]},
          x = ar[[1]] ;
          Do [ x = 1/x + ar[[1]] . {i, 2, Length[ar]}];
          x
      ]
```

**Exercise 0.2.** [P, M] What functions are given by the following *Mathematica* programs. Explain the algorithms used and how the program implements them.

```
MysteryOne[a_] :=
   Select[Take[#, Length[Union[#]]]& /@
          Map[NestList[a[[#]]&, #, Length[a]] &, a],
          #[[1]] == Min[#]&]

MysteryTwo[a_]:=
Last /@ Sort[Transpose[Flatten /@ {RotateRight /@ a, a}]]
```

**Exercise 0.3** [P, M] Write a function `SquareFreeQ` that returns `True` if $n$ is a squarefree integer, `False` otherwise. For example,

```
   SquareFreeQ[30] => True      SquareFreeQ[12] => False
```

**Exercise 0.4 [P]** Compare the running times of the four programs

```
Do[ , {10^3}]

For[i=1, i <= 10^3, i++, ]

For[i=1, i <= 1000, i++, ]

i = 1; While[i <= 1000, i++]
```

**Exercise 0.5** The total budget of the U.S. government is larger than $2^{32}$ dollars, so balancing the budget requires bignum arithmetic. Investigate how government agencies deal with multiple precision arithmetic.

# Contents

$$(1+a)(1+b)(1+c)$$

$$x^5 = x(x)$$

$$x(x^2)2$$

$$a^2c2$$

$$aaccbba$$

$$(1+a)(1+b)(1+c)(1+I)$$

$$(1+a)(1+b)(1+c)$$

$$1 = (p+1)(1+c)(1+b)(1+a)(1+I)$$

$$1 + a + b + c + d + ab + ac +$$

```
List @@ times @@
```

```
subsetsAux[Rest[x]]
```

```
({#, 1}& /@ x)
```

```
subsetsAux[Rest[x]], 1]
```

```
({#, 1}& /@ x)
```

```
subsetsAux[Rest[x]], 1]
```

```
@@ times
```

```
RunEncode[x
```

# Elegant Programming
# in *Mathematica*

# Chapter 1

# Elegant Programs in *Mathematica*

This chapter presents elegant *Mathematica* constructs by using them to solve some example problems. In order to get a better feeling for the solutions and to compare your own programming style to the one presented here, I have set these examples out as programming exercises.

**Question 1.** Construct the best *Mathematica* functions for run-length encoding and decoding. The function `RunEncode` should take a list of integers and return a list of pairs, each representing a contiguous "run" of identical integers in the original list. Each pair contains an integer and the length of a (maximal) run of that integer. The pairs must be in the same order as the runs. For

```
RunEncode[{2, 2, 1, 1, 1, 3, 1, 1, 2}]
```

should return

```
{{2, 2}, {1, 3}, {3, 1}, {1, 2}, {2, 1}}
```

**Question 2.** Write a *Mathematica* function `Subsets` that generates a list of all the subsets of a set. For example

```
In[1]:= Subsets[{a, b, c}]

Out[1]= {{},{a},{b},{c},{a,b},{a,c},{b,c},{a,b,c}}
```

(Note that a set, by definition, has no repeated elements.)

**Question 3.** Write a *Mathematica* function `FastPower` that evaluates powers $x^n$ efficiently, i.e., implement `Power[x, n]` directly in *Mathematica*.

**Question 4.** Write a *Mathematica* function that evaluates $x^k \pmod{n}$ efficiently for very large $x, k, n$, i.e., implement `PowerMod[x, k, n]` directly in *Mathematica*.

**Question 5.** Write a *Mathematica* function that returns the $n$'th element in the Conway sequence

$$3, 13, 1113, 3113, 132113, 1113122113, \ldots$$

## 1.1  An algebraic method in *Mathematica* programming

Some of the most frequently asked questions about *Mathematica* are whether it can do group theory, ring theory, etc. Well, it turns out that not only can *Mathematica* do this but that using these concepts can allow one to write more elegant programs. In particular an algebraic method can be used to solve Questions 1 and 2.

### 1.1.1  Answer to Question 1

This question was used for the programming competition of the 1990 *Mathematica* Conference. I will analyze what I consider the most elegant solution.

The key to this solution is to use the concept of a *free semigroup*. A semigroup consists of a set and an associative, possibly noncommutative product. So a semigroup is like a group but without an identity element and without inverses. A free semigroup is one with no relations, in other words no product ever simplifies to something simpler (in particular the multiplication is noncommutative). If you don't like group theory, you can think of a semigroup as a set of all *words*

$$a_1 a_2 a_3 \ldots a_n$$

with multiplication of two words given by concatenation, and a free semigroup has the extra property that there is never any reduction of words to simpler words (this is also true of English words).

The relation between run-length encoding and semigroups seems somewhat farfetched. However, consider the list $\{a, a, c, c, b, b, a\}$. If $a, b, c$ are elements of a semigroup then the product $aaccbba$ can be written as

$$a\,a\,c\,c\,b\,b\,a = a^2\,c^2\,b^2\,a\,.$$

This shows that RunEncode is just a model of a semigroup where the group operation $a^m \cdot a^n = a^{m+n}$ is modeled by $\{a, m\} \cdot \{a, n\} = \{a, m + n\}$, and singletons $a = a^1$ are always written as $\{a, 1\}$. To get a genuine semigroup multiplication one needs associativity. It turns out that the *Mathematica* attribute Flat has exactly the property of making a function associative. A program can therefore be given by

```
Attributes[times] = {Flat}
```

```
times[{a_, m_}, {a_, n_}]:= times[{a, m + n}]
```

```
RunEncode[x_List]:= List @@ times @@ ({#, 1}& /@ x)
```

This program has a number of nontrivial features. For example, one needs to specify times in the second line otherwise the program will return the wrong answer on input such as $\{a, a\}$. Second, the function NonCommutativeMultiply was not used since this function has no properties except that it is Flat, but is protected anyway! Using your own defined function times avoids conflicts with other possible uses of NonCommutativeMultiply.

To see how the program works one tries it step by step on an example, e.g., x = $\{$a, a, c, c, b, b, a$\}$

```
In[1]:= {#, 1}& /@ x
```

```
Out[1]= {{a, 1}, {a, 1}, {c, 1}, {c, 1}, {b, 1},
         {b, 1}, {a, 1}}
```

```
In[2]:= times @@ %
```

```
Out[2]= times[{a, 2}, {c, 2}, {b, 2}, {a, 1}]
```

```
In[3]:= List @@ %
```

```
Out[3]= {{a, 2}, {c, 2}, {b, 2}, {a, 1}}
```

This exact program was written by J. Wald and R. McGregor of Schlumberger Laboratory for Computer Science in Austin, Texas, but it only won second place in the competition. I suspect that one of the reasons it didn't win first place was that the algebraic meaning of the program was not realized at the time.

## 1.1.2   Answer to Question 2.

There are a number of obvious ways to write the Subsets program, for example, using recursion and the fact that Subsets of a set is just the union of its subsets that don't contain the first element with those that do:

```
SubsetsRecursive[{}]:= {{}}
```

```
SubsetsRecursive[x_]:=
  Block[{s = SubsetsRecursive[Rest[x]]},
        Join[s, Append[#, First[x]]& /@ s]]
```

Another possible method is to use the binary expansion of the numbers $1, \ldots, 2^n$, where $n$ is the number of elements in the set to generate all the subsets. However, this method is somewhat awkward to implement since one needs to pad the digit list of the integers involved and it seems that *Mathematica*'s list operations are not ideally suited to lists of 1's and 0's. I therefore leave this as an exercise. (A third method is given in Exercise 6.2)

It turns out that a very short program can be written using the ideas of the previous section, i.e., mapping the problem to an algebraic one.

Consider the list $\{a, b, c\}$. If the $a, b, c$ were in some arbitrary commutative ring then in the expansion

$$(1 + a)(1 + b)(1 + c) = 1 + a + b + c + ab + ac + bc + abc$$

each term on the right hand side corresponds to a subset of $\{a, b, c\}$. Now the expansion consists of distributing multiplication over addition and it turns out that the *Mathematica* function `Distribute` allows you to distribute any function over any other function and then replace these two with any other two in the result. The program

```
Subsets[x_List]:=
Distribute[{{}, {#}}& /@ x, List, List, List, Union]
```

will therefore generate all the subsets of a set. For example if x = $\{$a, b, c$\}$:

```
In[1]:= {{}, {#}}& /@ x
```

```
Out[1]= {{{}, {a}}, {{}, {b}}, {{}, {c}}}
```

```
In[2]:= Distribute[%, List, List, List, Union]
```

```
Out[2]=
  {{}, {c}, {b}, {b, c}, {a}, {a, c}, {a, b}, {a, b, c}}
```

Another way to think of this program is that it realizes the notion that the set of subsets of a set $S$ is the power set

$$\{0, 1\}^S ,$$

where the notation $x^y$, when $x$ and $y$ are sets, is used to denote the set of all functions $f : y \rightarrow x$.

**Exercise 1.1.**

**(a)** **[P]** **[M]** The Möbius inversion formula states that if two functions $f$ and $g$ are related by

$$f(n) = \sum_{d|n} g(n)$$

(where "$d|n$" expresses the condition that $d$ divides $n$) then one can express $g$ in terms of $f$ by

(1.1)
$$\sum_{d\,|\,n} \mu(d) f\left(\frac{n}{d}\right) ,$$

where $\mu(n)$ is the Möbius function given by

$$\mu(n) = \begin{cases} (-1)^r & \text{if } n = p_1 p_2 \cdots p_r \\ 0 & \text{if } n \text{ is not squarefree.} \end{cases}$$

(see [57, p. 236]). Write a program to implement the Möbius inversion formula. In other words `Moebius[f, n]` should return the sum in (1.1). For example

```
In[1]:= Moebius[f, 30]
```

```
Out[1]= -f[1] + f[2] + f[3] + f[5] -
          f[6] - f[10] - f[15] + f[30]
```

**(b) [P] [M]** Generalize this to more general operators than addition. For example use this to implement the *Mathematica* function `CyclotomicPolynomial` which gives the $n$th cyclotomic polynomial

$$\Phi_n(x) = \prod_{d|n} (1 - x^{n/d})^{\mu(d)} .$$

## 1.2   Efficient *Mathematica* programs

In the previous section the goal was to find elegant solutions without examining the running time. In this section I will show that efficient programs can also be written elegantly.

### 1.2.1   Answer to Question 3.

It is well known [66, Section 4.6.3] that there is a faster way to evaluate the power $x^n$ than just multiplying out

$$\overbrace{x \cdots x}^{n \text{ times}} .$$

The idea is to use repeated squarings. For example, if $n = 5$, then

$$x^5 = x (x^2)^2$$

takes three multiplications, instead of four. In general one uses the binary expansion of $n$ and this can be implemented in the short program

```
MyPower[x_, n_]:= Fold[#1^2 #2&, 1, x^Digits[n, 2]]
```

For example, evaluating $x^{13}$

```
In[1]:= Digits[13, 2]

Out[1]= {1, 1, 0, 1}

In[2]:= x^%

Out[2]={x, x, 1, x}

In[3]:= FoldList[#1^2 #2&, 1, %]

              3   6   13
Out[3]= {1, x, x , x , x   }

In[4]:= Last[%]

          13
Out[4]= x
```

where I have used `Last[FoldList[]]` instead of `Fold` to show the computation more clearly. This took five multiplications instead of twelve. Note that the program uses *Horner's rule* for fast polynomial evaluation to convert the binary expansion of a number back into the number:

$$a_d 2^d + a_{d-1} 2^{d-1} + \cdots + a_0 = ((a_d 2 + a_{d-1}) 2 + \cdots) 2 + a_0$$

which saves on multiplications, and allows one to write the argument of `Fold` in the more compact form `x^Digits[n, 2]`.

This program is quite efficient and in V1.2 it actually beat the built-in function for 4000-digit numbers since that version of *Mathematica* did not use Horner's rule.

## 1.2.2   Answer to Question 4.

The built-in `PowerMod` uses the repeated squaring method of Question 3, but also takes `Mod[ , n]` at each step in order to reduce the size of the partial results (this allows `PowerMod` to evaluate very large arguments quickly). A straightforward implementation is therefore

```
MyPowerMod[x_, k_, n_]:=
Fold[Mod[Mod[#1^2, n] #2, n]&, 1, x^Digits[k, 2]]
```

It turns out that for very large numbers there are theoretically faster methods (this is true of normal exponentiation as well). The simplest idea is to replace base two by base a power of two. Experience shows that using base $64 = 2^6$ seems optimal for the range range of 150–3000 digits [18].

First you precompute a table of $x^i$, for $i = 0, 1, 2, \ldots, 63$, so you immediately know the value of a power of $x$ for any digit in base 64. The table can be computed by

```
NestList[Mod[# x, n]&, 1, 63].
```

Instead of `x^Digits[k, 2]` as before, you use the table evaluated at all the digits of $k$, base 64, by writing

```
NestList[Mod[# x, n]&, 1, 63] [[Digits[k, 64] + 1]].
```

The rest of the program is similar to Question 3. The program is therefore

```
MyPowerMod[x_Integer, k_Integer, n_Integer]:=
Fold[Mod[PowerMod[#1, 64, n] #2, n]&, 1,
     NestList[Mod[# x, n]&, 1, 63] [[Digits[k, 64] + 1]]]
```

This program seems to run about 15% to 50% faster for number with more than 150 digits.

Another possible way that `PowerMod` can be speeded up is if the last argument has a known factorization. One can use Euler's theorem

$$(1.2) \qquad\qquad a^{\phi(n)} \equiv 1 \ (\mathrm{mod}\, n),$$

where $\phi(n)$, implemented by `EulerPhi` in *Mathematica*, is the number of integers less than $n$ and relatively prime to $n$, and $a$ and $n$ are relatively prime, to write the function

```
PowerModFactored[x_, k_, n_]:=
PowerMod[x, Mod[k, EulerPhi[n]], n] /; GCD[k, n] == 1
```

This will beat out `PowerMod` if $k$ is large compared to $n$,n but of course it won't run at all if $n$ is hard to factor. Another catch is that `PowerMod` with $k$ much larger than $n$ is mostly used when trying to factor $n$ in the first place, so it looks like this method is not useful in practice (though an application is given in Exercise 1.3 below).

**Exercise 1.2.** **[P]** Write a program to generate the minimal polynomial $f_n(x)$ of the square roots of the first $n$ primes $\sqrt{2}, \sqrt{3}, \sqrt{5}, \ldots, \sqrt{p_n}$. Note that a formula is given by

$$f_n(x) = \prod(x \pm \sqrt{2} \pm \sqrt{3} \pm \sqrt{5} \pm \cdots \pm \sqrt{p_n})$$

where the product is over all $2^n$ combinations of $\pm$'s. (This is the content of the package `SwinnertonDyer.m` of V2.0.)

**Exercise 1.3**

(a) **[P]** **[M]** Write a program to compute the "tower of power"

$$\left. a^{a^{\cdot^{\cdot^{a}}}} \right\}^a_k \quad \bmod n$$

For example, denoting this by `SuperPowerMod[a, k, n]` compute

```
SuperPowerMod[2354246773200, 235235356676221244402348,
              3235462343]
```

(b) **[P]** **[M]** Let $a \uparrow n = a^n$, and let $a \uparrow\uparrow n$ be the function of part (a), so that in general

$$a \uparrow^k n = a \uparrow^{k-1} \{a \uparrow^k (n-1)\}$$

(this notation was invented by D.E. Knuth [65]). Write programs to compute $a \uparrow^k n \pmod{m}$ and $n \uparrow^n n \pmod{m}$ (the last function is the *Ackerman function* $\bmod m$).

**(c)\* [HM]** Can you speed up the evaluation of $a \uparrow\uparrow n$?

**(d)** Eisenstein [27] showed that the limit $x^{x^{x^{\cdot^{\cdot^{\cdot}}}}}$ for $e^{-1/e} < x \leq 1$ converges to the inverse of the function $x^{1/x}$, and has the series expansion

$$1 + \log x + 3\,\frac{(\log x)^2}{2!} + 4^2\,\frac{(\log x)^3}{3!} + 5^3\,\frac{(\log x)^4}{4!} + \cdots$$

**(i)\* [HM]** (A. Wolf) Is there an analogue of this for matrices?

**(ii)\* [HM]** (D.B. Shapiro and S.D. Shapiro) Is there an analogue of Eisenstein's theorem for $p$-adic numbers?

**(e) [HM]** The infinite series

$$\sum \frac{1}{n}, \quad \sum \frac{1}{n \log n}, \quad \sum \frac{1}{n \log n \, \log \log n}, \ldots$$

all diverge more and more slowly (for example [64, pages 122–124])

**(i)** Show that if

$$f(n) = n \log n \, \log \log n \cdots \log_r(n)$$

where $\log_r(n)$ is the natural logarithm iterated $r$ times until $\log_r(n) \leq e$, then

$$\sum \frac{1}{f(n)}$$

diverges slower than any of the above series.

**(ii)\*** Generalize (i) and see how slow you can go.

## 1.3   Conclusion: Answer to Question 5

The idea here is to combine the results of Questions 1 and 3 (if you still don't understand the pattern you should work through this code). The sequence appears in a paper of Conway [20].

```
ConwaySequence[n_]:=
Fold[10 #1 + #2 &, 0,
     Nest[Flatten[Reverse /@ RunEncode[#]]&,
          {3}, n-1]]
```

Note that for the above program to work, no digit can ever occur more than nine times in a row. Actually, in [20] Conway proves that no digit occurs more than three times consecutively after the first iteration so this shows the correctness of the program.

An amazing result shown in Conway's paper is that the number of digits of the $n$'th term of this sequence is asymptotic to $C\lambda^n$, where $C$ is a constant and

$$\lambda = 1.30357726903429639125709911215255189073070250465940\ldots$$

is the largest root of the polynomial

$$
\begin{aligned}
f(x) \; &= x^{71} - x^{69} - 2\,x^{68} - x^{67} + 2\,x^{66} + 2\,x^{65} + x^{64} - x^{63} - x^{62} - x^{61} - x^{60} \\
&\quad - x^{59} + 2\,x^{58} + 5\,x^{57} + 3\,x^{56} - 2\,x^{55} - 10\,x^{54} - 3\,x^{53} - 2\,x^{52} + 6\,x^{51} + 6\,x^{50} \\
&\quad + x^{49} + 9\,x^{48} - 3\,x^{47} - 7\,x^{46} - 8\,x^{45} - 8\,x^{44} + 10\,x^{43} + 6\,x^{42} + 8\,x^{41} - 5\,x^{40} \\
&\quad - 12\,x^{39} + 7\,x^{38} - 7\,x^{37} + 7\,x^{36} + x^{35} - 3\,x^{34} + 10\,x^{33} + x^{32} - 6\,x^{31} - 2\,x^{30} \\
&\quad - 10\,x^{29} - 3\,x^{28} + 2\,x^{27} + 9\,x^{26} - 3\,x^{25} + 14\,x^{24} - 8\,x^{23} - 7\,x^{21} + 9\,x^{20} \\
&\quad + 3\,x^{19} - 4\,x^{18} - 10\,x^{17} - 7\,x^{16} + 12\,x^{15} + 7\,x^{14} + 2\,x^{13} - 12\,x^{12} - 4\,x^{11} - 2\,x^{10} \\
&\quad + 5\,x^{9} + x^{7} - 7x^{6} + 7x^{5} - 4x^{4} + 12x^{3} - 6x^{2} + 3x - 6\,.
\end{aligned}
$$

The value for $\lambda$ can be computed in a couple of seconds by

```
lambda:=
FindRoot[f, {x, 2}, AccuracyGoal -> 50,
                WorkingPrecision->500,
                MaxIterations-> 500]
```

**Exercise 1.4 [P]** It turns out that the polynomial given in Conway's article was incorrectly transcribed (one of the signs is wrong). The incorrect polynomial's largest root is

$$\lambda_2 = 1.30373208460257638390068004051191852322256526861420\ldots$$

Can you figure out which sign was incorrect?

**Exercise 1.5**

(i) [M] (W. Kolakoski) Show that there exists a unique infinite sequence $r_n$ of 1's and 2's satisfying $r_1 = 1$ and the sequence of run lengths of the sequence is equal to the sequence itself. In other words, if the sequence is represented by r then

```
First /@ RunEncode[r]
```

is also equal to r. Is this sequence periodic?

(ii)* What is the percentage of 2's in the sequence?

## 1.4 Notes

The error mentioned in Exercise 1.4 was introduced after A.O.L. Atkin had correctly computed the polynomial and its root [2].

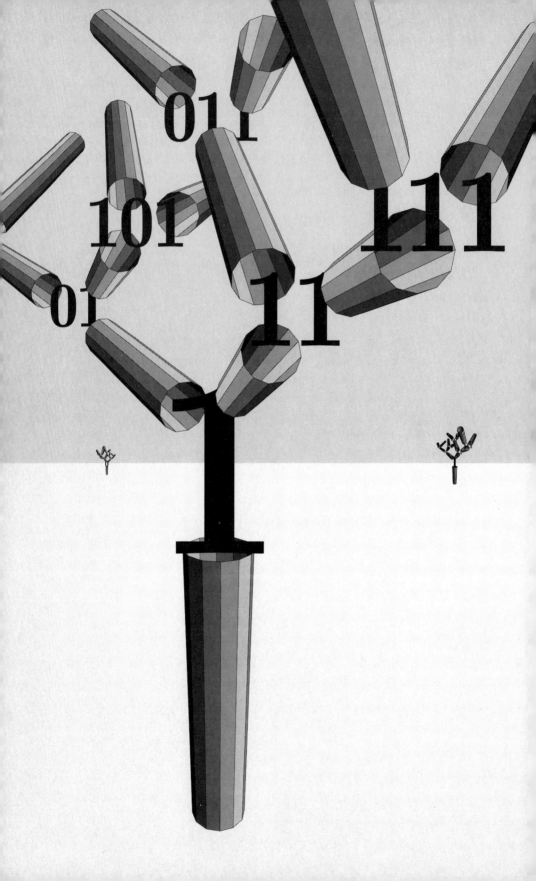

# 2

# Digital Computing

# Chapter 2

# Digital Computing

One of the most popular topics in recreational mathematics is the study of the properties of the digits of an integer. As a matter of fact many people are fascinated by digits, for example the infamous history of $2 \times 3 \times 3 \times 37$, and how many accidents were caused when the driver's attention was focused on the odometer turning to 111,111.1 miles?

A number of papers have been written on numbers with certain digital properties. For example, Kennedy and Cooper [21] have defined *Niven numbers* to be numbers divisible by the sum of their digits. Slightly more arcane are *Smith numbers* [40] which are composite numbers satisfying the property that the sum of their digits is equal to the sum of the sum of the digits of each their prime factors (taken with multiplicity). Strangely enough, $2 \times 3 \times 3 \times 37$ is a Smith number (which must prove something).

The reason that such properties are not studied in "serious" mathematics is because they do not reflect *intrinsic* properties of the integers. For example, $11111111111111111_2$ (131,071 in base two) is a prime and remains prime no matter what base it's written in.

As an example of an intrinsic set of integers consider *McNugget numbers* which are numbers of Chicken McNuggets which you can order at a McDonald's without throwing any away (recall that you must order McNuggets in sizes of 6, 9, or 20). Properties of these numbers lead to interesting questions in Diophantine analysis, some of which are quite deep.

19

**Exercise 2.1** [**M**] (David W. Wilson [134]) Are there infinitely many non-McNugget numbers? If not, what is the largest non-McNugget number?

**Exercise 2.2\*** [**HM**] (B. Ambati and J. Ambati) Are there infinitely many perfect squares like

$$1, 4, 9, 49, 144, \ldots$$

which only have the digits 1,4, and 9 in their decimal expansion?

## 2.1  The digits of $2^n$ in base three

Paul Erdös [28, p. 80] conjectured that for $n > 8$, $2^n$ is not a sum of distinct powers of 3. In terms of digits, this states that powers of 2 for $n > 8$ must always contain a "2" in their base 3 expansion. Unfortunately, proving such statements seems out of reach of current mathematical technique (see next section) but one can try to search for counterexamples.

  The first shortcut in doing such a search is to consider only the lower order base three digits of $2^n$, in other words computing $2^n \bmod 3^k$, for some $k$, in other words

```
Digits[PowerMod[2, n, 3^k], 3]
```

so that checking a specific power of two for the conjecture is done by looking at greater and greater values of $k$ until a "2" is found. Note that $2^n$ has roughly $n \log 2 / \log 3$ digits base three. The following program implements this

```
check[n_]:=
Block[{k = 20,   t = True,
       log = 4 + Ceiling[n N[Log[3, 2]]]},
  While[True,
        If[MemberQ[
            Digits[
              PowerMod[2, n, 3^k], 3], 2],
          t = False; Break[]];
```

```
        If[i > log, Break[]];
           k += 20];
   t]
```

To do a complete search of the powers $2^n$, $8 < n \le 3^k$, one computes $2^n \bmod 3^k$ by repeatedly multiplying by two and taking mod $3^k$. After removing those powers which have a "2" in their first $k$ digits, one uses check to eliminate the rest.

For example

```
checkrange[m_, k_]:=
Block[{list = {}, i, a, power = 3^k},
      For[i = 1; a = 2^8, i <= m, i++,
          a = Mod[2 a, power];
          If[!MemberQ[Union[Digits[a, 3]], 2],
             AppendTo[list, a]]];
      Select[list, check[#]&]]
```

This program examines every number $n$, $n = 9, \ldots, 3^k$ but one can do much better by using *sieve methods* which means eliminating certain arithmetic progressions.

## 2.1.1   Some facts about powers of 2 mod $3^k$

Euler's theorem says that

$$2^{\phi(3^k)} \equiv 1 \pmod{3^k}.$$

Now $\phi(3^k) = 2 \cdot 3^{k-1}$ since a number smaller than $3^k$ is relatively prime to $3^k$ if and only if its smallest digit is either one or two while the other $k - 1$ digits can be either $0, 1$, or $2$. This gives $2 \cdot 3^{k-1}$ choices. This gives that, for any integer $q$,

$$2^n \equiv 2^{n+2q3^{k-1}} \pmod{3^k},$$

which means that $2^n$ and $2^{n+2q3^{k-1}}$ have the same initial $k$ digits in base 3. Therefore, if $n$ is such that $2^n$ has a two in its first $k$ digits, one also has the same for $n + 2q3^{k-1}$ for all $r$, i.e., one can eliminate all numbers congruent to $n \bmod 2 \cdot 3^{k-1}$. Furthermore, any number $m$, $1 \leq m < 3^k$, relatively prime to $3^k$ is of the form $2^n \bmod 3^k$ for some $n$. This follows from a result of "elementary" number theory [107, page 82]

*If $p$ is a prime and $k \geq 2$, then the powers of the number $g$, namely $1, g, g^2, \ldots$, give all numbers $\bmod p^k$ if and only if they give all numbers $\bmod p$ and also $g^{p-1} \not\equiv 1 \pmod{p^2}$.*

Since $1, 2$ give are the numbers less than three and relatively prime to three, and since $2^{3-1} = 4 \not\equiv 1 \pmod 9$ this establishes the claim.

One can sum up the results of this section by saying that $2^n \bmod 3^k$ is periodic with period $2 \cdot 3^{k-1}$, but has no shorter period.

## 2.1.2   The algorithm

The algorithm will check all powers $2^n$ in the range $n = 9, \ldots, 2 \cdot 3^{k-1}$ by building up a set $s$ of candidates one level at a time. At level $r$, the set $s$ consists of the $2^r$ numbers less than $2 \cdot 3^{r-1}$ for which $2^n \bmod 3^r$ has only zeroes and ones. At the next level one lets

$$s \leftarrow s \cup \{n + 2 \cdot 3^{r-1} \mid n \in s\} \cup \{n + 4 \cdot 3^{r-1} \mid n \in s\}$$

One then computes $2^n \bmod 3^{r+1}$ for each $n$ in $s$ to see if the next digit is a "2", if it is then the number is stricken from $s$. This process generates a binary tree, see Figure 2.1 (the tree on the right represents the initial digits base 3 of powers of two of the corresponding elements of the tree on the left). The total number of survivors will be $2^{r+1}$. This part of the program requires

$$3(1 + 2 + 2^2 + 2^3 + \cdots + 2^k) = 3(2^{k+1} - 1)$$

operations. One then uses `check` to see whether any of these number generates a counterexample. The program therefore takes about $2^k$ steps to check all then numbers less than $2 \cdot 3^{k-1}$ which is a substantial savings even for moderate $k$.

The tree that is generated using this algorithm gets quite large and so can use up an excessive amount of memory. This can also slow the

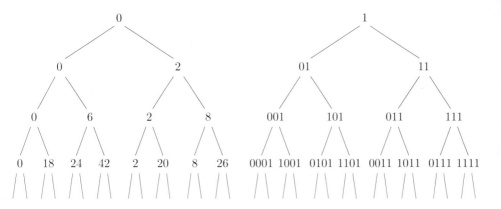

Figure 2.1: Binary tree of survivors

computation down since the program will have to start using virtual memory. In order to avoid this one uses the exact method as above to generate the tree in two stages: The first stage of generating tree of depth $n$ is to first generate the tree to depth $k$, and then *iteratively* generate the subtrees of depth $n - k$ for each leaf of the depth $k$ tree. This has the advantage of only needing to store trees of depth up to $\max\{k, n - k\}$.

The following program implements this. Note that, paradoxically, it is more efficient to reevaluate PowerMod[2, n, 3^k] from scratch at every level $k$, rather than trying to save the values somehow. This is due to the fact that the survivors of the sieve occur irregularly.

The first argument to checkrange is the total depth of the tree, while the second argument represents the depth of the initial tree as above (so the program iteratively generates trees of depth $m - k$).

```
CheckRangeTwo[m_, k_]:=
Block[{i, j, list={}, s, len = Length[powers[k]]},
     For[i = 1, i <= len, i++,
        s = {powers[k] [[i]]};
        For[j = k,  j < m, j++,
```

```
       s = Select[Join[s,
                        2 3^(j-1) + s,
                        4 3^(j-1) + s],
                   PowerMod[2, #, 3^(j+1)] < 2 3^j &]];
          list = Join[list, Select[s, check[#, m]&]]];
       list]
```

(* check[n, m] verifies that the terminal nodes of
   the tree are not counterexamples *)

```
check[n_, m_]:=
Block[{i = m + 10, t = True,
       log = 4 + Ceiling[n N[Log[2]/Log[3]]]},
       While[True,
              If[MemberQ[
                  Digits[PowerMod[2, n, 3^(4 i)],
                          3],
                        2],
                  t = False; Break[]];
              If[i > log, Break[]];
              i += 20];
       t]
```

(* powers[k] gives the initial tree *)

```
powers[1]:= {0}
```

```
powers[k_]:= powers[k] =
  Select[Join[powers[k-1],
             2 3^(k-2) + powers[k-1],
             4 3^(k-2) + powers[k-1]],
        PowerMod[2, #, 3^k] < 2 3^(k-1)&]
```

This program was run on an HP Risc workstation and checked the conjecture for $2^n$,

$$8 < n \le 2 \cdot 3^{20} = 6,973,568,802$$

in about five days of CPU time by running checkpowers[21, 14].

In the unlikely event that a very large candidate exists, i.e., with billions of digits not equal to 2, then *Mathematica* will have difficulty handling it with ordinary arithmetic. One therefore has to do a special purpose implementation of taking powers of 2 in base 3 (e.g., in C). This is not very difficult, you merely have to keep track of carries, and one can code in base three numbers fairly efficiently by using base $3^{10} = 59049$, which is very close to $2^{16} = 65536$.

## 2.2 Application to Binomial coefficients

Erdös [28, page 71] has also conjectured that for $n > 4$, the middle binomial coefficient $\binom{2n}{n}$ (see Section 4.1) is never squarefree. This result was essentially proved by A. Sárközy [108] who showed that there exists a number $n_0$ such that the conjecture is true for all $n > n_0$. In the other direction P. Goetgheluck [43] has shown that this is true for $4 < n \le 2^{42205184}$. Sárközy's method is indirect, he shows that if $s(n)$ is the square part of $\binom{2n}{n}$ then

$$\log s(n) \sim (\sqrt{2} - 2)\,\zeta(1/2)\,\sqrt{n}\,,$$

where $\zeta(s)$ is the Riemann zeta function of Chapter 8 (note that $\zeta(1/2) \approx -1.46035$ is negative). This quantity must be therefore positive for all sufficiently large $n$.

The relationship of this to the method of this Section is the result of Kummer [49, Exercise 5.36] that

*The power of a prime $p$ that divides $\binom{2n}{n}$ is the number of carries that occur when $n \Rightarrow 2n$ in base $p$.*

From this you can see that the power of 2 that divides $\binom{2n}{n}$ is the number of ones in the base 2 expansion of $n$. Therefore a necessary condition for $\binom{2n}{n}$ to be squarefree is that $n$ be a power of 2. The next thing to do is to check divisibility by 3, the next prime. One tries to show that $\binom{2n}{n}$ is not square free by showing that it is divisible by $3^2 = 9$, i.e., that two carries occur when $n \Rightarrow 2n$ is computed in base 3. The only way that two carries can occur is if the base 3 expansion of $n$ contains two 2's or if it contains a 2 preceded by a 1. So checking divisibility by 9 comes down to searching the base 3 expansion of $2^n$ for certain digit patterns. A simple modification of the algorithm of the previous section will do this (a similar tree to the one in Figure 2.1 is generated by this algorithm).

As before, the first argument represents the total depth of the tree and the second argument the depth of the initial part of the tree. To

```
CheckRangeNine[m_, k_]:=
Block[{i, j, list={}, a,
       len = Length[powers2[k]]},
       For[i = 1, i <= len, i++,
           a = {powers2[k] [[i]]};
           For[j = k,  j < m, j++,
               a = Select[Join[a,
                                2 3^(j-1) + a,
                                4 3^(j-1) + a],
                             dcheck2[#, j+1]&]];
           list = Join[list, Select[a, check2[#, m]&]]];
   list]

(* check2   verifies that the terminal nodes
   of the tree are not counterexamples    *)

check2[n_, m_]:=
Block[{i = m + 10, t = True,
   log = 4 + Ceiling[n N[Log[2]/Log[3]]]},
   While[True,
           If[!dcheck2[n, i], t = False; Break[]];
           If[i > log, Break[]];
              i += 20];
    t]

(* dcheck2 looks for a forbidden pattern of
   digits in 2^n mod 3^k *)

dcheck2[n_, k_]:=
Block[{dd = Digits[PowerMod[2, n, 3^k], 3], ct},
```

```
     ct = Count[dd, 2];
     If[ct > 1, False,
         ct == 0 ||
         First[dd] == 2 ||
         MemberQ[dd - RotateRight[dd], 2]]]


(*   powers2[k] gives the initial tree of depth k *)

powers2[1] := {1, 2}

powers2[k_] := powers2[k] =
  Select[Join[powers2[k-1],
            2 3^(k-2) + powers2[k-1],
            4 3^(k-2) + powers2[k-1]],
        dcheck2[#, k]&]
```

Running this program for six days on an Hewlett-Packard Risc work-station gave

```
In[1] := CheckRangeNine[19, 13]

Out[1]= {1, 2, 6, 8}
```

Now the computations

```
In[2] := FactorInteger[Binomial[2^7, 2^6]]

Out[2]= {{2, 1}, {3, 1}, {5, 3}, {11, 2}, {13, 1},
         {17, 1}, {23, 1}, {37, 1}, {41, 1}, {67, 1},
         {71, 1}, {73, 1}, {79, 1}, {83, 1}, {89, 1},
         {97, 1}, {101, 1}, {103, 1}, {107, 1}, {109, 1},
         {113, 1}, {127, 1}}

In[3] := FactorInteger[Binomial[2^9, 2^8]]

Out[3]= {{2, 1}, {7, 2}, {13, 2}, {17, 1}, {19, 1},
         {29, 1}, {37, 1}, {43, 1}, {53, 1}, {67, 1},
```

{71, 1}, {73, 1}, {89, 1}, {97, 1}, {101, 1},
{131, 1}, {137, 1}, {139, 1}, {149, 1}, {151, 1},
{157, 1}, {163, 1}, {167, 1}, {257, 1}, {263, 1},
{269, 1}, {271, 1}, {277, 1}, {281, 1}, {283, 1},
{293, 1}, {307, 1}, {311, 1}, {313, 1}, {317, 1},
{331, 1}, {337, 1}, {347, 1}, {349, 1}, {353, 1},
{359, 1}, {367, 1}, {373, 1}, {379, 1}, {383, 1},
{389, 1}, {397, 1}, {401, 1}, {409, 1}, {419, 1},
{421, 1}, {431, 1}, {433, 1}, {439, 1}, {443, 1},
{449, 1}, {457, 1}, {461, 1}, {463, 1}, {467, 1},
{479, 1}, {487, 1}, {491, 1}, {499, 1}, {503, 1},
{509, 1}}

show that the exceptional values 6 and 8 do not give squarefree $\binom{2n}{n}$ so the conjecture is true for all $n$, $4 < n \le 2^{774840978} = 2^{2 \cdot 3^{18}}$. Note that $2^{774840978} \approx 10^{2.3 \times 10^8}$.

**Exercise 2.3**

**(a)\* [HM]** (N.J. Sloane) Is it true that any power of $2^n$, $n > 15$, has a zero in its base 3 expansion?

**(b) [P]** Modify the methods of this section to verify this for some range of $n$.

## 2.3  Niven numbers

Somewhat surprisingly, one can make nontrivial statements about the distribution of Niven numbers (the question being how many numbers less than or equal to $x$ are Niven numbers). Even though the definition of a Niven number is somewhat strange, it turns out that there are many Niven numbers.

### 2.3.1  A lower bound

Denote the number of Niven numbers $\le x$ by $N(x)$ For each $n > 1$ consider the number whose base 10 expansion looks like

$$\overbrace{91\,00\ldots0}^{k}\overbrace{11\ldots1}^{k}\overbrace{22\ldots2}^{k}\overbrace{33\ldots3}^{k}\ldots\ldots\overbrace{88\ldots8}^{k}\overbrace{99\ldots9}^{k}\overbrace{00\ldots0}^{n}$$

where $10^n = 45k + 10$. Note that such a number can be constructed since $45 \,|\, (10^n - 10)$ for every $n \geq 2$.

Now, the digits of such a number add up to $45k + 10$ which divides the number itself, so every permutation of the middle $10k$ digits generates a different Niven number and this will give a lower bound on $N(X)$, where $X = 10^{10k+n+2}$. There are $(10k)!/(k!)^{10}$ permutations of the middle $10k$ digits. Now Stirling's asymptotic formula for $n!$ [49, p. 467]

$$n! \sim \sqrt{2\pi n} \, e^{n \log n - n} \, .$$

gives the estimate

$$\frac{(10k)!}{(k!)^{10}} \sim \sqrt{10} \, \frac{10^{10k}}{(2\pi k)^{9/2}} \, ,$$

so one gets the lower bound

$$N(X) > (1 + \varepsilon) \sqrt{10} \, \frac{10^{10k}}{(2\pi k)^{9/2}} \, ,$$

for any $\varepsilon > 0$, as $n \to \infty$.

Now,

$$\frac{X}{10^{10k}} = 10^{n+2} = 100(45k + 10) < \frac{5000 \log X}{\log 10} \, ,$$

for $n, k$ large enough. As well, one has that

$$k < \frac{\log X}{9 \log 10} \, .$$

The lower bound for $N(x)$ is therefore that

$$N(x) > \alpha \, \frac{x}{(\log x)^{11/2}}$$

holds for infinitely many $x$, in particular for all sufficiently large $x$ of the form $x = 10^{10k+n+2}$, $10^n = 45k + 10$, and $\alpha$ is a constant which can be given by

$$\alpha = \frac{\sqrt{10} \log 10}{5000(18 \log 10\pi)^{9/2}} \, .$$

## 2.3.2   An upper bound

Typical results of probability theory state that "almost all" sequences of length $m$ and elements $0, 1, 2, \ldots, 9$ have sum $4.5\,m$ with a variance $\sqrt{m}$ (see for example [31]). In the context of digits base 10 this says that almost all integers $n < x$ have digit sum

$$\mu = 4.5 \log_{10} x$$

with variance

$$\sigma = \sqrt{\log_{10} x}\,.$$

(Specific proofs for this case can be found in [21].)   Therefore if there are many Niven numbers almost all of them will be divisible by

$$k \in [4.5 \log_{10} x - (\log x)^{1/2-\varepsilon}, 4.5 \log_{10} x + (\log x)^{1/2+\varepsilon}]\,.$$

Each $k$ in this interval generates at most

$$(1 - \delta)\,\frac{x}{4.5 \log_{10} x}$$

Niven numbers, where $\delta > 0$ can be made arbitrarily small as $x \to \infty$,

The fact that there are at most $(\log x)^{1/2+\varepsilon}$ in the intervals gives the upper bound

$$N(x) < \beta \, \frac{x}{(\log x)^{1/2+\varepsilon}}\,,$$

for all sufficiently large $x$, where $\beta$ is a constant which can be given by

$$\beta = \frac{.99 \log 10}{4.5}\,.$$

**Exercise 2.4 [HM]** Use a more exact form of the Central Limit Theorem to improve the constant $1/2 + \varepsilon$ in the upper bound.

**Exercise 2.5\* [HM]** What is the true order of magnitude of $N(x)$?

## 2.4 Notes

The methods of Sections 1.1 and 1.2 were developed with Igor Rivin

The conjectures of Section 1.1 on the digits of $2^n$ base 3, follow from a general conjecture of H. Furstenburg [34, page 43].

Goetgheluck's method for checking the $\binom{2n}{n}$ conjecture was to check the last 256 digits base 3 of $2^n$, $8 < n < 42205184$ to see if a forbidden digit pattern occurred.

Kennedy and Cooper's paper [21] uses Chebyshev's inequality instead of the Central Limit Theorem to estimate $N(x)$, so they get the weaker bound

$$N(x) < C \frac{x}{(\log x)^{1/3}}, \qquad C \text{ a constant,}$$

which follows from equation (2.3) of their paper.

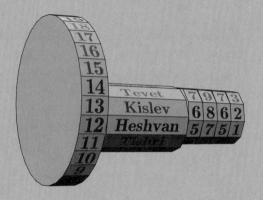

622

1582

1752

1792

# 3

# The Calendar

# Chapter 3

# The Calendar

It is easy to write a program that implements the basic calendar operations such as what day of the week a particular date is, how many days are there between two dates, etc. (Exercise 3.1). However, the fact that the western calendar is relatively simple encourages one to write an ad hoc program which obscures the overall picture. This chapter describes a general algorithm which can easily be adapted to most calendars.

## 3.1 The calendar as a number system

The approach here is to notice that the calendar keeps track of the number of days, so it can be regarded as a kind of positional number system. For example, if the date $\{1, 1, 1\}$, the first day of the first month of the first year, represents the number one, then $\{1, 2, 1\}$ would be the first day of the second month (day 32 in the ordinary calendar), $\{2, 1, 1\}$ would be the first day of the first month of the second year (day 366 in the ordinary calendar) and so forth. It will be seen below that this generalizes the concept of "mixed radix" representation. *Mathematica*'s object-oriented approach will enable one to write a single program to handle both ordinary number systems and the calendar.

Once the calendar is realized as a number system, one can easily implement calendar utility functions such as the day of the week. Thus assuming that one has functions

```
DateToNumber[date, calendar]
```

and

```
NumberToDate[n, calendar]
```

Using these function one has

```
DayOfWeek[date_List, calendar_]:=
  Mod[DateToNumber[date, calendar] +
     DayOfWeek[calendar], 7]
```

where the days of the week corresponding to Sunday, Monday,..., Saturday, are numbered $0, 1, 2, \ldots, 6$ and where DayOfWeek[calendar] gives a known day of the week for the specific calendar. Furthermore one can compute the number of days between two dates

```
DaysBetween[date1_List, date2_List, calendar_]:=
  DateToNumber[date2, calendar] -
  DateToNumber[date1, calendar]
```

```
DaysPlus[date_List, n_Integer, calendar_]:=
  NumberToDate[DateToNumber[date, calendar] + n,
              calendar]
```

This representation also allows easy transfer from one calendar to another

```
CalendarChange[date_, calendar1_, calendar2_]:=
  NumberToDate[DateToNumber[date, calendar1] +
        CalendarChange[calendar1, calendar2], calendar2]
```

where CalendarChange[calendar1, calendar2] is a constant computed by knowing a single date of calendar1 with respect to calendar2.

**Exercise 3.1.** [P] [M] Write a short program to compute the day of the week from any date after 1800. Recall the rule for leap year: Any year divisible by 4 is a leap year, except for centuries, which are leap years only when divisible by 400.

## 3.2   Positional Number Systems

First I'll review the basic theory of positional number systems and how to write *Mathematica* routines to handle them.

A number system represents an integer uniquely in a compact form. The most usual number systems are *fixed radix* number systems such as the usual base 10, base 2, and base 16 systems. Thus a number $n$ can be written uniquely in radix $b$ as

$$(3.1) \qquad a_0 + a_1 b + a_2 b^2 + \cdots + a_k b^k, \qquad 0 \le a_i < b, \, 0 < a_0,$$

yielding the representation (with $b$ suppressed)

$$(3.2) \qquad\qquad\qquad (a_k, \ldots, a_0).$$

The *Mathematica* function `Digits` allows one to find the representation of any integer $n$ in base $b$. For example

```
In[1]:= Digits[12345, 10]

Out[1]= {1, 2, 3, 4, 5}

In[2]:= Digits[666, 2]

Out[2]= {1, 0, 1, 0, 0, 1, 1, 0, 1, 0}
```

The "digits" themselves are in a base 10 representation, so one has to assume that there is an intrinsic notion of integers independent of any representation, which will be taken here as ordinary base 10 integers.

It is not difficult to write a *Mathematica* program for `Digits`. The function $\lfloor n/b \rfloor$ (`Quotient[n,b]` in *Mathematica*) acts as a "left shift" on the representation (3.1) and $n \pmod{b}$ (`Mod[n,b]`) picks out the least significant digit. So the simple recursive program

```
MyDigits[n_Integer, b_Integer] := {n}          /; 0 < n < b

MyDigits[n_Integer, b_Integer] :=
  Append[Digits[Quotient[n, b], b], Mod[n, b]]    /; n >= b
```

works.

The functional approach is to create a list of "left shifts" by using
`NestList` and then hit this list with the mod function using `Map`. The
only difficulty is that the length of the final list has to be figured out
in advance, but it turns out that this can be done using logarithms.

```
MyDigits[n_Integer, b_Integer] :=
Reverse[Mod[NestList[Quotient[#, b]&, n,
            Floor[N[Log[b, n]]]], b]] /; n > 1
```

This program uses the fact that `Range[0, x]` evaluates directly to
`Range[0, Round[N[x]]]`. One can recover the integer with the program

```
DigitsToNumber[digits_, b_]:= Fold[#1 b + #2 &, 0, digits]
```

using Horner's rule as in Section 1.2.

**Exercise 3.2** [P] Write the shortest possible implementation of `Digits`
without using this function directly.


## 3.3   Mixed radix representations

A slightly more general version of the previous section is the *mixed
radix* system in which the radix $b$ is replaced by a sequence $b_1, b_2, \ldots$
and the representation (3.1) is generalized to

$$(3.3)\quad a_0 + a_1 b_1 + a_2 b_1 b_2 + \cdots + a_k b_1 b_2 \cdots b_k, \quad 0 \le a_i < b_{i+1}, \quad 0 < a_0,$$

so that the fixed radix case is $b = b_1 = b_2 = \cdots$. As before one gets the
representation of (3.3) as

$$(a_k, \ldots, a_0).$$

These systems are used in many systems of measure, for example the
old non-decimal British currency of pounds, shillings,..., and more to
the point the time measure of weeks, days, hours, minutes, and seconds.
For example, {3, 2, 9, 22, 57} means "3 weeks, 2 days, 9 hours, 22
minutes, 57 seconds."

The sequence $b_1, b_2, \ldots$ could in principle be infinite (e.g., the *factorial number system* where $b_i = (i+1)!$, $i = 1, 2, 3, \ldots$) so one could also think of a *function* $b(n) = b_n$ for the radix (this will be applied to the calendar in Section 3.6).

Generalizing `Digits` is fairly straightforward. The "left shift" $\lfloor n/b \rfloor$ is replaced by $\lfloor n/b_i \rfloor$ and the least significant digit is found by $n \bmod b_i$ at "level" $i$, though one must take care to do the correct initialization step in the recursion. The program is

```
MyDigits[n_, b_List]:= {n} /; b == {} ||  0 < n < Last[b]
```

```
MyDigits[n_, b_List]:=
Append[MyDigits[Quotient[n, Last[b]], Drop[b, -1]],
      Mod[n, Last[b]]]
```

For example

```
In[1]:= MyDigits[10^6, {7, 24, 60, 60}]
```

```
Out[1]= {1, 4, 13, 46, 40}
```

i.e., a million seconds is 1 week, 4 days, 13 hours, 46 minutes, and 40 seconds.

Note how naturally *Mathematica* allows you to generalize the concept of an integer radix to a list radix since

```
MyDigits[n_, b_Integer]
```

is given by

```
MyDigits[n, Table[b, {Floor[N[Log[b, n]]]}]]
```

or, more compactly,

```
MyDigits[n, b Range[Log[b, n]]^0]
```

The functional approach doesn't seem as effective for the mixed radix case but perhaps the reader might find a good way to implement this.

As before, one can use Horner's rule to recover the number from its digits

```
DigitsToNumber[{n_}, b_]:= n

DigitsToNumber[digits_List, b_]:=
DigitsToNumber[Drop[digits, -1],
          Drop[b, -1]] Last[b] + Last[digits]
```

**Exercise 3.3.**
**(a)** **[P]** **[HM]** Show that every positive integer can be written uniquely as a sum of non consecutive Fibonnaci numbers (the Zeckendorf representation of a number). Write a *Mathematica* program that generates its Zeckendorf representation.

**(b)*** **[HM]** Part (a) is essentially a number system base $\phi = (\sqrt{5} + 1)/2$ (=GoldenRatio). Describe how a general real number can be written in $\phi$, and try to generalize such number systems to arbitrary algebraic numbers.

## 3.4   Generalizing to lists

The next idea in our implementation the calendar is to consider Quotient and Mod with respect to lists.   For example, assuming February has 28 days, then the list of months is

{31, 28, 31, 30, 31, 30, 31, 31, 30, 31, 30, 31}

To find the month and day for the 100th day of the year one sees that
$$31 + 28 + 30 \leq 100 < 31 + 28 + 30 + 31$$

in other words the "quotient" of 100 by the months is 3, and since $31+28+30 = 90$, the "remainder" is 10. Actually, one has the tradition that the first day of the year is in the first month, not month zero, so the definition of MyQuotient is increased by one so that

```
MyQuotient[n_Integer, list_List]:=
  Quotient[n, First[list]] + 1 /; Length[list] == 1
```

Of course one could just count the months from 0 to 11, but this method is much better suited to the way *Mathematica* handles lists, i.e., elements of lists in *Mathematica* are numbered starting at one, not zero. The definition of MyQuotient for lists is

```
MyQuotient[n_Integer, list_List]:=
Block[{s = First[list], q = 1},
      While[n > s, q++; s += list[[q]]]; q] /;
      Length[list] > 1
```

One has the corresponding definition for the remainder

```
MyMod[n_Integer, list_List]:=
   Mod[n, First[list]] /; Length[list] == 1
```

```
MyMod[n_Integer, list_List]:=
n - Fold[Plus, 0, Take[list, MyQuotient[n, list]-1]] /;
   Length[list] > 1
```

**Remark:** When the second argument in MyQuotient and MyMod is a list then the first argument has to be smaller than the total sum of the elements in the list unless the list only has one element. This means that all the lists we will consider will have first element a list consisting of one element only. This means that the calendars are assumed to all have one largest cycle (this will imply that the trees below have only one root).

These list functions allow one to implement mixed radix bases, where the radices are lists, for example the calendar with no leap years

```
{{1}, {31, 28, 31, 30, 31, 30, 31, 31, 30, 31, 30, 31}}
```

This can be done modulo two technical problems which lead us to change the `MyDigits` program and the above representation slightly.

First, the number of days in a month depend on what year it is, so that one needs to know what the higher "digits" are before being able to evaluate the lower "digits". In other words, one should develop the representation from left to right, instead of right to left.

The second point is that the base in the digit representation

$$a_0 + a_1 b + \cdots + a_k b^k$$

was just $\{b\}$, but in fact was shorthand for the "multiplied out" representation $\{b^k, b^{n-1}, \ldots, b, 1\}$. Similarly the mixed radix representation

$$a_0 + a_1 b_1 + a_2 b_1 b_2 + \cdots + a_k b_1 b_2 \cdots b_k \,,$$

was $\{b_k, b_{k-1}, \ldots, b_1\}$, but was shorthand for the multiplied out form $\{b_k b_{k-1} \cdots b_1, b_{k-1} b_{k-2} \cdots b_1, \ldots, b_1, 1\}$.  These longer representations are easily obtained by

```
b^Reverse[Range[0, k]]
```

and

```
Reverse[Accumulate[Times, {1, b[1], b[2], ...,b[k]}]]
```

respectively. For the purposes of the calendar, these full representations are difficult to produce, so that the complete, multiplied out, form is needed.

A program for digits for ordinary bases or for mixed radix bases using the multiplied out representation is

```
MyDigits1[n_, list_]:= {n}  /; Length[list] == 1
```

```
MyDigits1[n_, list_]:=
 Prepend[MyDigits1[Mod[n, First[list]], Rest[list]],
         Quotient[n, First[list]]] /; VectorQ[list]
```

so that "right shifts" have been replaced by "left shifts". The ordinary digits can therefore be written, using `MyDigits1` as

```
MyDigits[n_, b_Integer]:=
 MyDigits1[n, b^Reverse[Range[Log[b, n]]]]
```

and the mixed radix program can be recovered by

```
MyDigits[n_, b_List]:=
MyDigits1[n, Reverse[Select[Accumulate[Times,
                                        Reverse[b]],
                    # < n&]]] /; VectorQ[b]
```

The mixed list radix program is identical to the above program

```
MyDigitsLists[n_, {}]:= {n}

MyDigitsLists[n_, list_List]:=
  Prepend[MyDigitsLists[MyMod[n, First[list]], Rest[list]],
        MyQuotient[n, First[list]]]
```

For example, working with the simple calendar

```
SimplestCalendar =
{{365}, {31, 28, 31, 30, 31, 30, 31, 31, 30, 31, 30, 31}}
```

one computes

```
In[1]:= MyDigitsLists[100, SimplestCalendar]

Out[1]:= {1, 4, 10}
```

so that the 100th day of a non leap year is the 10th of April.

One must also convert back to numbers from the digital representation. This can be done by

```
DigitsToNumberLists[digits_, list_]:=
  (digits[[1]]-1) list[[1,1]] + Last[digits] +
  (Plus @@
  (Fold[Plus, 0, Take[list[[#]], digits[[#]]-1]]& /@
              Range[2, Length[list]]))
```

In this program one has to treat the first element of the list differently since its value may be greater than the first element in the radix list. The last element is also treated differently since one has actually cheated a little by replacing the list of lists

```
{Table[1, {31}], Table[1, {28}], Table[1, {31}],
 Table[1, {30}], Table[1, {31}], Table[1, {30}],
 Table[1, {31}], Table[1, {31}], Table[1, {30}],
 Table[1, {31}], Table[1, {30}], Table[1, {31}]}
```

with

```
{31, 28, 31, 30, 31, 30, 31, 31, 30, 31, 30, 31}
```

## 3.5    Rules for Some Calendars

Calendars are based on the basic celestial periods of the rotation of the earth about its axis, the rotation of the moon around the earth, and the rotation of the earth around the sun. The varying complexity of these calendars depends on how a culture decided to deal with these incommensurable quantities. Most calendars have abandoned one of these, for example months in the Christian calendars basically serve no purpose, while the Islamic calendar is a purely lunar calendar which does not correspond to the solar year. The only calendar that keeps track of both of these is the Jewish calendar (Exercise 3.7), but the analysis in this chapter is restricted to purely solar or purely lunar calendars.

### 3.5.1    The Julian Calendar

In 46 B.C. Julius Caesar reformed the Roman calendar so that each year would consist of 365 days, and that every fourth year would be a leap year of 366 days. During the reign of Augustus Caesar, the lengths of the months were readjusted to their present form. Due to difficulty with keeping track of leap years, the first normal leap year was in the year 8 A.D.[1] (see Exercise 3.4 (b)). Finally, there is no year zero: January 1, year 1 is preceded by December 31, 1 B.C.

---

[1]The UNIX "cal" function incorrectly lists the year 4 as a leap year.

## 3.5.2 The Gregorian Calendar

It turns out that the earth revolves around its own axis about 366.24...
times a year, not 366.25 as is assumed in the Julian system. This
disparity means that by 1582 the Julian calendar was 10 days off (i.e.,
the vernal equinox occurred roughly on March 11). To rectify this,
Pope Gregory XIII suppressed the ten days October 5–October 14,
1582, and declared that only centuries divisible by 400 would be leap
years. The Gregorian calendar was accepted by Catholic countries in
1582, but it was not adopted by Great Britain and its colonies until
1752. By that time, the Julian calendar was off by 11 days, so that the
British and American calendars omit September 3–September 13 1752.
In some countries (Greece, U.S.S.R.) the Gregorian calendar persisted
until World War II.

## 3.5.3 The Islamic Calendar

The Islamic calendar is computed from the *Hejira*, the flight of Mo-
hammed from Mecca to Medina, which is considered to be sunset July
16, 622 A.D. by the majority of Muslims.

The Islamic calendar is a purely lunar calendar with years of 12
months, each month alternatively having 29 or 30 days. This leads to
a year of 354 days, which means that the Islamic calendar "wanders"
around the solar year coming back full cycle every 30 years or so. This
leads to simple rules:

(i) The calendar has a 30 year cycle in which 11 of the 30 years are leap
years. These are years 2,5,7,10,13,16,18,21,24,26, and 29 of the 30 year
cycle.

(ii) There are twelve months which alternate between 30 and 29 days.
The last month has 30 days on leap years. The names are

Muharram, Safar, Rabia I, Rabia II, Jumada I, Jumada II, Rajab,
Sha'ban, Ramadan, Shawwal, Dhu al-Qada, Dhu al-Hijah

## 3.5.4 The French Revolutionary Calendar

This calendar was established in October 1793 by the National Conven-
tion of the French Republic. It was decided that the calendar should

start on September 22, 1792 (so that it was *continued proleptically* to that date). The calendar was used until December 31, 1805, when Napoleon reinstituted the Gregorian calendar.

The calendar consisted of 12 months of 30 days, with five days (six on leap years) added at the end to make it correspond to the solar year. Leap years were computed according to the Gregorian formula.[2] The names of the months were invented by Fabre D'Églantine, and were chosen to correspond to seasonal themes:

Fall: Vendémiaire, Brumaire, Frimaire,

Winter: Nivôse, Pluviôse, Ventôse,

Spring: Germinal, Floréal, Prairial,

Summer: Messidor, Thermidor, Fructidor.

Extra days: Sans Culottides.

For example, the first day of the calendar, September 22, 1792, was 1 Vendémiaire, year I, and July 7, 1794, corresponds to 9 Thermidor, year II.

## 3.6   Implementation of the calendars

The calendar will be a number system with list radix, as above, but where the list depends on earlier information in the date, since, for example, the length of the month can depend on what year you are in and what century you are in. This means that the calendar is a tree, i.e., that the list in the radix will change depending on the date (see Figure 3.1). For example, the Julian calendar can be represented by

```
{{1461},
 {{365, {31, 28, 31, 30, 31, 30, 31, 31, 30, 31, 30, 31}},
  {365, {31, 28, 31, 30, 31, 30, 31, 31, 30, 31, 30, 31}},
  {365, {31, 28, 31, 30, 31, 30, 31, 31, 30, 31, 30, 31}},
  {366, {31, 29, 31, 30, 31, 30, 31, 31, 30, 31, 30, 31}}
 }}
```

---

[2]This appears to be correct, though I have not seen this stated explicitly.

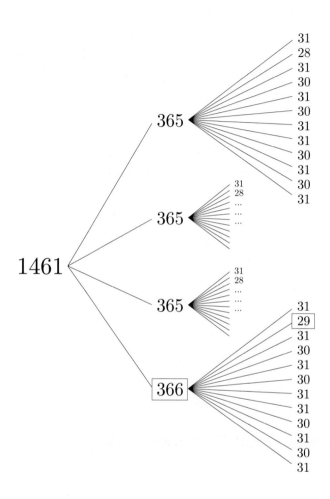

Figure 3.1: The Julian calendar

This tree can get quite large, for example, the Gregorian calendar has a period of 146097 days. The calendars in this chapter are very regular, so one can reduce the size of the representation a great deal as follows. One codes the tree by writing each level as a function giving the typical element and how it is modified by the path taken to that element.

For example, the Julian calendar has at its top level

```
JulianFourYears[_]:= {1461}
```

(as before, all list radix systems must have only one element at the root), and at the next level

```
JulianYears[_]:= {365, 365, 365, 366}
```

and the new feature occurs at the list of months

```
JulianMonths[path_]:=
{31, 28 + Quotient[path[[2]], 4],
 31, 30, 31, 30, 31, 31, 30, 31, 30, 31}
```

where `path[[2]]` gives the year in the four year cycle (this the fourth element representing a leap year).

The complete calendar is represented by the list of symbols

```
JulianCalendar =
 {JulianFourYears, JulianYears, JulianMonths}
```

Using this representation for the Julian calendar, a date will be a sequence $(y_4, y, m, d)$, where $y_4$ counts how many 4 year cycles occur, $y$ denotes which year in the cycle it is, $m$ is the month, and $d$ is the day. For example, September 3, 1752, is represented as $(438, 4, 9, 3)$, i.e., the 3d day of the 9th month of the 4th year in the 438th four year cycle of the Julian calendar.

Using this extended date representation, all one needs now is a generalization of `MyDigits` and `DigitsToNumber`. The implementation of `MyDigits` is similar to the the one in Section 3.4 except that one has to keep track of the date as it is being generated in order to find the path along the tree

```
MyDigits[n_, {}, _]:= {n}

MyDigits[n_, list_List, path_]:=
    Block[{r = MyQuotient[n, First[list][path]]},
    Prepend[MyDigits[MyMod[n, First[list] [path]],
                     Rest[list], Append[path, r]],
        MyQuotient[n, First[list] [path]]]]
```

and DigitsToNumber is almost identical except that one has to keep track of the path supplied with the date.

```
DigitsToNumber[date_, list_, path_]:=
 1 + date[[1]] list[[1]][path+1][[1]] + Last[date] +
 (Plus @@
   (Fold[Plus, 0, Take[list[[#]][path+1], date[[#]]]]& /@
        Range[2, Length[list]]))
```

Now that this works for extended dates, the final step is to convert the usual form for dates, i.e., in terms of year, month, day, into the longer form above. This is done by using the simpler mixed radix versions of MyDigits and DigitsToNumber

```
NumberToDate[n_, Julian]:=
  Prepend[Drop[#, 2],
          DigitsToNumber[Take[#-1, 2], {4}] + 1]& @
        MyDigits[n, JulianCalendar, {}]

DateToNumber[date_, Julian]:=
Block[{d = Join[MyDigits[First[date]-1, {4}] ,
               Rest[date]-1]},
      d = Join[Table[0, {4 - Length[d]}], d];
      DigitsToNumber[d, JulianCalendar, d]]
```

For example, one has that

```
In[1]:= DateToNumber[{1752, 9, 3}, Julian]

Out[1]= 639799
```

So that September 3, 1752, is day 639799 of the mythical Julian calendar starting on January 1, year 1.

## 3.6.1   The Gregorian Calendar

Implementation of the Gregorian calendar is quite similar, but one has to consider a 400 year cycle. The representation is

```
GregorianCalendar =
{GregorianFourCenturies, GregorianCentury,
 GregorianFourYears, GregorianYears, GregorianMonths}

GregorianFourCenturies[_]:= {146097}

GregorianCentury[_]:= {36524, 36524, 36524, 36525}

GregorianFourYears[path_]:=
 Append[Table[1461, {24}], 1460 + Quotient[path[[2]], 4]]

GregorianYears[path_]:=
 {365, 365, 365, 366 -
 (1-Quotient[path[[2]], 4]) Quotient[path[[3]], 25]}

GregorianMonths[path_]:=
{31, 28 + Quotient[path[[4]], 4] -
   (1 - Quotient[path[[2]], 4]) Quotient[path[[3]], 25],
 31, 30, 31, 30, 31, 31, 30, 31, 30, 31}
```

This calendar requires the more complicated extended representation $(y_{400}, y_{100}, y_{25}, y_4, m, d)$. For example September 14, 1752, is represented by $(5, 2, 13, 4, 9, 14)$, i.e., this date occurs on the 13th day of the 9th month of the 4th year in the 12th four year cycle of the 2nd century in the 5th four hundred year cycle!

As before, one has to convert the usual form for dates into the extended form in order to get the number system. This is done by

```
NumberToDate[n_, Gregorian]:=
Prepend[Drop[#, 4],
```

```
    DigitsToNumber[Take[#-1, 4], {4, 25, 4}] + 1]& @
    MyDigits[n, GregorianCalendar, {}]

DateToNumber[date_, Gregorian]:=
Block[{d = Join[MyDigits[First[date]-1, {4, 25, 4}],
              Rest[date]-1]},
      d = Join[Table[0, {6 - Length[d]}], d];
      DigitsToNumber[d, GregorianCalendar, d]]
```

Using these functions one has

```
In[1]:= DateToNumber[{1752, 9, 14}, Gregorian]

Out[1]= 639797
```

Now the rules for the Gregorian and Julian calendars in Section 3.5 indicate that September 3, 1752, Julian and September 14, 1752, Gregorian represent the same day, so that the difference of 2 between their numerical representations gives the constants

```
CalendarChange[Gregorian, Julian] = 2

CalendarChange[Julian, Gregorian] = -2
```

so that one can convert any date from Gregorian to Julian and back. For example,

```
In[2]:= CalendarChange[{1990, 10, 31}, Gregorian, Julian]

Out[2]:= {1990, 10, 18}
```

So that October 31, 1990 Gregorian, is October 18, 1990 in the Julian calendar.

Now one can use DateToNumber to normalize DayOfWeek. Since

```
In[3]:= DateToNumber[{1990, 10, 31}, Gregorian]
```

```
Out[3]= 726771
```

```
In[5]:= Mod[%, 7]
```

```
Out[5]= 3
```

and October 31, 1990, is a Wednesday, one has that
DayOfWeek[Gregorian] is 0. In general, assuming that a calendar is
valid for this date, one has

```
DayOfWeek[Gregorian] = 0
```

```
DayOfWeek[calendar_] := DayOfWeek[calendar] =
  Mod[3 -
    DateToNumber[
    CalendarChange[{1990, 10, 31}, Gregorian, calendar],
    calendar],
    7]
```

though one can obviously substitute any date with a known day of the
week.

## 3.6.2   The Islamic calendar

Implementing the Islamic calendar should now be routine.  First the
representation of the calendar is

```
IslamicCalendar = {IslamicThirtyYears,
                   IslamicYears,
                   IslamicMonths}
```

```
IslamicThirtyYears[_] := {30 354 + 11}
```

```
IslamicYears[_] := 354 +
    {0,1,0,0,1,0,1,0,0,1,0,0,1,0,0,
     1,0,1,0,0,1,0,0,1,0,1,0,0,1,0}
```

```
IslamicMonths[path_] :=
```

```
{30, 29, 30, 29, 30, 29, 30, 29, 30, 29, 30, 29 +
  {0,1,0,0,1,0,1,0,0,1,0,0,1,0,0,
   1,0,1,0,0,1,0,0,1,0,1,0,0,1,0}[[path[[2]]]]}
```

The extension to the usual representation of dates by years, months, and days is

```
NumberToDate[n_, Islamic]:=
 Prepend[Drop[#, 2],
         DigitsToNumber[Take[#-1, 2], {30}] + 1]& @
         MyDigits[n, IslamicCalendar, {}]
```

```
DateToNumber[date_, Islamic]:=
Block[{d = Join[MyDigits[First[date]-1, {30}] ,
             Rest[date]-1]},
      d = Join[Table[0, {4 - Length[d]}], d];
      DigitsToNumber[d, IslamicCalendar, d]]
```

Once again it is not hard to convert from Gregorian to Islamic and back. One must be careful to note that the first day of the Islamic calendar is July 16, 622, which is a *Julian* date, so that one must first do a calculation with respect to the Julian date
    Now

```
CalendarChange[Gregorian, Islamic] =
-DateToNumber[CalendarChange[{611, 7, 15},
                             Julian, Gregorian],
              Gregorian]
```

```
CalendarChange[Islamic, Gregorian] =
-CalendarChange[Gregorian, Islamic]
```

For example, one has

```
In[1]:= CalendarChange[{1990, 10, 31}, Gregorian, Islamic]
```

```
Out[1]= {1411, 4, 11}
```

So that October 31, 1990 is 11 Rabia II, 1411 in the Islamic calendar.

**Exercise 3.4.**

**(a) [P]** The programs in this chapter do not work for negative dates. Generalize the programs to include negative dates.

**Exercise (b)\*.** What day of the week was March 15, 44 B.C., an important date in the Julian calendar, i.e., how many days elapsed in the period March 15, 44 B.C.–October 31, 1990. (This is a good question for mentalists and others who challenge one to name a date for which they will identify the day of the week.)

**Exercise 3.5 [P]** Implement the French revolutionary calendar.

**Exercise 3.6\* [P] [M]** Implement addition and multiplication directly using calendar representations.

**Exercise 3.7**

**(a) [P]** Implement the Jewish calendar.

**(b)\*** Design a mechanical wristwatch that gives the day and month in the Jewish calendar. (This could be nontrivial as this calendar has a complete cycle of 689, 472 years [110, page 32].)

**(c)\* [HM]** Develop a theory of the calendar that keeps track of an arbitrary number of astronomical cycles.

**Exercise 3.8 [P]** Implement the *British regnal calendar*, for example, "The first year of Elizabeth II," was some time around 1952 (see [58]).

## 3.7   Notes

For a complete treatment of positional number systems see [66, Section 4.1].

Some simple algorithms have been developed for mental computation (e.g., the "Doomsday Algorithm" of J.H. Conway) but these are not optimal for computer programs. Many calendar computations can be found in *Winning Ways, Volume 2*, along with an excellent set of references (some of which are rather hard to locate).

From the fact that `CalendarChange[Gregorian, Julian]` is 2, one sees that these calendars in fact were the same only in the third and fourth centuries A.D. This is probably because the Christian Easter was first computed by the Nicaean council in 325. A.D., and the Gregorian calendar was created to conform to these computations.

Material on the French revolutionary calendar can be found in [88].

5 7 11

2 3 5 11

1 0 9 3 1

# 4

# Searching for Numbers

# Chapter 4

# Searching for Numbers

The state of knowledge about direct properties of numbers can be fairly discouraging. In a typical comment Erdös and Graham [28, page 71] state: "It is annoying that this problem is difficult." For example, Fermat's "little theorem" is the statement that for $p$ a prime and any $0 < a < p$

$$a^{p-1} \equiv 1 \pmod{p}.$$

So in particular

$$2^{p-1} \equiv 1 \pmod{p}$$

for all primes $p > 2$. One can now ask whether

$$(4.1) \qquad\qquad 2^{p-1} \equiv 1 \pmod{p^2},$$

also holds. It turns out that this can happen but exceedingly rarely since computations of D.H. Lehmer [80] showed that the only solutions to (4.1) with $p < 6 \times 10^9$ are $p = 1093$ and $p = 3511$. Almost nothing is known about the set of solutions to (4.1). For example, as far as we know every sufficiently large $p$ satisfies (4.1), or it could be possible that every sufficiently large $p$ does not satisfy (4.1). A heuristic argument does show that one should expect around $\log\log x$ solutions of (4.1) with $p < x$ [101, page 333], namely if the distribution of the numbers

$$\frac{2^{p-1} - 1}{p} \pmod{p}$$

is "random", that is, these numbers occur uniformly in the interval $[0, p-1]$, then the chance of this being 0 is $1/p$ so the expected number of hits $\leq x$ is

$$\sum_{p \text{ prime}} \frac{1}{p} \approx \log \log x .$$

In some sense the lack of knowledge about the solutions could indicate a lack of structure of the solutions and would support the randomness hypothesis.

However, our knowledge of *connections* between numbers is a lot better. The solutions to (4.1) are called *Wieferich primes* because Wieferich in 1909 [132] proved the difficult theorem that if the *first case of Fermat's Last Theorem* is false, i.e., there exists integers $x, y, z$ not divisible by $p$ satisfying

$$(4.2) \qquad\qquad x^p + y^p = z^p,$$

then $p$ is a solution of (4.1). Note that Wieferich's condition represents a great advance in the study of Fermat's Last Theorem, since it does not involve the variables $x, y, z$ in (4.2).

The Lehmer computation therefore shows that the first case of Fermat's Last Theorem is true for $p < 6 \times 10^9$ since 1093 and 3511 were ruled out much earlier. In fact immediately after Wieferich's result, Mirimanoff [86] was able to show that if the first case of Fermat's Last Theorem is false for $p$, then also

$$(4.3) \qquad\qquad 3^{p-1} \equiv 1 \ (\text{mod} \ p^2) ,$$

and this is not satisfied by 1093 or 3511. Actually, A. Granville and M. Monagan [52] have shown that conditions similar to (4.1) and (4.3) but with 2 and 3 replaced by $5, 7, 11, \ldots, 71$ hold if the first case of FLT is false for $p$. They used this to show that there is no counterexample to the first case of Fermat's last theorem less than or equal to $714, 591, 416, 091, 389$.

It is interesting to see what impact computers have had on computation of Wieferich primes. As soon as Wieferich published his result a search for Wieferich primes was undertaken, but it took until 1913 for

Meissner to discover that 1093 is a Wieferich prime. The next solution, 3511, took until 1922 to be discovered by Beeger.

Using a computer, and in particular *Mathematica* on a Sun workstation, one gets

```
In[1]:= Timing[
          For[i=2,
              PowerMod[2, Prime[i]-1, Prime[i]^2] != 1,
                  i++];
          Prime[i]]

Out[1]= {2.58333 Second, 1093}

In[2]:= Timing[
          For[i=1,
              If[Prime[i] == 1093, True,
              PowerMod[2, Prime[i]-1, Prime[i]^2] != 1],
                  i++];
          Prime[i]]

Out[2]= {10.5667 Second, 3511}
```

Another connection involving equation (4.1) is with *Mersenne numbers* $2^q - 1$, $q$ prime. Namely, a prime factor $p$ of a Mersenne number $2^q - 1$ is a Wieferich prime if and only if $p^2$ also divides $2^q - 1$ (see Exercise 4.1 (a)). In particular, Mersenne primes are *not* Wieferich primes, and so the first case of Fermat's Last Theorem is true for these numbers (and so is usually true for the world's largest known primes).

A similar result is true for *Fermat numbers* $2^{2^n} + 1$ (see Exercise 4.1 (a)). Thus old conjectures about whether there exists non squarefree Mersenne numbers and Fermat numbers [49, Exercises 4.65–66] are related to solutions of (4.1), and Wieferich primes are of interest independent of Fermat's Last Theorem.

No one has been able to prove anything definite about the distribution of Wieferich primes (see Exercise 4.1 (b) and (c) for conjectural information) but several mathematicians [62] have noted that 1092 and 3510 have the interesting base two expansions

$$1092 = 10001000100_2$$
$$3510 = 110110110110_2$$

so finding more Wieferich primes might reveal a true pattern (see Section 5.4).

It is quite difficult to search for Wieferich primes efficiently so I will turn my attention to some more tractable problems before returning to Wieferich in Section 5.4.

### Exercise 4.1 [HM]

**(a)** Show that if $p|2^n - 1$, $p$ and $n$ relatively prime, then $p$ is a Wieferich primes if and only if $p^2$ also divides $2^n - 1$. Show that this is also true for $2^n + 1$.

**(b)** (A. Granville [51])  Show that the conjecture that there are no 3 powerful numbers [87] implies that there are infinitely many Wieferich primes. A *powerful* number is one which is only divisible by squares of primes.

**(c)** (J. Silverman [118]) The *abc* conjecture of Masser and Oesterlé [72] states that for any $\varepsilon > 0$ there is a constant $C_\varepsilon$ such that for any three relatively primes integers $a, b, c$ satisfying

$$a + b = c$$

one has the inequality

$$\max\{|a|, |b|, |c|\} \le C_\varepsilon \prod_{p|abc} p^{1+\varepsilon}.$$

Show that this conjecture implies that there are at least $C \log x$ Wieferich primes $\le x$, for some constant $C$.

**Disclaimer:** This should not be taken as a personal endorsement by the author of this conjecture.

## 4.1  Binomial Coefficients

One of the most frequent numbers to come up in everyday mathematics are the binomial coefficients

$$\binom{n}{k} = \frac{n!}{k!(n-k)!}.$$

For example these count the number of ways of choosing $k$ objects from a set of $n$ objects. These numbers are fundamental to Discrete Mathematics and Chapter 5 of the book *Concrete Mathematics*, by Graham, Knuth, and Patashnik, is devoted to their study. Of most theoretical interest is the middle binomial coefficient

$$\binom{2n}{n} = \frac{(2n)!}{(n!)^2} = \frac{(n+1)(n+2)\cdots n}{1 \times 2 \times 3 \times \cdots \times n}$$

which has many amazing properties, for example it was used by Chebyshev to discover the correct order of primes less than or equal to a given number (see Exercise 4.2).

The next two sections investigate research problem 5.97 of [49]. This problem asks to characterize the numbers $n$ such that

(4.4)
$$\binom{n-1}{(n-1)/2} \equiv (-1)^{(n-1)/2} \pmod{n}.$$

R.W. Gosper noted that this is always the case when $n$ is prime, then conjectured that this was also a necessary condition. The reason for this is that

$$\binom{n-1}{(n-1)/2} = \frac{(n+1)/2 \times (n+2)/2 \times \cdots \times (n-1)}{1 \times 2 \times 3 \times \cdots \times (n-1)/2}$$

$$= \frac{(n-1)(n-2)(n-3)\cdots(n-(n-1)/2)}{1 \times 2 \times 3 \times \cdots \times (n-1)/2}$$

and so $\pmod{n}$ every term $k$ in the denominator will cancel with a term $n - k \equiv -k \pmod{n}$ in the numerator, as long as $k$ doesn't have a common factor with $n$. This is the case for all $k$ when $n$ is prime, giving the answer $(-1)^{(p-1)/2}$.

On the other hand, if $k$ has a common factor with $n$ then $(n-k)/k$ will not give $-1$, and there doesn't seem to be any indication that this number should ever be $\pm 1 \bmod n$, so in analogy to Wilson's theorem (see Exercise 4.2) Gosper conjectured that (4.4) can only hold for primes.

For example, let $n = pq$, where $p$ and $q$ are distinct primes. Writing

$$f(n) = \binom{n-1}{(n-1)/2}$$

one has that

$$f(pq) \equiv f(p)f(q) \pmod{pq}.$$

To see this, note that there are $(p-1)(q-1)/2$ terms not divisible by $p$ or $q$, so these contribute a factor of one. Each term divisible by $p$, i.e., of the form $ap$ contributes

$$\frac{pq - pa}{pa} = \frac{q - a}{a}$$

and all of these contribute a factor of $f(q)$, and similarly, the terms divisible by $q$ contribute a factor of $f(p)$.

S. Skiena (e.g., [120, page 262]) subsequently made a search of all numbers less than $20,000$ and found the example

$$n = 5907 = 3 \times 11 \times 179.$$

It turns out that one can construct a class of composite solutions to (4.4) since $n = p^2$ is a solution whenever $p$ is a Wieferich prime. I will show why this holds in the next section. In the following section I will describe faster methods of computing $\binom{n}{k} \pmod{p}$ and show that the only composite solutions $n$ of (1) with $n < 13 \times 10^6$ are $n = 5907, 1093^2$, and $3511^2$.

## 4.2   A class of solutions

The first result is that for $k \geq 1$ one always has

$$(4.5) \qquad \binom{p^k - 1}{(p^k - 1)/2} \equiv (-1)^{(p-1)/2} \binom{p^{k-1} - 1}{(p^{k-1} - 1)/2} \pmod{p^k},$$

i.e., $f(p^k) \equiv f(p^{k-1}) \pmod{p^k}$.

To see that (2) holds

(4.6)
$$\binom{p^k - 1}{(p^k - 1)/2} = \frac{(p^k + 1)/2 \times (p^k + 3)/2 \times \cdots \times (p^k - 1)}{1 \times 2 \times 3 \times \cdots \times (p^k - 1)/2}$$

$$= \frac{(p^k - 1)(p^k - 2)(p^k - 3) \cdots (p^k - (p^k - 1)/2)}{1 \times 2 \times 3 \times \cdots \times (p^k - 1)/2}$$

Now each term $a$ relatively prime to $p$ in the denominator corresponds to the term $p^k - a$ in the numerator and

$$\frac{p^k - a}{a} \equiv -1 \pmod{p^k}.$$

On the other hand each term $a = pb$, $b = 1, 2, \ldots, (p^{k-1} - 1)/2$ in the denominator gives

$$\frac{p^k - pb}{pb} = \frac{p^{k-1} - b}{b}.$$

Since there are $\phi(p^k)/2$ terms relatively prime to $p$ in the denominator of (4.6) and $\phi(p^k) = p^{k-1}(p - 1)$, and since $(-1)^{\text{odd} \times n} = (-1)^n$ this is

$$(-1)^{(p-1)/2} \frac{(p^{k-1} - 1)(p^k - 2)(p^k - 3) \cdots (p^{k-1}(p^{k-1} - 1)/2)}{1 \times 2 \times 3 \times \cdots \times (p^{k-1} - 1)/2},$$

which is exactly

$$(-1)^{(p-1)/2} \binom{p^{k-1} - 1}{(p^{k-1} - 1)/2}.$$

The next thing to do is look up some facts about binomial coefficients. In [57, Theorems 132, 133] it is proved that the theorem of Eisenstein

$$\frac{2^{p-1} - 1}{p} \equiv 1 + \frac{1}{3} + \frac{1}{5} + \cdots + \frac{1}{p - 2} \pmod{p},$$

where $1/k$ denotes the unique $0 < a < p - 1$ such that $ak \equiv 1 \pmod{p}$, implies that

(4.7)
$$\binom{p - 1}{(p - 1)/2} \equiv (-1)^{(p-1)/2} 4^{p-1} \pmod{p^2}.$$

From (4.5) and (4.6) it is seen that

$$2^{p-1} \equiv 1 \pmod{p^2}$$

is true if and only if (1) holds for $n = p^2$. Conversely, using (4.5), it follows that if (1) holds for $n = p^k$, then so does (4.1). Thus the question of which composite $n$ satisfy (4.4) is essentially characterized for $n = p^k$ a prime power by the theorem

**Theorem.** *Equation (4.4) is satisfied for $n = p^2$ if and only if $p$ is a Wieferich prime. Moreover, if $n = p^k$, $k > 3$ satisfies (4.4), then so does $n = p^{k-1}$.*

This gives that $1093^2$ and $3511^2$ are solutions of (4.4) but leaves unresolved the question of whether $1093^k$, $3511^k$, $k > 2$ satisfy (4.4). First one checks this for $k = 3$. Using (4.5) one reduces this to computing $\left(\begin{smallmatrix} p^2-1 \\ (p^2-1)/2 \end{smallmatrix}\right) \pmod{p^3}$, $p = 1093$ and $p = 3511$. Using the methods of the next section one gets that

```
In[1]:= BinomialMod[1093^3 - 1, (1093^3 -1)/2, 1093^3]

Out[1]= 1163588127

In[2]:= BinomialMod[3511^3 - 1, (3511^3 -1)/2, 3511^3]

Out[2]= 42023155488
```

so none of the higher powers satisfy (4.4).

**Exercise 4.2**

(a) [M] Show that if $p, q, r$ are distinct primes then

$$f(pqr)f(p)f(q)f(r) \equiv f(pq)f(pr)f(qr) \pmod{pqr}.$$

(b)* [HM] Is there a formula for $f(n)$ in terms of its prime factors?

# 4.3 Computing binomial coefficients

In this Section we'll search for composite solutions of (1) by speeding up the evaluation of $\binom{n}{k}$ $(\bmod\, m)$. Since the binomial is built into *Mathematica* this can be computed by

```
BinomialMod[n_, k_, m_]:= Mod[Binomial[n, k], m]
```

but we'll find ways to do this much more efficiently.

The simplest thing to consider is speeding up the evaluation of $\binom{n}{k}$. Using the definition

$$\binom{n}{k} = \frac{n(n-1)\cdots(n-k+1)}{k!}$$

gives the program

```
MyBinomial[n_, k_]:=
  Quotient[Times @@ (n + 1 - Range[k]), k!]
```

Note that since division is exact one uses `Quotient` in order to avoid the Euclidean algorithm that reduces fractions in lowest terms.

This method is the one used internally by *Mathematica* and it is fairly effective and is certainly of the right order of magnitude. However, one can win a $\log n$ factor by using the prime decomposition of $\binom{n}{k}$. One uses the fact that it is easy to find the exact power of a prime $p$ dividing $n!$ [49, Section 4.4] namely

$$\varepsilon_p(n) = \sum_{r \geq 0} \left\lfloor \frac{n}{p^r} \right\rfloor$$

for example, one can compute the number of trailing zeroes in 1990! directly by

```
In[1]:= Min[Last /@ FactorInteger[1990!][[{1,3}]]]
```

```
Out[2]= 495
```

or by the formula

```
FactorialExponent[p_, n_]:=
Block[{np = n/p, sum = 0},
      While[np >= 1,
              sum += Floor[np];
              np /= p];
      sum]
```

so that also

```
In[1]:= Min[FactorialExponent[2, 1990],
            FactorialExponent[5, 1990]]
```

```
Out[2]= 495
```

but the result returns much more quickly.

The prime factorization of $\binom{n}{k}$ is

$$\prod_{p \leq n} p^{\varepsilon_p(n)-\varepsilon_p(k)-\varepsilon_p(n-k)} \, .$$

To use this formula for computational purposes one needs a list of the primes less than or equal $n$, but this can readily be done in *Mathematica* since the function PrimePi gives the number of primes $\leq n$, and Prime will generate the primes up to $10^9$. In other words, the list of primes $\leq n$ can be generated by the incantation

```
Prime[Range[PrimePi[n]]]
```

since Prime is a listable function. Using this one has the program

```
FastBinomial[n_, k_]:= FastBinomial[k, n]  /; k > n
```

```
FastBinomial[n_, k_]:=
Times @@ (#^(e[#, n] - e[#, k] - e[#, n-k])&
          /@ Prime[Range[PrimePi[n]]])
```

This can be speeded up somewhat by noting that for every prime $\sqrt{n} < p \leq n$, $\varepsilon_p(n)$ is either zero or one, so

```
FastBinomial[n_, k_]:=
(Times @@
(#^(Quotient[n, #] - Quotient[k , #] -
    Quotient[n - k, #])& /@
 Prime[Range[PrimePi[N[Sqrt[n]]] + 1,
             PrimePi[n]]])) *
  Times @@ (#^(Plus @@
              (Block[{r = #^Range[Log[n]/Log[#]]},
 Quotient[n, r] - Quotient[k, r] -
 Quotient[n - k, r]]))& /@
 Prime[Range[PrimePi[N[Sqrt[n]]]]]])
```

You can do better for $\binom{2n}{n}$ since the prime factorization is somewhat more explicit

$$(4.8) \qquad \binom{2n}{n} = \prod_{k=1}^{n} \left( \prod_{2n/(2k)<p^m \leq 2n/(2k-1)} p \right).$$

In particular, the exact power of $p$ dividing $\binom{2n}{n}$ for $p \geq \sqrt{n}$ is one if $2n/(2k) < p \leq 2n/(2k-1)$ for some $k$, and zero otherwise. In the range considered here, it is efficient to use this formula only for $k = 2, 4$, so the resulting program is

```
FastBinomial[n_, k_]:=
Times @@ Prime[Range[PrimePi[k] + 1,
                PrimePi[n]]] *
Times @@ Prime[Range[PrimePi[k/2] + 1,
                PrimePi[2 k/3]]] *
(Times @@
  (#^(Quotient[2 k, #] - 2 Quotient[k , #]) & /@
   Prime[Range[PrimePi[N[Sqrt[2k]]] + 1,
             PrimePi[2 k/5]]])) *
Times @@
   (#^(Plus @@ (Block[{r = #^Range[Log[2 k]/Log[#]]},
```

```
Quotient[2 k, r] - 2 Quotient[k, r]]))& /@
Prime[Range[PrimePi[N[Sqrt[2 k]]]]]) /;
              n == 2 k
```

**Exercise 4.3** (Chebyshev) Use the factorization of $\binom{2n}{n}$ to show that the number of primes $\pi(n)$ which are less than or equal to $n$ satisfies

$$\log 2 \, \frac{n}{\log n} \leq \pi(n) \leq \log 4 \, \frac{n}{\log n} \, .$$

This is a first step towards the prime number theorem, see Section 8.2.

## 4.4    Binomials modulo an integer

As in the computation of `PowerMod` one can speed up the computation of $\binom{n}{k} \pmod{m}$ by repeatedly taking mod in the above program, since this keeps the size of the parameters small. However there is a theorem of E. Lucas that allows for a much more efficient method of evaluating these numbers

**Theorem.** (Lucas) If $p$ is a prime and $a = a_0 + a_1 p + \cdots + a_r p^r$, $b = b_0 + b_1 p + \cdots + b_s p^s$, then

$$\binom{a}{b} \equiv \binom{a_0}{b_0} \binom{a_1}{b_1} \cdots \binom{a_t}{b_t} \pmod{p}, \qquad t = \min(r, s).$$

This has a fairly simple proof: First note that if $f(x)$ is a polynomial considered with coefficients $\pmod{p}$ then $f(x)^{p^k} = f(x^{p^k})$ (this follows from the multinomial theorem since all middle terms are $\equiv 0 \pmod{p}$). So one has that

(4.9)          $(1+x)^a = (1+x)^{a_0}(1+x^p)^{a_1} \cdots (1+x^{p^t})^{a_t}$

and since the number $b$ has a unique digital representation the theorem follows by equating the coefficients of $x^b$ in (4.9).

Combining this with the method of the previous section one has the following fast computation of $\binom{2n}{n} \pmod{m}$.

```
BinomialMod[n_, k_, p_]:=
Block[{fi = First /@ FactorInteger[m]},
If[If[2 k >= fi[[-1]],
     Mod[Times @@ (#^(Plus @@
           (Block[{q = #^Range[Log[2 k]/Log[#]]},
             Quotient[2 k, q] - 2 Quotient[k, q]]))& /@
                fi), m] == 0,
   False],
     0,
Mod[Last[Accumulate[Mod[#1 #2, m]&,
     Mod[(Times @@ #)& /@
         partition[Prime[Range[PrimePi[k] + 1,
                       PrimePi[2 k]]], 20], m]]]*
Last[Accumulate[Mod[#1 #2, m]&,
     Mod[(Times @@ #)& /@
         partition[Prime[Range[PrimePi[k/2] + 1,
               PrimePi[2 k/3]]], 20],m]]] *
(Last[Accumulate[Mod[#1 #2, m]&,
   (#^(Quotient[2 k, #] - 2 Quotient[k , #]) & /@
           Prime[Range[PrimePi[N[Sqrt[2k]]] + 1,
                   PrimePi[2 k/5]]])]]) *
  Mod[Times @@
  (#^(Plus @@ (Block[{r = #^Range[Log[2 k]/Log[#]]},
             Quotient[2 k, r] - 2 Quotient[k, r]]))& /@
             Prime[Range[PrimePi[N[Sqrt[2 k]]]]]), m], m]]
   ] /; n == 2 k
```

**Exercise 4.4 [P]** Implement BinomialMod[n, k, m] for all $n, k$.

**Exercise 4.5 [M]** (H. Wilf) $\binom{2n}{n}$ (mod $p$) periodic for $p > 2$ a fixed prime, as $n$ runs over the integers?

**Exercise 4.6 [M]** For which $n$ are all $\binom{n}{k}$ odd, $k = 0, 1, \ldots, n$?

# 4.5 The search method

The basic idea of the search method is to avoid computing the complete value of $\binom{2n}{n}$ (mod $m$). Since this complete evaluation must be done when $n$ is a solution of (4.4), the first step is to not do any computation for $n$ which are known to satisfy (4.4). Using the results of Section 4.2 you can rule out all powers of primes, since it's true for primes and the prime powers are already characterized as coming from Wieferich primes.

Next, one uses the fact that a necessary condition for

$$\binom{n-1}{(n-1)/2} \equiv (-1)^{(n-1)/2} \pmod{n}$$

to hold is that

$$\binom{n-1}{(n-1)/2} \equiv (-1)^{(n-1)/2} \pmod{p}$$

also holds for all $p$ dividing $n$. Since $\binom{n-1}{(n-1)/2} \bmod p$ can be computed efficiently using Lucas' theorem, this will quickly eliminate most $n$ not satisfying (4.4), especially if this check is done in order of the size of the prime factors of $n$.

Here is an implementation of this method

```
BinomialSearchTest[n_] :=
Block[{fi= First /@ FactorInteger[n], dfi},
     dfi = MyDigits[(n-1)/2, #]& /@ fi;
     If[Select[fi - 2 (Max /@ dfi), # <= 0&] !={},
        False,
        If[Select[Mod[(Times @@ #[[1]]) - (-1)^((n-1)/2),
                  #[[2]]]& /@
              Transpose[{Binomial[2 dfi, dfi], fi}],
       # != 0&] == {},
    Mod[BinomialMod[n-1,(n-1)/2, n]
       - (-1)^((n-1)/2), n] == 0,
    False]]]
```

One can search a given range by removing the primes from this range and then using the above to test all odd numbers in the range. The following implements this method. Since the search for all numbers less than thirteen million takes at least a week of CPU time on a fast workstation, one has to plan for possible interruptions by saving results every hour or so.  Most of the following program consists of saving intermediate results.

```
BinomialSearch[a_, b_]:=
 Block[{r = Complement[Range[2 Quotient[a, 2] + 1,
                       2 Quotient[b, 2]-1, 2],
             Prime[Range[PrimePi[a], PrimePi[b]]]],
        i = 1, length, save = {}, info},
       length = Length[r];
       info = {a,b};
       Save["binomialsearch", info, length];
       While[i <= length,
             If[BinomialSearchTest[r[[i]]],
                AppendTo[save, r[[i]]]];
             If[Mod[i, 100] == 0,
                info = {i, r[[i]], save};
                Save["binomialsearch", info]];
             i++];
       info = {i, r[[i-1]], save};
       Save["binomialsearch", info];
       save]
```

**Exercise 4.7\*** **[P]** **[HM]** A *Wilson prime* is one which satisfies

$$(p-1)! \equiv -1 \;(\mathrm{mod}\,p^2),$$

(Recall that Wilson's theorem states that $(p-1)! \equiv -1 \;(\mathrm{mod}\,p)$ if and only if $p$ is prime.)

It turns out that 5,13, and 563 are the only Wilson primes $< 4 \times 10^6$ [101].  Can you find more?

## 4.6   Notes

A good reference for the material in this Chapter are Shank's book *Solved and Unsolved Problems in Number Theory* [114].  Another very helpful book is R.K. Guy's book *Unsolved Problems in Number Theory*

[53] (before trying to solve a problem, one should check if it's unsolved).


Historical material on Fermat's Last Theorem can be found in [100].

The function `PrimePi[x]` which implements the number of primes less than or equal to $x$, $\pi(x)$ in mathematical notation, is a built-in function for version 2.0 of *Mathematica* but not in earlier versions.

Since the $n$th prime $p(n)$ is implemented by the efficient built-in function `Prime[n]`, computing $\pi(x)$ is done by inverting $p(n)$. To do this one first uses the prime number theorem to guess a value of $n$ for which the $n$th prime is close to $x$. One then tries to home in on the exact largest value of $n$ for which $p(n) \leq x$ by using the local version of the prime number theorem.

The prime number theorem (see Section 8.2) states that

$$\pi(x) \approx \operatorname{Li}(x) = \int_2^x \frac{dt}{\log t}$$

with an error less than a constant multiple of $\sqrt{x} \log(x)$, assuming that the Riemann Hypothesis is true (an exact statement can be made for the range $x < 10^9$). $\operatorname{Li}(x)$ is implemented by the built-in function `LogIntegral`, and one could use this as a first guess. A more efficient method, however, is to use the *Gram series*

$$R(x) = 1 + \sum_{k=1}^{\infty} \frac{(\log x)^k}{k \, k! \zeta(k+1)},$$

which is generally ten times more accurate as an approximation to $\pi(x)$ than $\operatorname{Li}(x)$ in the range $2 \leq x < 10^9$ where this algorithm is valid (a celebrated theorem of Littlewood [60, Chapter 5] states that $R(x)$ is a worse approximation than $\operatorname{Li}(x)$ infinitely often, but this probably doesn't happen until you get to very large values of $x$). $R(x)$ can be easily computed using a table of the values $1/(k \, k! \zeta(k+1))$, $k = 1, 2, 3, \ldots, 100$. The evaluation is further simplified since one only needs an accuracy of $\pm 10$, for example, since one will have to do a search of at least $\pm 100$ in almost all cases at hand.

The search is done by using the local version of the prime number theorem. Locally the prime number theorem says that is one has that

$p(n) = y$ then $p(n + 1) \approx y + \log y$, so if $x - p(n) = d$ then $p(n + \lfloor d/\log x \rfloor)$ should be even closer to $x$. The problem with this is getting into "infinite loops" so one must also check that the error actually decreases at each step, so one combines the local PNT with binary search.

Here is *Mathematica* code for this program (written with J. Keiper)

```
rlist = Map[1/(#! # N[Zeta[# + 1]]) &, Range[100]]

(* In practice rlist can be stored directly *)

RiemannR[x_]:=
  1 + Round[rlist . (Log[N[x]]^Range[100])]

PrimePi[x_]:=
  PrimePi[Floor[x]] /;
         !IntegerQ[x] && IntegerQ[Floor[x]]

PrimePi[n_Integer]:= 0 /; n < 2

PrimePi[2] = 1

PrimePi[4] = PrimePi[3] = 2

PrimePi[6] = PrimePi[5] = 3

roundout[x_]:= Sign[x] Ceiling[Abs[x]]

PrimePi[n_Integer]:=
Block[{s = 1/Log[N[n]], t, diff,
       a, b = RiemannR[N[n]], sign},
     diff = roundout[(Prime[b] - n) s];
     sign = Sign[diff];
     a = b - diff;
     diff = Prime[a] - n;
     While[diff sign > 0,
           b = a;
```

```
            a -= roundout[diff s];
            diff = Prime[a] - n];
      If[diff == 0, Return[a]];
      t = a;
      If[a > b, diff = b; b = a; a = diff];

(* a and b are now lower and upper bounds.
   Search with mixed local PNT/binary search *)

   While[True,
          If[b == a+1, Return[a]];
          t -= Round[diff s];
          If[Not[a < t < b], t = Round[(a+b)/2]];
          diff = Prime[t] - n;
          Which[diff == 0, Return[t],
          diff  > 0, b = t,
          True, a = t]]] /; n > 6
```

# 5

# How not to use *Mathematica*

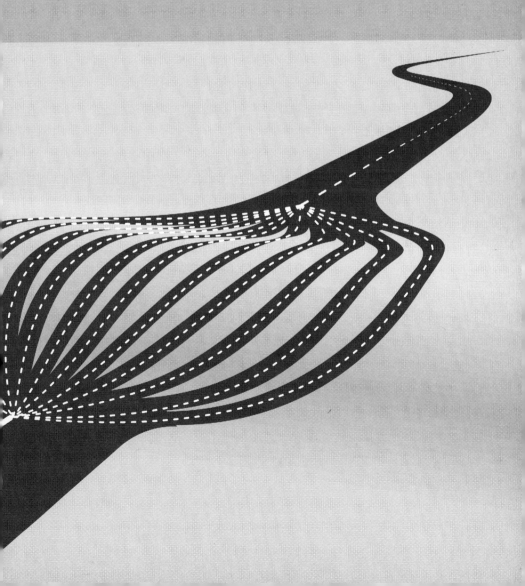

# Chapter 5

# How Not to Use *Mathematica*

*Mathematica* is a general purpose package for doing mathematics but when a world record is attempted it turns out that this generality may be somewhat of a disadvantage. This chapter will give examples of how to get substantial speedups by using C programs in conjunction with Mathematica. Since *Mathematica* is an *interpreted* language, control statements take longer to process than in a *compiled* languages such as C, Pascal, or Lisp, so I will give an example of a Lisp program that is somewhat faster than the equivalent *Mathematica* program. Since it is usually easier to write the programs in *Mathematica*, one can use it as a model and test of the special purpose programs.

For best results one can write everything in assembly language (actually, one could design a special purpose chip as has been done successfully for computer chess) The problem with this is that it is difficult for most people to write assembly language programs, and that, furthermore, different code has to be written for every machine. Another possibility is to run the program on the world's fastest machine. This seems unrealistic especially if your problem is not considered of vital importance. In any event, even on the fastest machines, days of uninterrupted time might be required.

Because of this I have limited myself to standardized languages that exist on various machines, namely C and Common Lisp.

**Exercise 5.1 [P]** (Bruce Smith) What does the following *Mathematica* program do?

```
If[#1 == 0, 1, #1 #0[#1-1]]&
```

(This is an example of a method that works but should never be used!)

## 5.1   Are all Euclid numbers squarefree?

Euclid's proof that there are an infinite number of primes is well known [29, Book IX, Proposition 20] If $p_1, p_2, \ldots, p_n$ represented all the primes, then $N = p_1 p_2 \cdots p_n + 1$ would not be divisible by any of $p_1, p_2, \ldots, p_n$, i.e., by *any* prime, which is a contradiction since every number bigger than one is divisible by a prime.

This proof is actually constructive in that one can generate an infinite sequence of primes $P_1, P_2, \ldots$ by multiplying all the existing $P_1, \ldots, P_n$ and then taking $P_{n+1}$ to be the smallest prime factor of $P_1 P_2 \cdots P_n + 1$ (of course this is impractical since one needs to factor very large numbers). An interesting question is whether Euclid actually thought of this as a constructive proof of an infinity of primes, or whether he just considered it as a proof by contradiction. One should keep in mind that he did invent the best algorithm in number theory!

Research problem 4.65 of "Concrete Mathematics" asks whether the sequence defined by

$$(5.1) \qquad e(0) = 2, \; e(n+1) = e(n)^2 - e(n) + 1,$$

contains a non squarefree term. This sequence arises from Euclid's proof of the infinitude of primes since (5.1) is equivalent to

$$e(0) = 2, \; e(n+1) = e(0)e(1) \cdots e(n) + 1$$

which is essentially Euclid's proof (i.e., the $e(n)$'s are pairwise relatively prime).

Now the $e(n)$'s grow very quickly, in fact [49, Exercise 4.37] there is a constant $E \approx 1.264$ such that

$$e(n) = \left\lfloor E^{2^{n+1}} + \frac{1}{2} \right\rfloor$$

so trying to factor $e(n)$, for $n > 10$ is not very realistic. However, one can check whether $p^2$ divides $e(n)$ by running the recursion (5.1) $\bmod p^2$. So letting $e(n, p)$ stand for $e(n) \bmod p$ one has that

$$(5.2) \quad e(0, p^2) = 2, \ e(n+1, p^2) = e(n, p^2)^2 - e(n, p^2) + 1 \ (\bmod p^2).$$

If a zero appears then a square factor of a Euclid number has been found.

Now running equation (5.2) for each prime $p$ in succession is a fairly expensive computation, but it can be speeded up considerably by noting that any solution of (5.2) must also be a solution $\bmod p$, and that such solutions only occur with probability $1/\sqrt{p}$. This follows (heuristically) from the theory of the Pollard-$\rho$ factoring algorithm:

**Pollard's factoring algorithm:**

(A) Let $x(0) = 2$

(B) Let $x(i+1) = x(i)^2 - x(i) + 1 \bmod n$.

(C) If $\text{GCD}(x(2i) - x(i), n) > 0$, then $n$ is factored

Since this iteration seems to behave like a random mapping this algorithm will usually produce a cycle within $\sqrt{p}$ steps and (C) will have a solution. To implement this one needs a cycle-finding algorithm. It turns out that an efficient algorithm has been discovered by R.W. Floyd [66, page 7], which was later improved by R. Brent [11] for the purposes of factorization. An implementation of this algorithm is given in the Notes at the end of this Chapter.

The Pollard-$\rho$ philosophy gives that

$$(5.3) \qquad e(0, p) = 2, \ e(n+1, p) = e(n, p)^2 - e(n, p) + 1 \ (\bmod p)$$

will have a cycle within $\sqrt{p}$ steps. This implies that one should detect a zero within $\sqrt{p}$ steps and that only about $1/\sqrt{x}$ of $p \leq x$ should give a zero.

The search for square factors of the $e(n)$ consists of:

(A) Find all $p$ which return 0 from (5.3) by using a cycle detection algorithm.

(B) Check these $p$ to see if they satisfy (5.2).

Another observation that speeds up the program by a factor of two is that if the recurrence ever gives $0 \pmod{p}$ then

$$x^2 - x + 1 \equiv 0 \pmod{p}$$

has a solution, so that by the quadratic formula

$$x = \frac{1 \pm \sqrt{-3}}{2} \pmod{p},$$

so that the above has a solution if and only if $-3$ is a perfect square $\bmod\, p$. By quadratic reciprocity this is true if and only if $p \equiv 1 \pmod{3}$.

One can therefore write a search program, where as usual a lot of care is taken to save intermediate results in a file (here `"euclid.data"`) in case the computer crashes

```
EuclidSearch[m_, n_]:=
Block[{i = m, j, a, p, q, r, plist = {},
   info={m,n}, answer=False, t},
   Save["euclid.data", info];
   While[i <= n,
       If[Mod[i, 1000]==0,
          Save["euclid.data", i, plist]];
          p = Prime[i];
          If[Mod[p, 3] != 1, i++; Continue[]];
          For[j=0; a=2; b = 2; t = 1,
             a != 0 &&
             If[2 t+2 - (t+1)/2 <= j <= 2 t + 1,
                a != b, True],
             j++,
             a = Mod[a^2-a+1,p];
                If[j == 2 t + 1, t = 2 t + 1; b = a]];
          If[a != 0, i++; Continue[]];
          AppendTo[plist, {j, p}];
          r = p^2;
          If[Nest[Mod[#^2-#+1, r]&, 2, j] == 0,
             answer={p, j};Break[]];
          i++];
```

```
info = {answer, plist};
Save["euclid.data", info];
info]
```

**Exercise 5.2 [HM]** One can win a further 25% speedup by removing the primes for which

$$(x^2 - x + 1)^2 - (x^2 - x + 1) + 1 = x^4 - 2x^3 + 2x^2 - x + 1 \equiv 0 \pmod{p}$$

has no solution. (These lie in an arithmetic progression, but finding which one requires understanding biquadratic reciprocity.)

**Exercise 5.3\* [HM]** Another sequence based on Euclid's method was defined by Shanks: Let $s(1) = 2$ and for $n \geq 1$, let $s(n+1) =$ smallest prime divisor of $s(1)s(2) \cdots s(n) + 1$. Do the $s(j)$ include all the primes?

**Exercise 5.4\* [HM]** Find a proof that the primes have density zero that could be understood by Euclid.

## 5.2   PowerMod **to the rescue**

The program of the last section turns out to be slow (10 hours to check the first 10,000 primes on a Sun3), and so is unrealistic if one wants to check the first million primes.

Most of the time lost is in doing very repetitive loops, and in using full bignum arithmetic in computing $x^2 \pmod{p}$, where $x, p < 10^7$. Now *Mathematica* is an interpreted language so it loses a lot of efficiency when doing repetitive loops, while its bignum package is very general, so inefficient for borderline numbers.

The solution is to use the **PowerMod** algorithm described in Section 1.2 to implement $x^2 \pmod{p}$, for $x, p$ double precision integers using repeated doubling. In other words, this is the additive analogue of **PowerMod**. The program below can evaluate $x^2 \bmod p$ in as little as 3 ordinary multiplication and remainder operations, and so will be much faster than any bignum package available.

The improved search method, therefore, is to create a list of primes using *Mathematica* (this is much more convenient than rewriting Prime in C!), and use this as input to a C program that selects the $p$ satisfying (5.3). Then checking (5.2) for these $p$ in *Mathematica*. This method can check $10,000$ primes in around 10 minutes on a Sun3 computer.

The C program computes $x^2 \bmod p$ differently depending on how close $p$ is to $2^{31} - 1$. The smaller $p$ is, the more efficiently this is computed.

```
#include <stdio.h>

main()

{int a, b, p, j, t, x, y, u, m;
 short i;

while (scanf("%d", &p) != EOF)
{if (p % 3 != 1) continue;
   a = 3; b = 2; j = 1; t = 1;
   while(a != 0)
             {if(a == b && t != j) break;
if ((2 * a) > p) m = p - a; else m = a;
if ((m >> 15) == 0) a = (m * m - a + 1) % p;

/*             p < 2^22                */

else if ((p >> 22) == 0)
  {y = m >> 7; x = m & 00000000177;
    a = (x * x  + ((x * y) << 8) +
    (((((y * y) % p) << 7) % p) << 7) - a + 1) % p;}

/*      '      p < 2^24                */

else    if ((p >> 24) == 0)
  {y = m >> 9; x = m & 00000000777;
    a = (x * x  + ((((x * y) << 5) % p) << 5)  +
   (((((((((y * y) % p) << 5) % p) << 5) % p)
                          << 5) % p) << 3)
        - a + 1) % p;}
```

```
/*          p < sqrt(2) 2^25, about 47 million  */

else
        {y = m >> 10;  x = m & 00000001777;
        u = y * y;
        for (i = 1; i <= 5; i++) {u %= p; u <<= 4;};
        a = (x * x  +
                ((((((x * y) << 4) % p) << 4) % p) << 3)
                     + u - a + 1) % p;}
             j++;
             if (j == 2 * t + 1) {t = j; b = a; }};
        if (a == 0)   printf("%d  %d  \n", j, p);
}
 }
```

Using these method, one finds 1166 primes $p$ out of the first three million primes (i.e., $p$ smaller than fifty million) which divide a Euclid number. However, none of these divides the Euclid number as a square! This shows that any square dividing a Euclid number must be greater than $2.5 \times 10^{15}$.

The largest value of $e(n)$ shown to be composite is $e(18547)$ which has the prime factor 35135167. The largest prime factor was 49967221 which divides $e(13957)$.

The following lists the pairs $(n, p)$ for $n \le 200$, i.e., the prime factors of $e(n)$, $0 \le n \le 200$ with $p \le 5 \times 10^7$. The list shows that all the $e(n)$, $5 < n \le 17$ are composite, except for $n = 8, 12$. Now

$$e(8) = 128649386832786717405371459983609615466653259485195807$$

and so

```
In[1]:= PrimeQ[e[18]]

Out[2]= False
```

returns very quickly. Moreover, running *Mathematica*'s factoring routine

In[2]:= FactorInteger[e[8], FactorComplete -> False]

Out[2]= {{5295435634831, 1},
      {24294391567445134205709156478940842221297, 1}}

(This only runs in V2.0 since one needs at least the Pollard-$\rho$ method
to obtain this factorization.) The 40 digit cofactor is also composite,
but is harder to factor (Exercise 5.5).

One must be slightly more careful if one wants to check that $e(12)$
is composite since $e(12) \approx 5.6 \times 10^{833}$. Instead of using PrimeQ one
checks whether PowerMod[2, e[12]-1, e[12]] == 1. This takes only
a couple of minutes to return False which proves compositeness (one
can speed this up by using the MyPowerMod function of Section 1.2).

The following list therefore extends by one the set of composite $e_n$
given in [49, p. 108] up to $n = 17$ (the definition of $e(n)$ in [49] is
denoted by $e(n-1)$ here). By running the recurrence directly mod $p$,
$p < 200,000,000$, I have checked that $e_{18}$ and $e_{19}$ are not divisible by
any prime less than $2 \times 10^8$.

| 0 | 2 | 45 | 51769 | 114 | 473611 |
|---|---|----|-------|-----|--------|
| 1 | 3 | 47 | 429547 | 115 | 6906223 |
| 2 | 7 | 53 | 9829 | 116 | 148207 |
| 3 | 43 | 59 | 2029 | 117 | 17977 |
| 4 | 13 | 59 | 38329 | 119 | 54919 |
| 4 | 139 | 59 | 320329 | 123 | 1944721 |
| 5 | 3263443 | 59 | 3567469 | 126 | 32779 |
| 6 | 547 | 61 | 50023 | 130 | 26778949 |
| 6 | 607 | 64 | 1459 | 131 | 36680803 |
| 6 | 1033 | 64 | 11234941 | 136 | 27031 |
| 6 | 31051 | 65 | 72091 | 137 | 8221 |
| 7 | 29881 | 65 | 609421 | 137 | 149197 |
| 7 | 67003 | 67 | 245563 | 139 | 46380739 |
| 7 | 9119521 | 67 | 3346633 | 140 | 6469 |
| 9 | 181 | 68 | 6367063 | 141 | 6886081 |
| 9 | 1987 | 69 | 12763 | 142 | 1182253 |
| 10 | 2287 | 70 | 384061 | 142 | 2211019 |
| 10 | 2271427 | 71 | 3799489 | 144 | 615721 |

| | | | | | |
|---|---|---|---|---|---|
| 11 | 73 | 71 | 8401963 | 145 | 2564857 |
| 13 | 52387 | 73 | 11844787 | 146 | 13147 |
| 13 | 5020387 | 74 | 35869 | 146 | 8186719 |
| 14 | 13999 | 75 | 20161 | 148 | 7205893 |
| 14 | 74203 | 75 | 42428887 | 151 | 2686393 |
| 14 | 9638659 | 76 | 123427 | 156 | 232051 |
| 15 | 17881 | 79 | 51973 | 161 | 64621 |
| 16 | 128551 | 80 | 2437 | 161 | 1530229 |
| 17 | 635263 | 82 | 6230971 | 161 | 8244391 |
| 17 | 1286773 | 86 | 9436201 | 166 | 1763911 |
| 17 | 21269959 | 88 | 151477 | 169 | 695131 |
| 20 | 352867 | 89 | 41077 | 170 | 215899 |
| 23 | 74587 | 89 | 2171593 | 172 | 35099257 |
| 26 | 27061 | 92 | 15373 | 173 | 839437 |
| 27 | 164299 | 92 | 21661 | 176 | 31159 |
| 27 | 3229081 | 92 | 1386013 | 176 | 28384141 |
| 28 | 20929 | 94 | 12593197 | 180 | 57853 |
| 29 | 1171 | 95 | 535879 | 183 | 107053 |
| 29 | 298483 | 96 | 1407223 | 184 | 60919 |
| 31 | 1679143 | 98 | 20479 | 184 | 505123 |
| 34 | 120823 | 100 | 537037 | 185 | 39360469 |
| 34 | 447841 | 103 | 4519 | 188 | 7948981 |
| 35 | 2408563 | 104 | 13291 | 193 | 12436189 |
| 36 | 38218903 | 105 | 9123469 | 194 | 80173 |
| 37 | 333457 | 106 | 97549 | 194 | 11073379 |
| 38 | 30241 | 107 | 1101733 | 197 | 562909 |
| 39 | 4219 | 108 | 297589 | 198 | 13163791 |
| 40 | 1085443 | 108 | 549733 | 198 | 24518173 |
| 41 | 7603 | 110 | 943567 | 199 | 19597 |
| 42 | 1861 | 111 | 1285633 | 199 | 150649 |
| 44 | 23773 | 113 | 132637 | 200 | 765241 |
| 44 | 290791 | 113 | 45352921 | | |

**Exercise 5.5 [P]** (F. Morain)
Factor 242943915674451342057091564789408422129 7.

## 5.3   American Science

This Section examines the concept of "golygon" discovered and named by L. Sallows. These were studied by M. Gardner, R.K. Guy, and D.E. Knuth [42] and immortalized in the July 1990 Scientific American column "Mathematical Recreations" by A.K. Dewdeney.

A "golygon" is a lattice path in the plane where you start at the origin and move 1 unit to the north or south, then 2 units to the east or west, 3 units to the north or south, etc, always increasing step length by one, and alternating between up and down and sideways, until you come back to the origin (with an even number of steps).

For example the simplest golygon consists of the path

$$(0,0) \Rightarrow (0,1) \Rightarrow (2,1) \Rightarrow (2,-2) \Rightarrow$$
$$(-2,-2) \Rightarrow (-2,-7) \Rightarrow (-8,-7) \Rightarrow (-8,0)$$
$$\Rightarrow (0,0)$$

which forms an eight sided polygon.

The golygon condition can therefore be stated as finding an even integer $n$ such that

(5.4) $$\pm 1 \pm 3 \pm \cdots \pm (n-1) = 0$$

(5.5) $$\pm 2 \pm 4 \pm \cdots \pm n = 0$$

The problem is therefore not really 2-dimensional (these are not simultaneous equations). Note that the definition has left the possibility of the summands $-1$ and $-2$ which increases the number of solutions by a factor of 4, but makes point B. below more symmetric.

The Scientific American article consists mostly of showing that all golygons must have $8k$ sides. This was a conjecture of Sallows and was proved by Martin Gardner.

Actually, showing that $n = 8k$ is true is fairly easy: Condition (5.4) taken $(\bmod 2)$ implies that $n/2$ is even. Dividing (5.5) by 2 implies that

$$\pm 1 \pm 2 \pm \cdots \pm n/2 = 0 \; (\bmod 2)$$

so that the number of odd numbers $< n/2$ is even, which shows that $n/2$ is divisible by 4.

One can easily construct solutions to (5.4) and (5.5) by using the identity

$$1 - 3 - 5 + 7 = 0,$$

since it implies that

$$(n+1) - (n+3) - (n+5) + (n+7) = 0$$

for any integer $n$.

To compute the number of golygons of a certain length one uses the observation of D.E. Knuth [42] that the number of solutions to (5.4) and (5.5) can be computed using generating functions. For example, the number of solutions to (5.4) is the constant term in

$$(5.6) \qquad \left(x + \frac{1}{x}\right)\left(x^3 + \frac{1}{x^3}\right)\cdots\left(x^{n-1} + \frac{1}{x^{n-1}}\right).$$

To see this observe that expanding this product out gives the sum of all terms

$$x^{\pm 1}x^{\pm 3}\cdots x^{\pm(n-1)} = x^{\pm 1 \pm 3 \pm \cdots \pm (n-1)}$$

so the coefficient of $x^k$ gives the number of solutions to

$$\pm 1 \pm 3 \pm \cdots \pm (n-1) = k.$$

Expanding (5.6) by writing

$$\left(x^k + \frac{1}{x^k}\right) = \frac{1}{x^{2k}}\left(1 + x^{2k}\right)$$

gives

$$\frac{1}{x^{1+3+5+\cdots+n-1}}(1 + x^2)(1 + x^6)\cdots(1 + x^{2(n-1)})$$

which, on noting that

$$1 + 3 + 5 + \cdots + n - 1 = \frac{n^2}{4}$$

can be written as

$$(5.7) \qquad \frac{1}{x^{n^2/4}} (1+x^2)(1+x^6) \cdots (1+x^{2(n-1)}).$$

The coefficient of the constant term in (5.6) is therefore the coefficient of $x^{n^2/4}$ in (5.7). Finally, since all the terms in (5.7) are powers of $x^2$, one can let $x \to \sqrt{x}$ to get that the coefficient of $x^{n^2/4}$ in (5.7) is the coefficient of $x^{n^2/8}$ in

$$(1+x)(1+x^3) \cdots (1+x^{n-1}).$$

Similarly, the number of solutions to (5.5) is the coefficient of $x^{n(n/2+1)/8}$ in

$$(1+x)(1+x^2) \cdots (1+x^{n/2}).$$

This analysis can be summarized as

**Theorem.** *The number of golygons of length $n$, $n$ even, (with every initial direction counted as different) is the product of the coefficient of $x^{n^2/8}$ in*

$$(1+x)(1+x^3) \cdots (1+x^{n-1})$$

*with the coefficient of $x^{n(n/2+1)/8}$ in*

$$(1+x)(1+x^2) \cdots (1+x^{n/2}).$$

Since *Mathematica* has built-in polynomial arithmetic this can be easily implemented

```
GolygonNumber[n_]:=
Coefficient[Expand[
     Times @@ (1 + x^Range[n/2]), x, n (n/2+1)/8]] *
Coefficient[Expand[
     Times @@ (1 + x^Range[1, n-1, 2]), x, n^2/8]] \;
     n < 250
```

For example it only takes a couple of minutes to compute

```
In[1]:= GolygonNumber[64]

Out[1]=  510696155882492

In[2]:= solutions[200]

Out[2]= 15094388394882262487936954 2821
>          315428093031043194977 3968
```

Computing larger values has extensive memory requirements due to symbolic computations involving polynomials so one must use some other method. An efficient alternative is to use a modular method i.e., evaluate all the polynomials (mod $p$) for the an initial set of primes and then reconstruct the answer using the Chinese remainder theorem. This has the further advantage that the computational intensive steps can be done in small precision arithmetic, i.e., in C. Generating the primes and reconstructing the solution is done very easily in *Mathematica* and using the program below one obtains for example

```
In[3]:= GolygonNumber[400]

Out[3]= 30570282505903591014509519 3455<
          12930202078980538433541792 4922<
          1105980639338 9155773047468813<
          8636122581265015300957624

In[4]:= GolygonNumber[1000]

Out[4]= 81587626119077969765846115 7552<
          23755335925199901868109678 2768<
          74056977730002764168651730 5095<
          26416239097618592883244411 2053<
          27644821305531145546445802 4858<
          99122746285874596340551638 8565<
          76631488366840003652093037 2500<
```

```
67281388974398727787786033159<
61845759531468328878271466144<
0018765080207563965235
```

Here is the *Mathematica* and C code for solution[1000]. You first generate the file "primelist" by running PrimeList[1000]. This file contains a sufficient number of primes to compute solution[1000] using the Chinese remainer theorem (one needs the bound given by Exercise 5.6). The next step is to use this file as input for the C program and then output the result to a file "primesolutions". In the Unix operating system this is easily done by the command

```
%cprogram < primelist > primesolutions
```

Finally, one inputs the file "primesolutions" into *Mathematica* and then runs ChineseRemainderTheorem on it. The *Mathematica* part of the code is

```
PrimeList[n_]:=
Block[{i, product = 1, x},
      For[i = 1, product <=  2^n, i++,
          product *= Prime[i];
          Prime[i] >>> "primelist"]]

ChineseRemainderTheorem:=
Block[{sum = 0, product, i, a},
 prime = ReadList["primesolutions", {Number, Number}];
 product = Times @@ (First /@ prime);
 For[i = 1, i <= Length[prime], i++,
    a = Quotient[product, prime[[i, 1]]];
    If[prime[[i, 2]] == 0, Continue[],
    sum +=
      prime[[i, 2]]  PowerMod[a, -1, prime[[i, 1]]] a]
];
Mod[sum, product]]
```

Writing the C program is not exceedingly difficult but you do have to convert the polynomial multiplication method into a non symbolic

method. Because of the simplicity of the polynomials involved this is
very easy. Here is a non-modular *Mathematica* program which uses the
C method to compute the number of solutions.

```
RotateRightD[list_, n_]:=
Join[Table[0, {n}], Drop[RotateRight[list, n], n]]

GolygonNumberC[n_]:=
Block[{a, b, i, t1, t2},
      t1 = n (n/2 + 1)/8; t2 = n^2/8;
      a = Prepend[Table[0, {t1}], 1];
      b = Prepend[Table[0, {t2}], 1];
      For[i = 1, i <= n/2, i++,
          a += RotateRightD[a, i];
          b += RotateRightD[b, 2 i -1]];
      a[[t1+1]] b[[t2+1]]]]
```

Note that `RotateRightD` is a right shift which destroys elements instead
of wrapping around the left.

The following is the C program for $n = 1000$.

```
#include <stdio.h>
#include <math.h>

main()

{int   p, i, j, n, min;
 int a[130000], b[130000];

while (scanf("%d", &p) != EOF)
{for (i = 1; i <= 130000; i++) {a[i] = 0; b[i] = 0;};
 a[0] = 1; b[0] = 1;
n = 1000;
for (i = 1; i <= (n/2); i++)
  {if (4 * i * i < (n * (n /2  + 1)/8))
        min = 4 * i * i + 2;
      else min = n * (n / 2 + 1)/8;
```

```
for (j = min; j >= i; j--)
    a[j] = (a[j] +  a[j - i]) % p ;
if (4 * i * i < (n * n /8)) min = 4 * i * i + 2;
else min = n * n /8 + 2;
for (j = min; j >= (2 * i - 1); j--)
b[j] = (b[j] +  b[j - ((2 * i) - 1)]) % p ;
 };
  printf("%d %d \n", p,
         (a[n * (n/2 + 1)/8] * b[(n * n) / 8]) % p);
}}
```

**Exercise 5.6 [HM]** (R.K. Guy [42]) Show that the number of golygons of length $n$ is asymptotic to

$$\frac{3 \cdot 2^{8n-4}}{\pi\, n^2(4n+1)}.$$

## 5.4   Wieferich

First some remarks about what level of efficiency one needs in order to make a serious search for more Wieferich primes, i.e., increase the record by a factor of two at least. The present record is $6 \cdot 10^9$, so a factor of 2 would represent checking another $6 \cdot 10^9$ numbers. Now assuming that a month of computer time is realistic, this would require being able to check about 8 million numbers an hour. It turns out that the size of numbers in this range are awkward for *Mathematica* to handle and the best we have been able to obtain is 250,000 numbers an hour. The numbers in this range are too large for a direct implementation in C (see Exercis 5.8) but Lisp has infinite precision arithmetic, and, unlike *Mathematica*, it can be compiled to reduce overhead. Included below is a Lisp implementation of a Wieferich search algorithm that achieves the rate of a million numbers per hour. This program would therefore take about 8 months to check the conjecture up to $12 \cdot 10^9$.

**Remark:** This program has not been run for any extended period of time so I leave the search for Wieferich primes to readers with a lot of free computer time, or with a surplus of machines (the search can be done in parallel on many machines in order to reduce running time).

The program is based on the method of [13]. The first point is to test only primes. In order to approximate this, one does a sieve by $2, 3, 5, 7, 11, 13, 17, 19, 23$ which means you only look at 16% of all numbers. This still leaves you with roughly 3.7 times the number of real primes when you are around $10^9$, so [13] do a pseudo prime test $2^{n-1} \equiv 1 \pmod{n}$ before checking $\pmod{n^2}$.

It turns out that one can actually calculate whether the extra pseudo prime test makes sense: One wants to compare the cost of testing $2^n \equiv 1 \pmod{n}$ before doing $2^n \pmod{n^2}$, so let $2^n \pmod{n^2}$ have unit cost on average in this range, and denote the average cost of $2^n \pmod{n}$ by $x$.

Now the percentage of numbers surviving the sieve is about

$$\frac{1}{2} \times \frac{2}{3} \times \cdots \times \frac{22}{23} \approx .163588$$

which is computed easily by

```
Times @@ (1 - 1/N[Prime[Range[9]]])
```

Since passing the $(\bmod\, n)$ test will essentially only return primes, one compares the efficiency of the combined $n, n^2$ method to the $n^2$ method by using the fact that, by the Prime Number Theorem, the probability that $n$ is prime in the neighborhood of $6 \cdot 10^9$ is about

$$\frac{1}{\log(6 \cdot 10^9)} \approx .044441$$

So the average cost of the combined test per number is

$$x + \frac{.044441}{.163588},$$

and the break even point occurs when this quantity is one, i.e., when $x \approx .728336$. Thus it makes sense to pretest $(\bmod\, n)$ only if this can be done 27% faster than the $(\bmod\, n^2)$ test. For the Lisp implementation below testing $2^n \pmod{n}$ was only about 10% faster so it was not used in the final program.

## 5.4.1   The program

*Mathematica* has a difficult time with this problem since the numbers are too small for the built-in functions to really kick in. A *Mathematica* implementation on a Risc machine could only check about $250,000$ numbers per hour (Exercise 5.7). Being able to compile the program is a big advantage in this range and the following Lisp program is able to check about a million primes an hour using Allegro Common Lisp on a NeXT machine.

The most important factor in the efficiency of arithmetic operations is whether these are done using primitive hardware operations (fixnums) or by a software routine (bignums), so one tries to maximize the number of fixnum operations versus bignum operations. On almost all computers the cutoff occurs at about $2^{32}$ and one tries to restrict as many operations to numbers smaller than this. The program below was written in Allegro Common Lisp which has $2^{29} - 1$ as its most positive fixnum (`most-positive-fixnum`).

The program checks for Wieferich primes in the range $m \leq p \leq n$ using the 9 prime sieve and checking whether

$$2^{p-1} \equiv 1 \; (\mathrm{mod}\, p^2)$$

on the survivors. The program has the following features

1. The 9 prime sieve can be done quickly by iterating modulo the small primes and only getting into bignums if you survive the sieve.

2. You can compute $2^n \; (\mathrm{mod}\, n^2)$ more quickly than by a direct `PowerMod` algorithm (Exercise 5.8) since multiplying by powers of 2 is just binary shifts. One can therefore use the analog of the `MyPowerMod` program of Section 1.2 to speed up this operation, since doing a binary shift is just as cheap an operation as table lookup. This wins a factor of 33% on average.

3. One can save a single multiplication as follows. Since $n - 1$ is even, checking for
$$2^{n-1} \equiv 1 \; (\mathrm{mod}\, n)$$

is equivalent to checking that

$$2^{(n-1)/2} \equiv \pm 1 \ (\mathrm{mod}\, n)$$

in other words, that

$$2^{(n-1)/2} + 1 \equiv \begin{cases} 2 \\ 0 \end{cases} \quad (\mathrm{mod}\, n).$$

This only saves one multiplication out of 30, but is so easy to implement and does not complicate the program.

```
; First set up array of numbers PHI210
; relatively prime to 210. Next get BOT
; which is the largest multiple of 210 < m.
; We will check divisibility by
; 11, 13, 17, 19, 23, so you set up an array
; of values of BOT mod these primes,
; and then increase by 210 at every
; iteration (MODCHECK).
;
;;;;; (wieferich m n) tests for any solutions
;;;;; of 2^(p-1) = 1 (mod p^2) for m <= p <= n.
;;;;;

(defun wieferich (m n)

  (setf BOT (* 210 (floor (/ m 210))))
  (setf TOP (+ (floor (/ (- n m) 210)) 1))

;; How much to iterate.

  (setf PHI210 (make-array '(48)
    :initial-contents
   '(1 11 13 17 19 23 29 31 37
     41 43 47 53 59 61 67 71
     73 79 83 89 97 101 103
     107 109 113 121 127 131
```

```
      137 139 143 149 151 157
      163 167 169 173 179 181
      187 191 193 197 199 209)))
   (setf PRIMES (make-array '(5)
     :initial-contents '(11 13 17 19 23)))
   (setf MODCHECK (make-array '(5)))
   (setf FLAG NIL)
   (setf TEMP NIL)
;
;    Beginning of program
;
;    Initialize MODCHECK
;
   (do ((j 0 (1+ j))) ((= j 5))
    (setf (aref MODCHECK j)
          (mod bot (aref primes j))))


;
;;    The main loop
;
   (do ((i 0 (1+ i))) ((or FLAG (> i TOP)))
    (cond ((zerop (mod i 100)) (print i)) (T Nil))
    (do ((j 0 (1+ j))) ((or FLAG (= j 48)))
     (setf TEMP (aref PHI210 j))
;; Don't recompute array element
     (setf FLAG
        (not (or
   (zerop (mod (+ TEMP (aref MODCHECK 0)) 2))
   (zerop (mod (+ TEMP (aref MODCHECK 1)) 3))
   (zerop (mod (+ TEMP (aref MODCHECK 2)) 5))
   (zerop (mod (+ TEMP (aref MODCHECK 3)) 7))
   (zerop (mod (+ TEMP (aref MODCHECK 4)) 11))
   (cond ((zerop alt) Nil)
          (T (pms (+ BOT (* 210 i) TEMP) 1)))
     (pms (+ BOT (* 210 i) TEMP) 2))))
   (cond (FLAG (setf ANSWER (+ BOT (* 210 i) TEMP))
          (setf j 5) (setf i (1+ TOP))) (T Nil)))
```

```
    (do ((j 0 (1+ j))) ((= j 5))
        (setf (aref MODCHECK j)
    (mod (+ (aref MODCHECK j) 210) (aref primes j)))))
    (cond (FLAG (print Answer)) (T Nil))
)
;
; pms is a specialized PowerMod to compute
; 2^p-1 (mod p^2). It uses the MyPowerMod
; algorithm of Section 1.2.
;
; You save one multiplication by checking whether
; (powermod 2 (p-1)/2  (p or p^2)) = 1 or -1.
;
; So the most efficient check is whether
;
;   2^((p-1)/2) + 1 != 0,2 (mod p or p^2)


(defun pms (p exp)              ;; exp = 1 or 2
  (let* ((ptemp Nil)
         (psq (expt p exp))
 (p-1 (ash (1- p) -1))
 (power (mod (ash 1 (* 64
            (logand (ash p-1  -30) 63))) PSQ)))
    (do ((k -24 (+ k 6))) ((= k 0))
    (setf power (ash power (logand (ash p-1 k) 63)))
(do ((s 1 (1+ s))) ((> s 6))
;;;
;;; This has evaluated (powermod Power 64 PSQ)
;;;

    (setf power (mod (* power power) psq)))
    )
  (setf ptemp (mod (1+ (ash power
          (logand p-1 63))) psq))
  (not (or (equalp ptemp 0)
          (equalp ptemp 2)))))
```

**Exercise 5.7** [P] Write the program `wieferich` in *Mathematica*.

**Exercise 5.8** [P] Implement `PowerMod` in Lisp.

**Exercise 5.9** [P] [M] ([13]) Implement the test $2^{n-1} \equiv 1 \pmod{n^2}$ efficiently.

## 5.5   Notes

A good reference to the material in this Chapter is the book *Computers in Number Theory* [3]. Especially relevant is D.H. Lehmer's article *The Economics of Number Theoretic Computation* [79].

The following implementation of Pollard's $\rho$ method is based on the exposition in [12, Section 5.3]. Note that the `FactorInteger` function V2.0 of *Mathematica* uses this implementation of the Pollard-$\rho$ method. This should be able to factor in reasonable time any number with less than 30 digits

```
PollardRho[n_]:= PollardRho[n, 2]  /; !PrimeQ[n]

PollardRho[n_, c_]:=
  Block[{x1 = 2, x2 = 2^2 + c, i = 0, j, gcd,
         max = Min[Round[2 Power[N[n], 1/4]],
                   3 10^7],
         range = 1, prod = 1, factor = 1},
        While[i <= max && factor == 1,
              For[j = 1,
                  j <= range && factor == 1,
                  j++,
                  x2 = Mod[x2^2 + c, n];
                  prod = Mod[prod (x1 - x2), n];
                  If[prod == 0,
                      gcd = GCD[x1 - x2, n];
                             If[1 < gcd < n,
                                factor = gcd;
                                Break[]]];
```

```
            i++;
            If[Mod[i, 10] == 0,
                gcd = GCD[n, prod];
                If[1 < gcd < n, factor = gcd;
                                Break[],
                                prod = 1]]];
        x1 = x2; range *= 2;
        x2 = Nest[Mod[#^2 + c, n]&, x2, range]];
    If[factor > 1, factor, PollardRho[n, c+1]]]]
```

D.E. Knuth has written a short Macsyma program to implement the generating function method for counting golygons evaluating their number up to $n = 64$.

R. Schroeppel has noted that using the sieve of Erathostenes to produce only primes in a certain range is more efficient than using the 9 prime sieve.

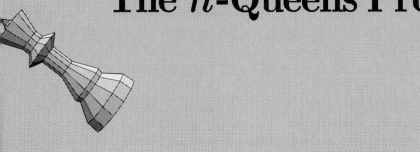

# 6

# The $n$-Queens Problem

# Chapter 6

# The $n$-Queens Problem

A canonical homework assignment in introductory programming classes is to compute how many ways eight queens can be arranged on a chess board so that no two queens attack each other. In other words, how to put eight elements on an $8 \times 8$ grid so that no two are on the same row, column or diagonal.

The technique (usually outlined on the problem sheet) is to construct all solutions by the use of *backtracking* which basically eliminates subconfigurations which do not result in a completed solution.

Obviously this problem can be generalized to an $n \times n$ chessboard though it turns out that showing that even *one* solution exists is somewhat nontrivial. The disadvantage of the backtracking method is that its running time will be at least the total number of solutions, which could be very large, and backtracking can be very very inefficient, for example, the related problem of nonattacking *rooks* on a $n \times n$ chessboard which has exactly $n!$ solutions. Recently, an algebraic algorithm for computing the number of queens solutions was proposed by I. Rivin and R. Zabih [104], which is theoretically faster than backtracking, modulo some conjectures on the number of queens solutions [105].

The algebraic methods of [104] can be reduced to the computation of a *permanent*. A permanent is similar to a determinant but where all the signs are positive, for example

$$
\text{perm} \begin{pmatrix} a_{11} & a_{12} & a_{13} \\ a_{21} & a_{22} & a_{23} \\ a_{31} & a_{32} & a_{33} \end{pmatrix}
$$

$$
= a_{11}a_{22}a_{33} + a_{11}a_{32}a_{23} + a_{21}a_{13}a_{33}
$$

$$
+ a_{21}a_{32}a_{13} + a_{31}a_{22}a_{13} + a_{31}a_{12}a_{23} \, .
$$

Note that each term can be thought of generating a $3 \times 3$ rook solution, in the sense that the subscripts give the coordinates of three nonattacking rooks on a $3 \times 3$ chessboard. The basic observation, due to S. Günther in 1874, is that if $x_1, \ldots, x_{2n}, y_1, \ldots, y_{2n}$ are independent variables then the number of queens solution is the sum of the coefficients of the squarefree terms in the permanent

$$
\text{perm}\,(x_{i+j}y_{i-j}), \qquad i = 1, \ldots, n, \; j = 1, \ldots, n \, .
$$

To see this note that, as before, each term in the expansion of the permanent represents a rook solution, and each squarefree term represents a rook solution in which no two rooks at $(i_1, j_1)$ and $(i_2, j_2)$ have $i_1 + j_1 = i_2 + j_2$ or $i_1 - j_1 = i_2 - j_2$, which are exactly the conditions that the rooks are not on the same positive or negative diagonals, i.e., that the solution is also a queens solution.

This can be implemented in *Mathematica* as follows. First, one adds the rule that every power of $x(i, j)$ is immediately reduced to zero (this will save many intermediate terms in the result).

```
In[1]:= x /:  x[__]^_:= 0
```

Next, one sets up the matrix using the `Array` (I have let $n = 5$ to show how the computation progresses)

```
In[2]:= Array[x[#1 - #2,1] x[#1 + #2,2]&, {5, 5}]

Out[2]= {{x[0, 1] x[2, 2], x[-1, 1] x[3, 2],
```

```
    x[-2, 1] x[4, 2], x[-3, 1] x[5, 2],
    x[-4, 1] x[6, 2]},
   {x[1, 1] x[3, 2], x[0, 1] x[4, 2],
    x[-1, 1] x[5, 2], x[-2, 1] x[6, 2],
    x[-3, 1] x[7, 2]},
   {x[2, 1] x[4, 2], x[1, 1] x[5, 2],
    x[0, 1] x[6, 2], x[-1, 1] x[7, 2],
    x[-2, 1] x[8, 2]},
   {x[3, 1] x[5, 2], x[2, 1] x[6, 2],
    x[1, 1] x[7, 2], x[0, 1] x[8, 2],
    x[-1, 1] x[9, 2]},
   {x[4, 1] x[6, 2], x[3, 1] x[7, 2],
    x[2, 1] x[8, 2], x[1, 1] x[9, 2],
    x[0, 1] x[10, 2]}}
```

and one evaluates the permanent of this

```
In[3]:= Permanent[%]

Out[4]= 2 x[-4, 1] x[-1, 1] x[0, 1] x[2, 1] x[3, 1] *
          x[4, 2] x[5, 2] x[6, 2] x[7, 2] x[8, 2] +
        2 x[-3, 1] x[-2, 1] x[0, 1] x[1, 1] x[4, 1] *
          x[4, 2]  x[5, 2] x[6, 2] x[7, 2] x[8, 2] +
        2 x[-3, 1] x[-1, 1] x[0, 1] x[1, 1] x[3, 1] *
          x[3, 2] x[5, 2] x[6, 2] x[7, 2] x[9, 2] +
        2 x[-2, 1] x[-1, 1] x[0, 1] x[1, 1] x[2, 1] *
          x[2, 2]  x[5, 2] x[6, 2] x[8, 2] x[9, 2] +
        2 x[-2, 1] x[-1, 1] x[0, 1] x[1, 1] x[2, 1] *
          x[3, 2] x[4, 2] x[6, 2] x[7, 2] x[10, 2]
```

Finally, one lets all the $x(i,j)$ terms go to one

```
In[5]:= % /. x[__]-> 1

Out[5]= 10
```

The program is therefore given by

```
x /:  x[__]^_ := 0
```

```
Queens[n_]:=
Expand[Permanent[
        Array[x[#1 - #2, 1] x[#1 + #2, 2]&,
              {n,n}]]] /. x[__]-> 1
```

This program will run in time about $16^n$ since evaluation of the permanent by the methods of the next section takes $2^n$ multiplications, and one is multiplying polynomials in $2n$ variables of degree $\leq 2n$, so that there are at most $2^{2n}$ terms, so a multiplication takes time $8^n$.

**Exercise 6.1 [P]** Write a short *Mathematica* program to generate all $n \times n$ queens solutions.

## 6.1   Permanents

For the program Queens to run, one needs an an implementation of the permanent function. For the algorithm to run in reasonable time, one needs an efficient evaluation of the permanent. Indeed one can improve on $n!$ operations to $2^n$ operations as can be seen by the following method: perm $(a_{ij})$ is the coefficient of $x_1 \cdots x_n$ in

$$(6.1)\qquad\qquad \prod_{i=1}^{n}(a_{i1}x_1 + a_{i2}x_2 + \cdots + a_{in}x_n).$$

This can be implemented as

```
y /: y[_]^_ = 0
```

```
Permanent1[a_]:=
Expand[Times @@ (y /@ Range[Length[a]] . #& /@ a)] /.
       y[_] -> 1
```

This method will take about $2^n$ multiplications but has the disadvantage that the partial results are polynomials in the variables $y_1, \ldots, y_n$ and so there will be up to $\binom{n}{\lfloor n/2 \rfloor} \approx 2^n/\sqrt{n}$ terms in the partial results, so a great deal of memory is required. The use of symbolic algebra, i.e., polynomials instead of just arithmetic operations, will slow you down as well.

A more efficient method relies on the *Ryser formula* for permanents [66, page 497]. This formula is

$$\text{perm}\,(a_{ij}) = (-1)^n \sum_{s \subseteq \{1,\ldots,n\}} (-1)^{|s|} \prod_{i=1}^{n} \sum_{j \in s} a_{ij}$$

where the sum is over all subsets $s$ of $\{1,\ldots,n\}$, and $|s|$ denotes the number of elements in $s$.

This method also takes $2^n$ steps but only uses storage $n$. A direct implementation of this can be done rather elegantly in *Mathematica*

```
Permanent2[a_]:=
  (-1)^Length[a] Plus @@
  ((-1)^Length[#] Times @@ Plus @@ a[[#]]& /@
  Subsets[Range[Length[a]]])
```

One can improve on this by choosing the subsets of $\{1,\ldots,n\}$ in such a way that only one element is ever added or deleted. In this way only $n$ additions per set will occur, instead of $n^2$ additions. Choosing subsets in such a way is called the *Gray code*. The Gray code occurs in many recreational problems such as the Tower of Hanoi or the Chinese rings [38, Chapter 2]. For example, if the Tower of Hanoi consists of $n$ disks numbered $1, 2, \ldots, n$ from smallest to largest, then the disk moved in step $k$ is the same as the element that needs to be added or deleted in the $k$th summand of the Ryser formula (see [41, pages 180–182] for generalizations of this).

There is a simple formula that computes which element has to be moved at step $k$: write $k = 2^{j-1}\,q$, where $q$ is odd and $j \geq 1$. Then element $j$ is moved and is inserted if $q-1$ is divisible by four, and deleted otherwise. Writing the ordered pair $\{j, \pm 1\}$ to mean that element $j$ is moved and inserted if the second element is 1 and deleted if it's $-1$, a program is given by

```
GrayInsert[n_]:=
Block[{q = n, j = 1},
      While[EvenQ[q], q /= 2; j++];
        {j, (-1)^((q-1)/2)}]
```

Using this function one has the program

```
Permanent[a_]:=
Block[{d = Length[a],
       i, rowsum, sum = 0, j = 1},
       rowsum = Table[0, {d}];
       Do[gi = GrayInsert[i];
          rowsum += gi[[2]] m[[gi[[1]]]];
          sum += (-1)^i (Times @@ rowsum);
          {i, 2^d-1}];
       (-1)^d sum]
```

**Exercise 6.2 [P]** Write a program `Gray[n]` which lists the subsets of $\{1, 2, \ldots, n\}$ in Gray code order.

## 6.2  Toroidal Semiqueens

Now it turns out a more tractable problem than the ordinary queens problem is the *toroidal* $n$ queens problem. Consider an $n \times n$ chess board, $n$ odd, a toroidal queen is a piece that moves like a rook and like a bishop on positive and negative broken diagonals, i.e., wraps around the board. The diagonals now contain $n$ elements each and are all of the same type (i.e., are just like rows and columns). The reason why this is easier is that one can use modular arithmetic $\bmod n$, and give the characterization of a solution with coordinates $(i, f(i))$, $i = 1, \ldots, n$,

**(i)** $i \mapsto f(i)$ is a one to one map,

**(ii)** $i \mapsto f(i) - i \bmod n$ is a one to one map,

**(iii)** $i \mapsto f(i) + i \bmod n$ is a one to one map

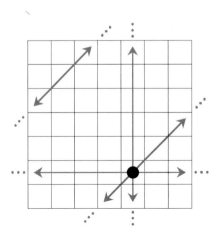

Figure 6.1: Toroidal semiqueen

For example, a simple program to generate all toroidal solutions on an $n \times n$ board is

```
ToroidalQueens[n_]:=
Block[{r = Range[n]},
      Select[Permutations[Range[n]],
             Mod[# - r, n] == Mod[# + r, n] == r&]]
```

and using the method below one has a time $8^n$ algorithm to generate all toroidal solutions.

It turns out that the $n$-queens and toroidal queens problems have received a lot of attention so, to be different, I will instead examine the question for a new chess piece, the *toroidal semiqueens*, which moves like a rook and like a bishop but only on positive broken diagonals (see Figure 6.1). One writes $S(n)$ for the number of toroidal semiqueens solutions on an $n \times n$ chessboard.

As before one can compute $S(n)$ using permanents, and in fact this is simply the constant term in

$$\text{perm}\,(y_{i-j \bmod n}) \qquad 0 \le i, j < n\,,$$

where $y_0, \ldots, y_{n-1}$ are independent variables. The matrix $(x_{i-j \bmod n})$ has the property that each row is a cyclic shift of the previous row, for example if $n = 5$,

$$\begin{pmatrix} y_0 & y_1 & y_2 & y_3 & y_4 \\ y_4 & y_0 & y_1 & y_2 & y_3 \\ y_3 & y_4 & y_0 & y_1 & y_2 \\ y_2 & y_3 & y_4 & y_0 & y_1 \\ y_1 & y_2 & y_3 & y_4 & y_0 \end{pmatrix}.$$

These matrices have many interesting properties and are referred to as a *circulant matrix* in the literature. I will denote the circulant matrix with first row $(y_0, \ldots, y_{n-1})$ by $\mathrm{circ}\,(y_0, \ldots, y_{n-1})$.

The above permanent program for ordinary queens can be adapted to count toroidal semiqueens, and will take about $4^n$ multiplications. One can use the greater amount of symmetry due to the fact the problem is on a torus to speed up the algorithm. The method is intriguing in that it uses the `PowerMod` algorithm in an unexpected context.

One uses the formula (6.1) to compute the permanent

$$\mathrm{perm}\,(\mathrm{circ}\,(y_0, \ldots, y_{n-1}))$$

so that, introducing the independent variables $x_0, \ldots, x_{n-1}$, one computes the squarefree term in

$$\prod_{i=0}^{n-1} \sum_{j=0}^{n-1} y_{i-j \bmod n} x_j.$$

Note that, as one expands the permanent row by row, the partial products represent the product of the first $k$ rows, for $k < n$, and so the fact that the rows are cyclic shifts of each other implies that the partial product of any consecutive $k$ rows is just a cyclic shift of the first $k$ rows product. This means that one essentially can do repeated squaring to evaluate the permanent (using the first method above).

By Exercise 6.3, there are no solutions for even $n$, so a program is given by

```
(* keep only squarefree terms *)
```

```
x /: x[_]^_:= 0; y /: y[_]^_:= 0

ToroidalSemiQueens[n_]:= 0     /; EvenQ[n]

ToroidalSemiQueens[n_]:=
Block[{poly =
      (x /@ Range[0,n-1]) . (y /@ Range[0, n-1]),
        digits=Digits[n, 2], num = 1, j},
        For[i = 2, i <= Length[digits], i++,
    poly = Expand[poly (poly /.
        Table[y[j] -> y[Mod[j + num, n]],{j,0,n-1}])];
    num *= 2;
    If[digits[[i]] == 1,
       poly = Expand[poly
                    ((x /@ Range[0,n-1]) .
                     (y /@ Mod[Range[0,n-1] + num, n]))];
       num++]];
    poly /. {x[_]-> 1, y[_]->1}
    ]
```

For example on a $5 \times 5$ board, one gets the polynomial by expanding $5 = 2^2 + 1 = 2 \times (2 \times 1) + 1$, i.e., the sequence will be row 1, then rows 1 up to $2 \times 1 = 2$, rows 1 up to $2 \times (2 \times 1) = 4$, and then all rows. By printing out intermediate steps in the computation of semi[5] one has the polynomials

Row 1:

```
x[0] y[0] + x[1] y[1] +x[2] y[2] +
x[3] y[3] + x[4] y[4]
```

Rows 1 to 2:

```
x[0] x[1] y[0] y[2] + x[0] x[2] y[1] y[2]
x[0] x[2] y[0] y[3] + x[1] x[2] y[1] y[3]
x[0] x[3] y[1] y[3] + x[0] x[3] y[0] y[4]
x[1] x[3] y[2] y[3] + x[1] x[3] y[1] y[4]
```

```
x[2] x[3] y[2] y[4] + x[0] x[4] y[1] y[4]
x[1] x[4] y[0] y[1] + x[1] x[4] y[2] y[4]
x[2] x[4] y[0] y[2] + x[2] x[4] y[3] y[4]
x[3] x[4] y[0] y[3]
```

Rows 1 to 4:

```
3 x[0] x[1] x[2] x[3] y[0] y[1] y[2] y[4] +
3 x[0] x[1] x[2] x[4] y[0] y[1] y[3] y[4] +
3 x[0] x[1] x[3] x[4] y[0] y[2] y[3] y[4] +
3 x[0] x[2] x[3] x[4] y[1] y[2] y[3] y[4] +
3 x[1] x[2] x[3] x[4] y[0] y[1] y[2] y[3]
```

Rows 1 to 5

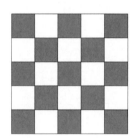

```
15 x[0] x[1] x[2] x[3] x[4] *
   y[0] y[1] y[2] y[3] y[4]
```

and the number of toroidal semiqueen solutions on a 5 × 5 chessboard is 15. These can easily be found using a program similar to `ToroidalQueens` (see Figure 6.2).

The algorithm spends most of its time computing the last squaring operation of a squarefree polynomial of $2n$ and degree $n$. The number of terms in this polynomial is at most $\binom{2n}{n} \approx 4^n$ and so a direct multiplication will take about $8^n$ steps. However, since one only needs to keep the squarefree terms in the product, this multiplication can be done in (essentially) *linear time* as follows. Each term in the polynomial is of the form

$$a_{i_1,i_2,\ldots,i_{(n-1)/2};j_1,j_2,\ldots,j_{(n-1)/2}}\, x_{i_1} x_{i_2} \cdots x_{i_{(n-1)/2}}\, y_{j_1} y_{j_2} \cdots y_{(n-1)/2} \,.$$

The contribution of this term to the squarefree part of the product comes only from being multiplied by the *complementary terms*

$$a_{i'_1,i'_2,\ldots,i'_{(n-1)/2};j'_1,j'_2,\ldots,j'_{(n-1)/2}}\, x_{i'_1} x_{i'_2} \cdots x_{i'_{(n-1)/2}}\, y_{j'_1} y_{j'_2} \cdots y_{j'_{(n-1)/2}} \,,$$

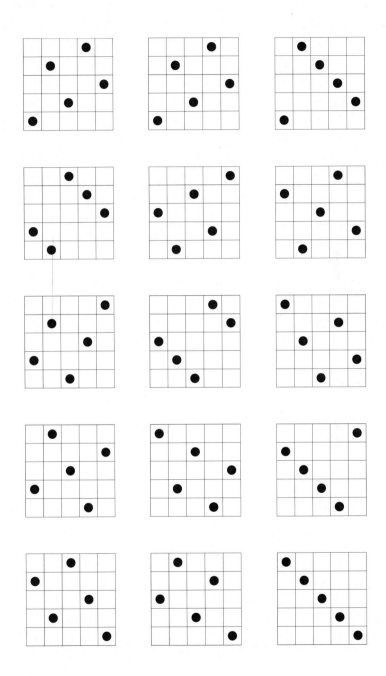

Figure 6.2: Toroidal semiqueens solutions on a $5 \times 5$.

where $i_r \neq i'_s$, $j_r \neq j'_s$, $1 \leq r, s \leq (n-1)/2$. Each term has at most $n$ complementary terms. Moreover, these can can be found efficiently (i.e., time $n$) by using a tree data structure for the polynomial. One therefore has that *the number of toroidal semiqueens can be computed in time $4^n$ and space $4^n$.*

Unfortunately, it seems that implementing the last squaring step along these lines is extremely difficult to do in *Mathematica*. One needs very tight control of list processing, so it seems that such an implementation should probably be done in some dialect of Lisp.

**Remark:** If the number of toroidal semiqueens on an $n \times n$ chessboard grows more quickly than $4^n$ then this algorithm will eventually beat the backtracking method. (In the next section I conjecture that the number actually grows like $e^{\alpha n \log n}$, where $\alpha$ is close to one.)

As before the above method requires a lot of storage and is slowed down because of the symbolic computation involved. For small values of $n$ it turns out that using a backtracking program in C is faster. I. Rivin implemented this and found the values

| | |
|---|---|
| 1 | 1 |
| 3 | 3 |
| 5 | 15 |
| 7 | 133 |
| 9 | 2025 |
| 11 | 37851 |
| 13 | 1030367 |
| 15 | 36362925 |
| 17 | 1606008513 |

**Exercise 6.3 [HM]** Show that $S(n) = 0$ if $n$ is even.

# 6.3   Determinants and permanents

The important open question in the $n$-queens problem is what is the approximate order of the number of solutions. In [R–V–Z] we conjecture that the answer is $e^{\alpha n \log n}$ for $0 < \alpha < 1$. For toroidal semiqueens we conjecture that the order of magnitude is

$$S(n) \approx n!/\beta^n$$

for some $\beta$, and this would imply, by Stirling's formula that

$$S(n) > e^{(1-\varepsilon)\, n \log n}$$

for any $\varepsilon > 0$ (a heuristic argument for this is given in Exercise 6.4 (c)).

One can use the properties of circulant matrices to try to estimate $S(n)$ as follows. Since all the terms in the product expansion of a permanent are positive, it follows that every coefficient in

$$\mathrm{perm}\,(\mathrm{circ}\,(y_0, \ldots, y_{n-1}))$$

is greater in absolute value than in the expansion of the determinant

(6.2) $$\det(\mathrm{circ}\,(y_0, \ldots, y_{n-1}))\,.$$

But it turns out that one can evaluate the determinant of circulant matrices explicitly as

$$\det \mathrm{circ}\,(y_0, \ldots, y_{n-1}) = \prod_{k=0}^{n-1} \left( \sum_{m=0}^{n-1} \xi^{m\,k}\, y_m \right),$$

where $\xi = e^{2\pi i/n}$. This can be easily shown by noting that each vector

$$(\xi^0, \xi^k, \xi^{2k}, \ldots, \xi^{(n-1)k})$$

is an eigenvector of $\mathrm{circ}\,(y_0, \ldots, y_{n-1})$ with eigenvalue $\sum_{m=0}^{n-1} \xi^{mk} y_m$, and that the determinant is just the product of the eigenvalues.

Now the coefficient of $y_0 y_1 \cdots y_{p-1}$ in (6.2) is, by (6.1)

$$\mathrm{perm}\,(\xi^{mk})\,, \qquad 0 \le m, k < n\,.$$

This permanent has been studied by Graham and Lehmer [50], where they call the matrix $\mathrm{Sc}(n) = (\xi^{mk})$ the *Schur matrix*. The reason is that the evaluation

$$\det \mathrm{Sc}(p) = \varepsilon_p\, p^{p/2}, \qquad \varepsilon_p = \begin{cases} 1 & \text{if } p \equiv 1 \ (\mathrm{mod}\ 4) \\ i & \text{if } p \equiv 3 \ (\mathrm{mod}\ 4) \end{cases}$$

for $p$ an odd prime was used by Schur to prove quadratic reciprocity [76, pages 207–212]. This matrix is also the FFT matrix, in the sense that the Fourier coefficients corresponding to $a_1, \ldots, a_n$ are given by $(a_1, \ldots, a_n)\,\mathrm{Sc}(n)$.

The above steps show that one has the lower bound

$$S(n) > |\mathrm{perm}\,\mathrm{Sc}(n)|$$

and one would like to use the properties of the Schur matrix to get a genuine lower bound.

Unfortunately, finding a lower bound for the permanent of the Schur matrix is not that easy, but one can get an upper bound using the theory of permanents. A theorem of Marcus and Newman [85, page 25] states that if $M$ is a *unitary* matrix, i.e., $M\bar{M}^T = I$, where $\bar{M}^T$ represents the conjugate transpose and $I$ is the identity matrix, then

$$|\mathrm{perm}\,M| \leq 1.$$

Now one has that

$$\mathrm{Sc}(n)\overline{\mathrm{Sc}(n)}^T = (\xi^{mk})\,(\xi^{-k\ell}) = \left(\sum_{k=0}^{n-1} \xi^{mk}\bar{\xi}^{k\ell}\right)$$

$$= \left(\sum_{k=0}^{n-1} \xi^{mk-k\ell}\right) = \left(\sum_{k=0}^{n-1} \xi^{(m-\ell)k}\right)$$

$$= \left(\begin{cases} n & \text{if } k = \ell \\ 0 & \text{otherwise} \end{cases}\right)$$

$$= n\,I$$

so that $\mathrm{Sc}(n)/n^{n/2}$ is a unitary matrix. The conclusion is that

$$|\mathrm{perm}\mathrm{Sc}(n)| < n^{n/2}.$$

One conjectures that this is actually the right order of magnitude when $n$ a prime.

Finally, one can try to find some pattern by computing $\mathrm{perm}\,\mathrm{Sc}(n)$ for odd values of $n$. The following is a table of values for $n \leq 25$

| | |
|---|---|
| 1 | 1 |
| 3 | -3 |
| 5 | -5 |
| 7 | -105 |
| 9 | 81 |
| 11 | 6765 |
| 13 | 175747 |
| 15 | 30375 |
| 17 | 25219857 |
| 19 | 142901109 |
| 21 | 4548104883 |
| 23 | -31152650265 |
| 25 | -5198937484375 |

The values for $n \leq 23$ were computed by N.J. Sloane [50] using an improvement of Ryser's formula due to Nijenhuis and Wilf (see Notes at the end of this Chapter).

The last value was computed by implementing in *Mathematica* the Nijenhuis-Wilf method and the following tricks (the running time was five days on an IBM workstation).

One first notes that if $Sc'(n)$ is the Schur matrix $Sc(n)$ with first row and first column deleted then

$$\text{perm } Sc(n) = n \, \text{perm } Sc'(n) \, ,$$

so one can save a factor of two in the computation.

Next, one notes that the Ryser formula applied to $C'(n)$ will involve products of the form

(6.3)
$$\prod_{k=1}^{n-1} \sum_{m=1}^{n} \varepsilon_m \zeta^{mk} \, ,$$

where the $\varepsilon_m$ are either zero or one. Since

$$\sum_{m=1}^{n} \varepsilon_m \zeta^{m(n-k)}$$

is the complex conjugate of

$$\sum_{m=1}^{n} \varepsilon_m \zeta^{mk}$$

one can compute the product in (6.1) using only $(n-1)/2$ complex multiplications by

$$\left| \prod_{k=1}^{(n-1)/2} \sum_{m=1}^{n} \varepsilon_m \zeta^{mk} \right|^2 .$$

One therefore computes the permanent of the Schur matrix by the *Mathematica* program

```
Schur[n_, prec_]:=
Block[{xi = N[E^(2 Pi I/n), prec], m,
       i, j, rowsum, sum = 0},
      m = Table[xi^Mod[i j, n],
               {i, n-2}, {j, (n-1)/2}];
      rowsum = Table[xi^(-j) + N[1/2, prec],
                    {j, (n-1)/2}];
      sum = abs2[Times @@ rowsum];
      Do[gi = GrayInsert[i];
         rowsum += gi[[2]] m[[gi[[1]]]];
         sum += (-1)^i abs2[Times @@ rowsum],
         {i, 2^(n-2)-1}];
           -Round[n 2 sum]] /; OddQ[n]

abs2[x_]:= Re[x]^2 + Im[x]^2
```

The value for $n = 25$ was computed using Schur[25, 20].

## Exercise 6.4 [M]

One can count the number of rooks on certain restricted chess boards. For every subset $s$ of $\{1, \ldots, n\}$ one has restricted chess board where one cannot put a rook on column $s + j \pmod{n}$ when on row $j$, where rows are counted from $0, 1, \ldots, n-1$. For example, if $n = 6$, $s = \{0, 2\}$,

```
X . X . . .
. X . X . .
. . X . X .
. . . X . X
X . . . X .
. X . . . X
```

you can't put rooks on the **x**'s.

Denote the number of such restricted rook solutions by rook $(s, n)$. This number be computed by evaluating the $0, 1$ permanent

$$\text{perm}\, (a_{ij}),$$

where $a_{ij} = 0$ if $(i, j)$ is a restricted position, and $a_{ij} = 1$ otherwise.

For $s = \{1\}$ this is the usual problem of the number of *derangements* (permutations that leave no element fixed) and so

$$\text{rook}\, (\{1\}, n) = \left\lfloor \frac{n!}{e} \right\rfloor,$$

(for example, see [123, page 67]). For $s = \{1, 2\}$ this is known as the *problème des ménages* [82]. Touchard [128] has given the formula

$$\text{rook}\, (\{1, 2\}, n) = \sum_{k=0}^{n} \frac{2n}{2n - k} \binom{2n - k}{k} (n - k)!(-1)^{k}.$$

There do not seem to be simple formulas for general $\{1, \ldots, p\}$ but there are recurrence relations for $p = 3, \ldots, 6$ which allow you to compute rook $(\{1, \ldots, p\}, n)$ in polynomial time [84] [85, Section 3.1].

**(a)\* [HM]** Is there a polynomial time algorithm to compute rook $(s, n)$? If this is true then (b) would give a time $2^n$ algorithm for computing the number of toroidal semiqueens.

**Remark:** A famous theorem of L. Valiant [130] shows that computing the general $0, 1$ permanent (i.e., non circulant rook problems) is a $\#P$-complete problem, in particular one does not expect a subexponential algorithm.

**(b) [M]** Show that the number of toroidal semiqueens is

$$\sum_{s \subseteq \{1, \ldots, n\}} (-1)^{|s|} \text{rook}\, (n, s),$$

where the sum runs over all subsets of $\{1, \ldots, n\}$.

**(c)\* [HM]** (P. Flajolet) Show that rook $(s, n) \sim n!/e^{|s|}$ for fixed $s$ as $N \to \infty$.

**Remark:** This result would gives the heuristic estimate

$$S(n) \approx \sum_{s \subseteq \{1,\ldots,n\}} (-1)^{|s|} \frac{n!}{e^{|s|}}$$

$$= n! \left( \sum_{k=0}^{n} (-1)^k \binom{n}{k} / e^k \right) = n! \left( 1 - \frac{1}{e} \right)^n$$

which supports the conjecture of Section 6.3 that $S(n) > e^{(1-\varepsilon) n \log n}$.

**Exercise 6.5\* [HM]** One can implement the determinant of circ $(a_0, \ldots, a_{n-1})$ easily as

```
DetCirculant[a_]:= Times @@ Fourier[a]
```

If the $a_j$ are integers, then as above one can reduce the number of complex multiplications by taking the product of the first $n/2$ terms and then multiplying by the complex conjugate.

  This method takes $n \log(n)$ steps for the FFT and uses $n/2$ complex multiplications. Is there a faster algorithm to compute this determinant?

**Exercise 6.6**

**(a) [M]** Show that $\mathrm{Sc}(n) = n\,\mathrm{Sc}'(n)$.

**(b) [M]** (Graham-Lehmer [50]) Show that

$$\mathrm{perm}\,\mathrm{Sc}(n) = \frac{1}{2^n} \sum_{s_1 = \pm 1, \ldots, s_n = \pm 1} (-1)^{w(s_1,\ldots,s_n)} \det \mathrm{circ}\,(s_1, \ldots, s_n),$$

where the sum ranges over all $2^n$ sequences of $\pm 1$'s and $w(s_1, \ldots, s_n)$ denotes the number of $s_i$'s equal to $-1$.

**(c)\* [HM]** (W. Duke) Let $n$ be an odd prime. Is there a closed form for

$$\det(\xi^{(mk)^2}), \qquad 0 < m, k \le (n-1)/2.$$

**(d)\* [HM]** The FFT algorithm depends on the factorization of $\mathrm{Sc}(n)$. Use this to get good bounds for $\mathrm{perm}\,\mathrm{Sc}(n)$.

## 6.4  Notes

The material in this Chapter was done jointly with Igor Rivin.

Nijenhuis and Wilf manage to save a further factor of two in the computation of Ryser's formula as follows [91, Chapter 19]

```
Permanent[a_]:=
Block[{d = Length[a], m = Drop[a, -1],
       i, rowsum, sum = 0, j = 1},
       rowsum = Last /@ a - .5 (Plus @@ a);
       sum = Times @@ rowsum;
       Do[gi = GrayInsert[i];
          rowsum += gi[[2]] m[[gi[[1]]]];
          sum += (-1)^i (Times @@ rowsum);
          {i, 2^(d-1)-1}];
       (-1)^(d-1) 2 sum]
```

The theory of rook placement on restricted chessboards was developed by Riordan, for example [103, Chapters 7,8].

# 7

# The $3x+1$ Problem

# Chapter 7

# The $3x + 1$ Problem

One of the most notorious questions in computational number theory is the $3x + 1$ problem, also known as the Collatz problem, named after its originator L. Collatz, which asks whether, for any integer $n$, iterating $f(x)$ where

$$f(x) = \begin{cases} x/2 & x \text{ even} \\ 3x + 1 & x \text{ odd} \end{cases}$$

always returns to 1. This is has been shown to hold for every number tested and for all numbers $< 10^{15}$.

For example, starting with $n = 7$ gives the sequence

$$7 \to 22 \to 11 \to 34 \to 17 \to 52 \to 26 \to 13$$

$$\to 40 \to 20 \to 10 \to 5 \to 16 \to 8 \to 4 \to 2 \to 1 \,.$$

This question has defeated all attempts at solution and even Erdös stated that "Mathematics is not ready for such problems" [73]. Many partial results have been obtained, most notably by R. Crandall [22] and R. Terras [125] [126]. A very complete survey of the problem has been written by J. Lagarias [73].

One can use *Mathematica* to study this problem computationally but one must be careful to use it where it is most appropriate. Due to the use of binary shifts this problem can very easily be coded into machine specific language which allows for large searches for $n$ in the realistic range $n$ up to $10^{20}$. Obviously, *Mathematica* loses big here, so I have chosen to write an efficient *Mathematica* program to check the conjecture for very large $n$.

## 7.1   Using some ideas of Terras

R. Terras [125] and C. Everett independently [30] made the important
observation that the correct function to look at was not the original
$3x + 1$ function $f(x)$ but the function $T(x)$ given by

$$T(x) = \begin{cases} x/2 & x \text{ even} \\ (3x + 1)/2 & x \text{ odd.} \end{cases}$$

The reason is that if $x$ is an odd number, then $3x + 1$ is even and is
automatically mapped to $(3x + 1)/2$. So the behavior of the $3x + 1$
map is that if a number is odd it gets mapped to a number roughly
$3/2$ times as big, and if it's even it gets mapped to a number $1/2$ times
as big. The map $T(x)$ is therefore strongly weighted towards reducing
the size of $x$, so it seems reasonable that the iterates of $x$ eventually
become less than $x$ (see below).

The next observation is that an understanding of the first $k$ iterates of the function $T$ can be gained from knowing the first $k$ binary
digits of $x$. The function $T(x)$ is determined by the parity of $x$, i.e.,
$x \pmod 2$. Similarly the function $T^2(x)$ is determined by $x \pmod 4$,
and in general $T^k(x)$ is determined by knowing $x \pmod k$. In other
words if $x$ and $y$ have the same lower $k$ bits, i.e., $x \equiv y \pmod{2^k}$, then
the iterates $T(x), T^2(x), \ldots, T^k(x)$ and $T(y), T^2(y), \ldots, T^k(y)$ have the
same parity, and so define the same function. This function consists
of a set $2^k$ linear functions $T^k(x) = ax + b$, where $a, b$ depend only on
$x \bmod 2^k$. In fact, one can compute $a, b$ explicitly [73] as

(7.1)
$$a = \frac{3^{t_0(x) + \cdots + t_{k-1}(x)}}{2^k}$$

$$b = \sum_{i=0}^{k-1} t_i(x) \frac{3^{t_{i+1}(x) + \cdots + t_{k-1}(x)}}{2^{k-i}}$$

where $t_i(x) = T^i(x) \bmod 2$, the parity of the $i$th iterate of $x$, is uniquely
determined by $x \bmod 2^k$, for $i < k$. One codes these linear maps
as ordered pairs of rational numbers $(a, b)$ so that $ax + b = (a, b) \cdot
(x, 1)$, where "$\cdot$" is the usual inner product of vectors. For example, the
ordered pair corresponding to $k = 4, x = 666$ is $(3/16, 1/8)$.

For each $k$ one can construct a table of the $(a,b)$'s corresponding to $x = 0, 1, \ldots, 2^k - 1$. The essence of Terras' results on the Collatz problem is the following: Most of the $(a,b)$'s in this table satisfy $a < 1$ (Exercise 7.1), and so $ay + b < y$ for all sufficiently large $y \equiv x \pmod{2^k}$, where $x$ is the number corresponding to $(a,b)$. This implies that for a fixed $k$ almost all number $y$ satisfy $T^k(y) < y$.

**Exercise 7.1 [M]** Show that each $0 \le x < 2^k$ determines a unique $k$ vector of ones and zeroes by $(t_0(x), t_1(x), \ldots, t_{k-1}(x))$. Use this to estimate the number of $(a,b)$ with $a < 1$.

## 7.2 The algorithm

Note that, to check the conjecture, one doesn't have to find the exact sequence of iterates, just know that the length of this sequence is finite. This quantity is the *total stopping time* of $n$, and is in fact much easier to compute than the explicit sequence.

The first step in the algorithm is to pick a fixed $k$ (I have used $k = 10$) and create a list of the corresponding $(a,b)$'s for each $T^k(x)$, $x = 0, \ldots, 2^k - 1$. This table takes a while to be created, but the computation is only done once.

Now given the last $2k$ digits of $x$ one can compute the ordered pair corresponding to $T^{2k}(x)$ as follows: From the last $k$ digits of $x$ one uses the table to find the corresponding $(a,b)$. Let $y = x \bmod 2^{2k}$, the last $2k$ digits of $x$, then $ay + b \equiv T^k(x) \pmod{2^k}$ so that the last $k$ digits of $ay + b$ will determine an ordered pair $(c,d)$ corresponding to the map $T^k(x) \mapsto T^k(T^k(x))$. One uses the table to get the ordered pair $(c,d)$. The combined effect on $x$ is to compose the two linear maps given by $(a,b)$ and $(c,d)$ to get the linear map

$$c(ax + b) + d = acx + bc + d$$

so the ordered pair corresponding to the function $T^{2k}(x)$ is given by the "semi-product"

$$(a,b) * (c,d) \Rightarrow (ac, bc + d).$$

In general if one knows the lowest order $mk$ digits of $x$, then one can compute the map $T^{mk}(x)$ by doing $r$ such computations involving only numbers mod $2^{rk}$, and semi-products from the table.

So this method allows one to compute $T^{rk}(x)$ by only working with the first $rk$ binary digits of $x$, and then doing only two arithmetic operations with $x$ itself. The advantage of this is that when dealing with an integer $n$ with tens of thousands of digits one wants to minimize the actual number of operations involving $n$ directly. For example, if $n$ has $100,000$ digits in base two, one first extracts the least significant $1000$ digits in base two. One computes the ordered pair $(a, b)$ corresponding to the first $1000$ iterations of $T$ exclusively by computation with these $1000$ digits, and with only $100$ semi-products of elements of the table of $T^{10}(x)$. Only when this $(a, b)$ has been computed does one actually do a computation involving $n$. In the meantime one gets the value of the total stopping time for free since it is simply increased by $1000$.

This simple method increases the efficiency of computation fairly dramatically and will routinely verify the conjecture for a given number $\leq 2^{100000}$.

## 7.3   The program

The first part of the program is the basic computation of the iterates of $T(x)$ up to the first cycle. The function $T$ is the first to be implemented

```
CollatzT[n_]:= If[EvenQ[n], n/2, (3 n + 1)/2]
```

The next remark is that one should include negative arguments since negative integers are important to understanding the Collatz problem (for example the fact that $2^k - 1$ increases for the first $k$ iterates follows from the fact that $-1$ is a fixed point of $T$).

The known cycles over the positive and negative integers are

$$(1, 2), \ (-1), \ (-5, -7, -10, -5),$$

$$(-17, -25, -37, -55, -82, -41, -61, -91, -136, -68, -34)$$

so when $n = 1, -1, -5, -17$ the list of iterates is well understood. One therefore sets

```
Collatz[1] := {1}

Collatz[-1] := {-1};

Collatz[-5] := {-5};

Collatz[-17] := {-17};
```

For small $n$ (here $n < 2^{11} + 2$) one computes the iterates of $n$ using a simple recursive program

```
Collatz[n_Integer] := Prepend[Collatz[CollatzT[n]], n] /;
                    Abs[n] < 2050
```

The first step to more efficient algorithm is to build up a table, as in the last section, of the ordered pairs $(a, b)$ corresponding to all $T^{10}(x)$, $x = 0, 1, \ldots, 2^{10} - 1$.

For large $n$ one uses the method of the previous section to compute the table of ordered pairs $(a, b)$. A direct implementation of formula (7.1) gives

```
CollatzTable[k_Integer] :=
  RotateRight[
     Map[Function[x,
          {3^Apply[Plus, x] / 2^Length[x],
             Reverse[x] .
             Accumulate[#1 #2 &,
                 1/2 Prepend[3^Reverse[Rest[x]],1]]}],
             Mod[Map[NestList[CollatzT,
                          #, k-1] &,
             Range[1, 2^k]], 2]]]
```

The pair $(a, b)$ corresponding to $T^k(x)$ is given by

```
CollatzTable[k][[Mod[x+1, 2^k]]]
```

and if the table already exists one can compute $T^k(x)$ very quickly by

```
CollatzTable[k][[Mod[x+1, 2^k]]] . {x, 1}
```

For example, to compute $T^4(666)$, one has that $666 \equiv 10 \pmod{16}$ and

```
In[1] := CollatzTable[4]
```

```
Out[1]= {{1/16, 0}, {9/16, 7/16}, {9/16, 7/8},
         {9/16, 5/16}, {3/16, 1/4}, {3/16, 1/16},
         {9/16, 5/8}, {27/16, 19/16}, {3/16, 1/2},
         {27/16, 29/16}, {3/16, 1/8}, {27/16, 23/16},
         {9/16, 5/4}, {9/16, 11/16}, {27/16, 19/8},
         {81/16, 65/16}}
```

```
In[2] := %[[11]] . {666, 1}
```

```
Out[2]= 125
```

This can be verified by

```
In[3] := Collatz[666]
```

```
Out[3]= {666, 333, 500, 250, 125, 188, 94, 47,
         71, 107, 161, 242, 121, 182, 91, 137,
         206, 103, 155, 233, 350, 175, 263, 395,
         593, 890, 445, 668, 334, 167, 251, 377,
         566, 283, 425, 638, 319, 479, 719, 1079,
         1619, 2429, 3644, 1822, 911, 1367, 2051,
         3077, 4616, 2308, 1154, 577, 866, 433,
         650, 325, 488, 244, 122, 61, 92, 46, 23,
         35, 53, 80, 40, 20, 10, 5, 8, 4, 2, 1}
```

```
In[4] := %[[5]]
```

```
Out[4]= 125
```

For the algorithm I will use $k = 10$ in CollatzTable and for convenience define the constant

```
CollatzTable10 = CollatzTable[10]
```

so that computing $T^{10}(x)$ is done very quickly. To speed up the computation of the Collatz function one uses the table for larger $n$ by only computing every tenth iterate,

```
CollatzIterate[n_Integer] := {}       /; n < 2055

CollatzIterate[n_Integer] :=
  Prepend[CollatzIterate[{n, 1} .
          CollatzTable10[[1 + Mod[n, 1024]]]], n]
```

and Collatz can now be computed using this by filling in the the missing nine iterates

```
Collatz[n_Integer] :=
 Block[{cr},
       cr = Flatten[NestList[CollatzT, #, 9]& /@
                    CollatzIterate[n]];
       Join[cr, Rest[Collatz[Last[cr]]]]]
```

This will speed up the computation of Collatz[n] and so similar results can be obtained for $\sigma_\infty(n)$, denoted by TotalStoppingTime, the length of Collatz[n].

```
TotalStoppingTime[n_Integer] :=
   Length[Collatz[n]] - 1       /; n < 2055

TotalStoppingTime[n_Integer] :=
   10 + TotalStoppingTime[{n, 1} .
   CollatzTable10[[1 + Mod[n, 1024]]]] /;
            2055 <= n <= 2^1002
```

However, this can be improved for large $n$ using the method of the previous section which only does a computation involving $n$ directly every 1000 iterations

```
TotalStoppingTime[n_Integer] :=
  1000 +
  TotalStoppingTime[
```

```
NestList[Block[
      {a = CollatzTable10[[1+Mod[#[[2]], 1024]]]},
      {SemiProduct[#[[1]], a], Mod[{#[[2]], 1} . a,
            2^1000]}]&,
        {{1, 0}, Mod[n, 2^1000]},
          100] [[-1, 1]] . {n, 1}]           /;
                        n > 2^1002
```

```
SemiProduct[{a_, b_}, {c_, d_}]:= {a c, b c + d}
```

Finally, these algorithms will require a high level of recursion so one
needs

```
$RecursionLimit = Infinity
```

As examples of the speed these computations took in version 2.0 of
*Mathematica* on a DEC 3100 workstation:

```
In[1]:= Timing[<<CollatzProblem.m]
```

```
Out[1]= {55.5667 Second, Null}
```

It takes a while to build up `CollatzTable10`.

```
In[2]:= TotalStoppingTime[2^50 -1]//Timing
```

```
Out[2]= {0.383333 Second, 383}
```

```
In[3]:= TotalStoppingTime[2^500 - 1]//Timing
```

```
Out[3]= {1.86667 Second, 4331}
```

```
In[4]:= TotalStoppingTime[2^5000 - 1]//Timing
```

```
Out[4]= {44.8667 Second, 43247}
```

```
In[5]:= TotalStoppingTime[2^50000 - 1]//Timing
```

```
Out[5]= {622.767 Second, 428838}

In[6]:= TotalStoppingTime[2^100000 - 1]//Timing

Out[6]= {1563.97 Second, 863323}
```

**Exercise 7.2** [**P**] CollatzTable[k] consists of ordered pairs $(a/2^k, b/2^k)$, where $a$ and $b$ are integers. Since the construction guarantees that $2^k \mid ax + b$, this division is

```
Quotient[a x + b, 2^k]
```

and so three greatest common divisor operations are saved. Speed up TotalStoppingTime by using 2^k CollatzTable[k] instead of CollatzTable[k].

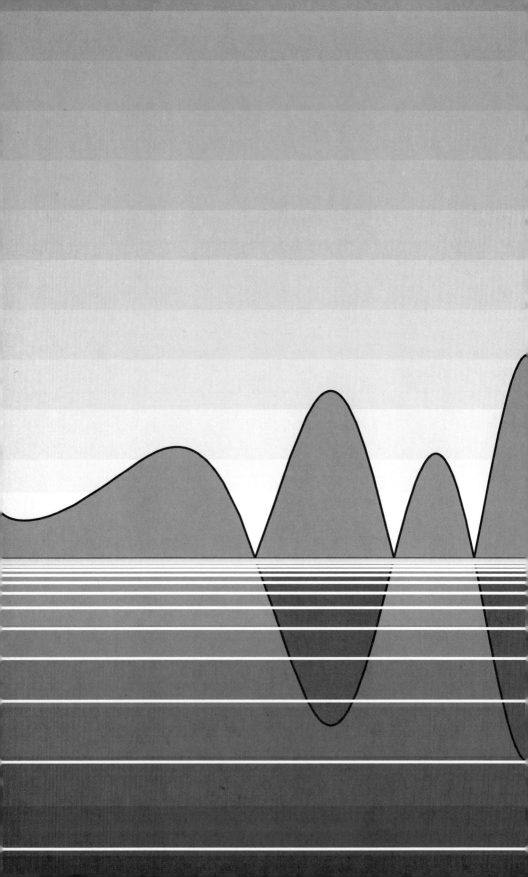

# 8

# The Riemann Zeta Function

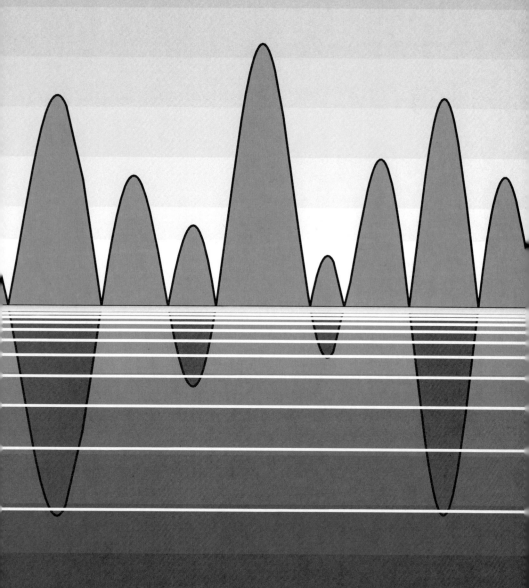

# Chapter 8

# The Riemann Zeta Function

In 1859, Georg Riemann astounded the mathematical world by publishing the eight-page paper *Ueber die Anzahl der Primzahlen unter einer gegebenen Grösse* (On the Number of Primes Less Than a Given Magnitude). In this paper he outlined a method to prove the prime number theorem conjectured by Gauss and others. The prime number theorem states that the number of primes numbers less than or equal to a number $x$ is roughly $x/\log x$ (see the next section). There were many gaps in Riemann's outline that needed to be filled, but much effort by various mathematicians finally culminated in independent proofs by Hadamard and de la Vallée-Poussin in 1896.

Riemann's method is based on the function

$$\zeta(s) = \sum_{k=1}^{\infty} \frac{1}{k^s}.$$

Euler had studied this function earlier and had proved the remarkable identity

$$\sum_{k=1}^{\infty} \frac{1}{k^s} = \prod_{p \text{ prime}} \frac{1}{1 - \frac{1}{p^s}},$$

where the product runs over all prime numbers. It is this formula that allows one to use analytic methods in the study of prime numbers. Euler had only considered the $\zeta$ function for real values of $s$. Riemann's great insight was to study this function for *complex* values of $s$ and to use the powerful methods of complex analysis. This enabled him to discover a remarkable connection between the complex zeros of this function and prime numbers. Riemann showed that the complex values of $s$ seen as arguments to $\zeta(s)$ essentially form a "frequency domain" for prime numbers, and that information about the complex zeros of $\zeta(s)$ would lead to a result about the distribution of prime numbers. In fact it was subsequently shown that the prime number theorem is equivalent to the fact that the $\zeta$ function has no complex zeros $s$ with $\operatorname{Re}(s) \geq 1$.

Riemann's paper contains one of the most celebrated of all mathematical problems—the so-called Riemann Hypothesis (RH). Though there are many equivalent formulations (e.g., Exercise 8.3) the RH is now usually stated in terms of the $\zeta$ function: *all the complex zeros of* $\zeta(s)$ *lie on the so-called "critical line"* $\operatorname{Re}(s) = 1/2$. The real importance of this problem is not as a property of a complex valued function but the fact that it is equivalent to the statement that the prime numbers are distributed as evenly as possible (see the next section for details). Little progress towards this result has been achieved since Riemann first conjectured it, although many first-class mathematicians since Riemann have worked on it at some time in their careers.

Results about the complex zeroes of the $\zeta$ function comprise some the most technically difficult theorems in mathematics and are due to the most talented mathematicians of the century most notably Hardy, Littlewood, Weyl, Siegel, Vinogradov, and Selberg. For example, work of Hardy, Selberg, Levinson, and Conrey has established that there are an infinite number of zeroes on the critical line, and in fact these comprise at least 40% of all zeroes.

Most mathematicians do believe the RH to be true. One reason is purely aesthetic—prime numbers are the building blocks of the natural numbers, and, unless a compelling reason can be found, one does not expect any hidden irregularities in their distribution. Another reason is the vast numerical evidence compiled in the last 130 years: it is known that each of the first 1,500,000,001 complex zeros has real part exactly equal to $1/2$. It is also known that the next $10^9$ zeros beyond the $10^{20}$th zero also satisfy the RH [92].

Interestingly enough, all of these computations are also based on Riemann's work. The most efficient way known to compute a single value of $\zeta(s)$ "far up" in the critical strip was published in 1932 by Carl Ludwig Siegel who reconstructed it from Riemann's unpublished notes; the method is now known as the Riemann-Siegel formula. For $t$ real and positive, one defines the functions

$$\vartheta(t) = \arg \Gamma\left(\frac{1}{4} + \frac{it}{2}\right) - \frac{t \log \pi}{2}$$

and

$$Z(t) = \zeta\left(\frac{1}{2} + it\right) e^{i\vartheta(t)}.$$

It turns out that the "functional equation" relating $\zeta(1-s)$ to $\zeta(s)$ via the more elementary functions $\sin, \Gamma, e^s$,

$$\zeta(1-s) = 2^s \pi^{s-1} \sin\frac{1}{2}s\pi\Gamma(1-s)\zeta(s)$$

implies that $Z(t)$ is actually real valued for $t$ real. Also $Z(t)$ has the same zeroes as $\zeta(1/2 + it)$. Since

$$\left|\zeta\left(\frac{1}{2} + it\right)\right| = |Z(t)|,$$

one can think of $Z(t)$ as the graph of $|\zeta(1/2+it)|$ but with the negative parts where they belong, see Figure 8.1.

Since $Z(t)$ is real for real values of $t$ (along the "critical line") complex arithmetic can be completely avoided and, by the intermediate value theorem, the zeros of $Z(t)$ (and therefore the zeros of $\zeta(1/2+it)$) can readily be found by locating the sign changes of $Z(t)$.

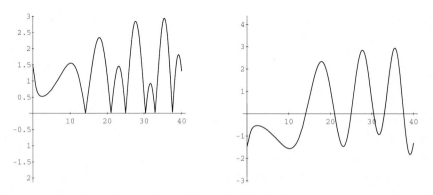

Figure 8.1: $Z(t)$ versus $|\zeta(1/2+it)|$, $0 < t < 40$.

Computationally, the Riemann-Siegel formula requires about $\sqrt{t}$ steps to compute $\zeta(1/2 + it)$ while the previously known method, the Euler-Maclaurin formula (`NSum`, see Section 8.2 of this Chapter) increased as $t$, and one can extend $\zeta(1/2 + it)$ calculations to *much* larger values of $t$. (The Euler-Maclaurin formula is still superior if one requires accurate values of $\zeta(1/2 + it)$.)

An exciting possibility in doing large scale computations is to become the world's most famous mathematician by finding a counterexample to the RH. One way of doing this would be to find a positive local minimum of $Z(t)$ or a negative local maximum of $Z(t)$ since this is known to violate RH. One could also cause quite a stir by discovering evidence for a double zero of $Z(t)$ (a maximum or minimum that occurs right at a zero), since these have also been conjectured never to occur. Even for the less ambitious, it can be fascinating to actually see the zeros of the $\zeta$ function, since these in some way represent the "fundamental harmonics" of the prime numbers.

## 8.1 The distribution of primes

The distribution of primes has fascinated mathematicians for thousands of years, but unfortunately some important aspects of the subject are known only to specialists in analytic number theory. Examples are the following

**Principle I:** There are a lot of prime numbers.

**Principle II:** In technical work on the distribution of primes

**(a)** The primes should be counted using their logarithms.

**(b)** You should consider primes and prime powers together (prime powers are the squares, cubes, etc. of primes).

To understand Principle I, one has to know the prime number theorem which implies that the number of primes less than or equal to a number $x$ is about $x/\log x$.

This says that the sequence of primes is much more dense than many other common sequences. For example, the number of perfect squares less than $x$ is about $\sqrt{x}$ and the number of powers of 10 about

$\log x / \log 10$, and both these quantities grow much slower than $x / \log x$, which is basically just $x$ divided by the number of its digits.

From this point of view Lagrange's theorem, taught in basic undergraduate algebra, that every positive integer can be written as a sum of four squares is much more surprising than the extremely difficult result of Vinogradov that every sufficiently large number is the sum of four primes.

Similarly, every heuristic argument and computational result indicates that the number of twin primes less than $x$ is about $x / \log^2 x$ though every attempt at proving that there are an infinite number has failed (twin primes are primes like 17 and 19 which only differ by two from the nearest other prime). So the conjectured density of twin primes is much larger than that of squares or powers of 10. Nevertheless, twin primes are often cited in popular accounts as being "exceedingly rare".

The difficulty in dealing with sums of primes and twin primes comes not from the fact that the results are at the limit of what is true, but from a lack of technical tools. Sparser sequences such as squares are easier to handle since they have many algebraic properties which allow you to "talk" about them. For example the fact that $a^2 + b^2 + c^2 + d^2$ is the norm of the quaternion $a + bi + cj + dk$ can be used very effectively to prove Lagrange's theorem.

Principles II (a) and (b) are mostly empirical observations about the techniques used in the theory (so a totally new idea might invalidate them). The following "philosophy" might explain Principle II (a): Since every integer is a unique product of distinct primes, one can write $\log n$ in a unique way as

$$\log n = a_1 \log p_2 + a_2 \log p_2 + \cdots$$

where $p_1, p_2, \ldots$ are the first primes and $a_1, a_2, \ldots$ are integers (so almost all the $a_r$'s are zero). This converts the multiplicative structure of the problem into a linear one, which is more tractable. For example, since the $\log p$ are linearly independent, one can think of

$$\sum_{n \leq x} \log n$$

as asking how many lattice points there are in a certain region. This type of consideration naturally leads to Chebyshev's estimate of Exercise 4.3.

This type of analysis occurs in other branches of number theory, for example in studying numbers of the form

$$(8.1) \qquad\qquad a + \sqrt{2}b, \qquad a, b, \text{ integers}.$$

it can be shown [57, page 209] that any *unit* $a + \sqrt{2}b$, i.e., satisfying

$$(a + \sqrt{2}b)(a - \sqrt{2}b) = \pm 1$$

can be written as

$$a + \sqrt{2}b = \pm\varepsilon^r,$$

where $r$ is an integer and

$$\varepsilon = 1 + \sqrt{2}.$$

One can therefore think of the log of any unit (ignoring the factor of $\pm$) as being an integer multiple of $\log \varepsilon$. It turns out that the number $\log \varepsilon$ is a very important invariant called the *regulator* of the ring of algebraic numbers of the form (8.1).

The technical realization of Principle II is that the right function for studying the distribution of primes is not $\pi(x)$, the number of primes less than or equal $x$, but the function $\psi(x)$, the sum function of the von Mangoldt function $\Lambda(n)$ defined by

$$\Lambda(n) = \begin{cases} \log p & \text{if } n = p^k, \, p \text{ a prime,} \\ 0 & \text{otherwise.} \end{cases}$$

$\psi(x)$ is therefore given by

$$\psi(x) = \sum_{n \leq x} \Lambda(n).$$

It turns out that proofs in the theory of the distribution of primes are technically much easier when dealing with $\psi(x)$ instead of $\pi(x)$. For example, the usual statement of the prime number theorem is

$$(8.2) \qquad\qquad \pi(x) = \frac{x}{\log x} + R_\pi(x),$$

where
$$\frac{R_\pi(x)}{x/\log x} \to 0 \qquad \text{as } x \to \infty.$$

But expressed in terms of $\psi(x)$ this is
$$\psi(x) = x + R_\psi(x),$$

where
$$\frac{R_\psi(x)}{x} \to 0 \qquad \text{as } x \to \infty.$$

This is a somewhat simpler expression of the result, but in fact it is much more informative than (8.2) as will be seen below.

The deeper one delves, the more important Principle II becomes. For example, the integral formula expressing $\pi(x)$ in terms of the zeta function is[1]

$$(8.3) \qquad \pi(x) = \frac{1}{2\pi i} \int_{2-i\infty}^{2+i\infty} \left( \sum_{n=1}^{\log x/\log 2} \frac{\mu(n)x^{s/n}}{n} \right) \log \zeta(s) \, \frac{ds}{s},$$

where $\mu(n)$ is the Möbius function of Exercise 1.1 The analogous formula expressing $\psi(x)$ in terms of the Riemann zeta function is[2]

$$(8.4) \qquad \psi(x) = \frac{1}{2\pi i} \int_{2-i\infty}^{2+i\infty} -\frac{\zeta'(s)}{\zeta(s)} \frac{x^s}{x} \, ds.$$

Note that formula (8.3) is rather awkward: the inner sum occurs because you consider primes as distinct from prime powers in $\pi(x)$ (Principle II (b)). Moreover, the asymptotic behavior of these integrals is determined by the singularities of the functions in the integrand (the asymptotics behavior is what you're interested in!) and the function $\log \zeta(s)$ has logarithmic singularities while $\zeta'(s)/\zeta(s)$ only has poles, which are easier to deal with (Principle I (a)).

**Remark:** Formula (8.4) can be used to prove the "explicit formula" of von Mangoldt which was alluded to above

$$\psi(x) = x - \sum_\rho \frac{x^\rho}{\rho} - \log 2\pi - \frac{1}{2}\log(1-x^2),$$

---

[1] This has to be modified slightly when $x$ is an integer.
[2] $\psi(x)$ is replaced by $\psi(x) - \Lambda(x)/2$ when $x$ is an integer.

where the second sum is over all complex zeroes $\rho$ of $\zeta(s)$ and taken to mean

$$\lim_{t \to \infty} \sum_{|\mathrm{Im}(\rho)| < t} \frac{x^\rho}{\rho}$$

(with a similar condition to (8.4) when $x$ is an integer). The explicit formula is reminiscent of a Fourier expansion of a function and it is in this sense that the zeroes of $\zeta(s)$ represent the "spectrum" of the primes.

The general reason why Principle II (b) works is that there are very few prime powers relative to primes. An example of this principle in action is the following: Consider the definition of $\psi(x)$

(8.5) $$\psi(x) = \sum_{n \le x} \Lambda(n) = \sum_{p^n \le x} \log p$$

then contributions due to prime powers can only occur if $p^n \le x$, which means that $p \le \sqrt{x}$ and $n \le \log x / \log 2$. So all these terms only contribute at most $\sqrt{x} \log^2 x / \log 2$ to (8.5). This immediately gives that if

$$\theta(x) = \sum_{p \le x} \log p$$

then the prime number theorem can be stated for $\theta(x)$ as

$$\theta(x) = x + R_\theta(x),$$

with $R_\theta(x)/x \to 0$. So the asymptotics for the sum of logarithms of the primes is also clearer than for the number of primes (Principle II (a)).

Technically, Principles II (a) and (b) hold because any statement about $\psi(x)$ can be translated to one about $\pi(x)$ by *partial summation*, the analogue for sums of integrations by parts [49, page 54]. Informally, one can see this as follows. Let $\chi(n)$ be the characteristic function of the primes so that

$$\chi(n) = \begin{cases} 1 & \text{if } n \text{ is prime} \\ 0 & \text{otherwise} \end{cases}$$

and as is usual in this theory, let $f(x) = O(g(x))$ mean that there is a constant $C$ such that $|f(x)| \le g(x)$ say for all $x > 2$ [49, Section 9.2].

If $\chi(n)$ could be integrated just like a continuous function one would have that

$$\pi(x) = \int_2^x \chi(t)dt$$

and

$$\theta(x) = \int_2^x \chi(t)\log(t)dt \, .$$

Integration by parts would give

$$\pi(x) = \int_2^x \frac{\chi(t)\log t}{\log t}dt$$

$$= \int_2^x \frac{1}{\log t}\frac{d}{dt}\theta(t)$$

$$= \frac{\theta(x)}{\log x} - \frac{\theta(2)}{\log 2} + \int_2^x \frac{\theta(t)}{t\log^2 t}dt$$

$$(8.6) \qquad = \frac{x}{\log x} + \frac{R_\theta(x)}{\log x} + \int_2^x \frac{1}{\log^2 t}dt + \int_2^x \frac{R_\theta(t)}{t\log^2 t}dt - 1$$

upon substituting $\theta(t) = t + R_\theta(t)$, $\theta(2) = \log 2$. A further integration by parts gives

$$(8.7) \qquad \int_2^x \frac{1}{\log^2 t}dt = \int_2^x t\frac{d}{dt}\left(-\frac{1}{\log t}\right)dt$$

$$= -\frac{x}{\log x} + \int_2^x \frac{dt}{\log t} + \frac{2}{\log 2} \, .$$

Putting this back into (8.6) gives

$$\pi(x) = \frac{x}{\log x} + \frac{R_\theta}{\log x} - \frac{x}{\log x} + \int_2^x \frac{dt}{\log t}$$

$$(8.8) \qquad + \frac{2}{\log 2} + \int_2^x \frac{R_\theta(t)}{t\log^2 t}dt - 1$$

$$= \int_2^x \frac{dt}{\log t} + \frac{R_\theta(x)}{\log x} + \int_2^x \frac{R_\theta(t)}{t\log^2 t}dt$$

(in this informal description you can drop the constant term $\frac{2}{\log 2} - 1$ since it is too small to affect the asymptotics).

The term

$$\int_2^x \frac{R_\theta(t)}{t \log^2 t}\, dt$$

is estimated by substituting $R_\theta(t)$ inside the integral with the largest value it can take. For the purposes of this argument, one can assume that $R_\theta(x)$ is increasing, so

$$\max_{a < t < x} R_\theta(t) = R_\theta(x).$$

Actually you have to do one more trick in order to get the right answer, i.e., split up the integral as

$$\int_2^x = \int_2^{\sqrt{x}} + \int_{\sqrt{x}}^x.$$

This gives

$$\int_2^x \frac{R_\theta(t)}{t \log^2 t}\, dt = \int_2^{\sqrt{x}} \frac{R_\theta(t)}{t \log^2 t}\, dt + \int_{\sqrt{x}}^x \frac{R_\theta(t)}{t \log^2 t}\, dt$$

$$\leq \max_{2 \leq t \leq \sqrt{x}} \{R_\theta(t)\} \int_2^{\sqrt{x}} \frac{1}{t \log^2 t}\, dt$$

$$+ \max_{\sqrt{x} \leq t \leq x} \{R_\theta(t)\} \int_2^x \frac{1}{t \log^2 t}\, dt$$

$$(8.9) \qquad \leq R_\theta(\sqrt{x}) \int_2^{\sqrt{x}} \frac{1}{t \log^2 t}\, dt + R_\theta(x) \int_{\sqrt{x}}^x \frac{1}{t \log^2 t}\, dt$$

$$= \frac{R_\theta(\sqrt{x})}{\log 2} - \frac{R_\theta(\sqrt{x})}{\log \sqrt{x}} + \frac{R_\theta(x)}{\log \sqrt{x}} - \frac{R_\theta(x)}{\log x}$$

$$\leq \frac{2\sqrt{x}}{\log 2} + \frac{R_\theta(x)}{\log x}$$

$$= O\left(\frac{R_\theta(x)}{\log x}\right),$$

since $\pi(\sqrt{x}) \leq \sqrt{x}$ implies that

$$R_\theta(\sqrt{x}) \leq 2\sqrt{x},$$

and since I have assumed, for the purposes of this discussion, that $R_\theta(x) > \sqrt{x}\log x$ so that the $2\sqrt{x}/\log 2$ term gets absorbed into the $O(\ )$ term. (This method can be refined to drop these assumptions, see below.)

Splitting up the integral into two pieces was necessary, otherwise the fifth line of (8.9) would have given the term $R_\theta(x)/\log 2$ instead of $R_\theta(\sqrt{x})/\log 2$.

Putting the estimate of (8.9) into formula (8.8) gives

$$\pi(x) = \int_2^x \frac{dt}{\log t} + O\left(\frac{R_\theta(x)}{\log x}\right).$$

Well, it turns out that one can define integrals so that functions like $\chi(n)$ can be treated just like continuous functions (the Stieltjes integral) so the above argument is easily made exact [23] [24]. In fact one also has the analogous

(8.10)
$$\pi(x) = \int_2^x \frac{dt}{\log t} + O\left(\frac{R_\psi(x)}{\log x}\right),$$

where $R_\psi(x)$ is the error term $\psi(x) - x$ (Principle II (b)).

Note that the main term in (8.10) is not $x/\log x$ as in (8.2). The function in (8.10) is the *logarithmic integral* Li$(x)$

$$\mathrm{Li}\,(x) = \int_2^x \frac{dt}{\log t}\, dt\,.$$

The distinction between these two forms of the prime number theorem is crucial but somewhat confusing. The point is that the prime number theorem says that the density of primes in an interval around $x$ is about $1/\log x$, while the error term in the prime number theorem tells you in how short an interval this behavior still dominates. The formulation of (8.2) states that this density result holds in the interval $(0, x)$, which only corresponds to the weakest form of the error term. On the other hand, the Riemann hypothesis, which is essentially the strongest form of the error term (see below), states that the density result holds in much shorter intervals of the form $(x, x + x^{1/2+\varepsilon})$, for any fixed $\varepsilon > 0$.

It is in this sense that the Riemann hypothesis says that the primes are distributed as regularly as possible.

Actually, one can show that $x/\log x$ is an approximation to $\pi(x)$, but a very bad one! To see this, first find an asymptotic formula for $\mathrm{Li}\,(x)$ by using integration by parts, namely

$$\int \frac{dx}{\log x} = \frac{x}{\log x} + \int \frac{dx}{\log^2 x}$$

$$= \frac{x}{\log x} + \frac{x}{\log^2 x} + \int_2^x \frac{dx}{\log^3 x}$$

which implies

$$\mathrm{Li}\,(x) = \frac{x}{\log x} + \frac{x}{\log^2 x} + O\left(\frac{x}{\log^3 x}\right).$$

Next, invoke de la Vallée Poussin's version of the prime number theorem (for example [23, page 110]) which says that

$$\psi(x) = x + O(x\, e^{-a\,\sqrt{\log x}}),$$

for some constant $a$. Converting to $\pi(x)$ as above gives

(8.11)                    $$\pi(x) = \mathrm{Li}\,(x) + O\left(\frac{x}{\log x}\, e^{-a\,\sqrt{\log x}}\right).$$

The observation that

$$e^{-a\sqrt{\log x}} = O\left(\frac{1}{\log^3 x}\right)$$

yields that

$$\pi(x) = \frac{x}{\log x} + \frac{x}{\log^2 x} + O\left(\frac{x}{\log^3 x}\right).$$

This means that the error term $R_\pi(x)$ in

$$\pi(x) = \frac{x}{\log x} + R_\pi(x)$$

is asymptotic to $x/\log^2 x$. Note that this is much weaker than the de la Valée Poussin error term in (8.11). As a matter of fact, one can keep on integrating by parts to get the complete asymptotic expansion for $\mathrm{Li}\,(x)$ as

$$\mathrm{Li}\,(x) = \frac{x}{\log x} + \frac{x}{\log^2 x} + 2!\,\frac{x}{\log^3 x} + \cdots$$

Since the de la Valée Poussin error term also satisfies

$$e^{-a\sqrt{\log x}} = O\left(\frac{1}{\log^m x}\right)$$

for any fixed $m$, one gets the asymptotic expansion (e.g., [66, page 366])

$$\pi(x) = \frac{x}{\log x} + \frac{x}{\log^2 x} + 2!\,\frac{x}{\log^3 x} + \cdots$$

but even this form is much weaker than (8.11).

The conclusion is that the most accurate way to state the prime number theorem simply is to say that the probability that integer $n$ is prime is about $1/\log n$ since this says that the expected number of primes $\leq x$ is

$$\int_2^x \frac{dn}{\log n} = \mathrm{Li}\,(x)$$

which is the correct main term.

The Riemann Hypothesis fits into the theory by being equivalent to the statement

(8.12) $$\psi(x) = x + O(\sqrt{x}\log^2 x)$$

(e.g., [23, page 114]). The $\sqrt{x}$ term in the $O(\ )$ is of the right order [111], for example formula (8.4) can be "inverted" (see [75, page 127]) to give

$$-\frac{\zeta'(s)}{\zeta(s)} = \frac{s}{s-1} + s\int_1^\infty \frac{\psi(x) - x}{x^{s+1}}\,dx$$

so that a bound $\psi(x) - x = O(x^\alpha)$, $\alpha < 1/2$, would imply that $\zeta(s)$ has no zeroes with $\mathrm{Re}(s) = 1/2$ (which is false!). What is not known is whether the $\log^2 x$ factor in (8.12) is optimal (assuming RH, of course).

A celebrated theorem of Littlewood states that the error term $R_\psi(x) = \psi(x) - x$ satisfies

$$R_\psi(x) > A\sqrt{x}\log\log\log x$$

and

$$R_\psi(x) < -B\sqrt{x}\log\log\log x$$

infinitely often, where $A, B$ are positive constants (see [60]). This implies the analogous statements for the error

$$R(x) = \pi(x) - \text{Li}(x)$$

though the transition is more tricky since one can no longer assume that $R_\psi(x)$ is monotonically increasing or that $|R_\psi(x)| > \sqrt{x}\log x$. The result is that

$$R(x) > A'\frac{\sqrt{x}\log\log\log x}{\log x}$$

and

$$R(x) < -B'\frac{\sqrt{x}\log\log\log x}{\log x}$$

infinitely often, for positive constants $A', B'$.

So even assuming RH, there is a discrepancy between the upper and lower bounds for $R(x)$, but H.L. Montgomery has suggested [60, page xiv], based on some further conjectures regarding the zeroes of the Riemann zeta function, that

$$\limsup \frac{R_\psi(x)}{\sqrt{x}(\log\log\log x)^2} = \frac{1}{2\pi}$$

and

$$\liminf \frac{R_\psi(x)}{\sqrt{x}(\log\log\log x)^2} = -\frac{1}{2\pi}$$

so there is reason to believe that

$$\pi(x) = \text{Li}(x) + O\left(\frac{\sqrt{x}(\log\log\log x)^2}{\log x}\right)$$

is the best possible form of the prime number theorem.

**Exercise 8.1\*** [HM] Prove the Riemann Hypothesis.

**Exercise 8.2**
(a) [P] [M] Implement $\Lambda(n)$ in *Mathematica*.
(b) [P] [M] Implement $\psi(x)$.
(c) [M] Show that

$$\log\lfloor x \rfloor! = \psi(x) + \psi(x/2) + \psi(x/3) + \cdots$$

**Exercise 8.3** [HM] Consider the prime counting function

$$\pi^*(x) = \# \left\{ \frac{x}{2k} < p \le \frac{x}{2k-1}, \ p \text{ prime}, \ k = 1, 2, \ldots, \lfloor x/2 \rfloor \right\}.$$

Show that $\pi^*$ satisfies

$$\pi^*(x) = \log 2 \int_2^x \frac{dx}{\log x} + O(\sqrt{x}\,\log x).$$

Explain why the analogue of the Riemann Hypothesis is true for this function.

**Exercise 8.4** The Farey sequence $\mathcal{F}_n$ consists of the fractions $a/b$, with $0 \le a \le b \le n$, $a$ and $b$ relatively prime, ordered according to size. For example, for $n = 5$ this is

$$\left\{ 0, \frac{1}{5}, \frac{1}{4}, \frac{1}{3}, \frac{2}{5}, \frac{1}{2}, \frac{3}{5}, \frac{2}{3}, \frac{3}{4}, \frac{4}{5}, 1 \right\}.$$

(a) [P] [HM] Write a program to generate the $n$th Farey sequence.
(b) [HM]
(i) Show that the number of pairs of relatively prime integers $(a, b)$, $1 \le a, b, \le N$, is asymptotic to $6\,N^2/\pi^2$. (So that $\Phi(n)$, the number of elements in $\mathcal{F}_n$, is asymptotic to $3\,n^2/\pi^2$.)
(ii) (S. Lang) Generalize (i) to sequences of integers $(a_1, \ldots, a_n)$ with no common factor and $0 < a_i \le N$, $i = 1, \ldots, n$.
(c) [HM] A sequence of real numbers $x_1, x_2, \ldots, 0 \le x_n \le 1$, is *equidis-tributed* if the "probability" of finding $x_n$ in a subinterval $[\alpha, \beta]$ is the

length of the subinterval (see [69] [97, page 88] for general facts about equidistribution). More precisely this says that for any $S \subseteq [0, 1]$

$$\lim_{N \to \infty} \frac{1}{N} \#\{n \le N \mid \alpha \le x_n \le \alpha \in S\} = \beta - \alpha.$$

**(i)** Show that the Farey sequence is equidistributed. In order to make this into a sequence $x_1, x_2, \ldots$, you will have to modify the Farey sequence slightly so that it is ordered according to size of numerators and denominators, i.e.,

$$\left\{ 0, 1, \frac{1}{2}, \frac{1}{3}, \frac{2}{3}, \frac{1}{4}, \frac{3}{4}, \frac{1}{5}, \frac{2}{5}, \ldots \right\}.$$

**Hint:** The main technique in the theory of equidistribution is *Weyl's criterion* (see [97]) which states that $x_1, x_2, \ldots$ is equidistributed if and only if

(8.13)          $$\lim_{N \to \infty} \frac{1}{N} \sum_{n < N} e^{2\pi i m \, x_n} = 0$$

for each $m = 1, 2, \ldots$.

**(ii)** What is the *discrepancy* in the equidistribution of the Farey series? In other words, measure the deviation from equidistribution by giving a quantitative form of the limit (8.13) in the case of the Farey sequence.

**(iii)** Generalize (i) to elliptic curves.

**(d)\* [HM]** Does the Farey sequence appears in the Mandelbrot set?

**Exercise 8.5 [P]** Write a program to locate the complex zeroes of $\zeta(s)$.

## 8.2   A more pedestrian application of $\zeta$

The deepest relations between the $\zeta$-function and prime numbers seems limited to the complex arguments of $\zeta(s)$. The $\zeta$ function does have some moderately interesting properties at other values, for example I will show how someone armed with a table of zeta values at the integers can accelerate convergence of many common series (of course the *Mathematica* user is such a person since he has access to the built-in function `Zeta[n]`).

It is well known that Gregory's series for $\pi$

$$\frac{\pi}{4} = 1 - \frac{1}{3} + \frac{1}{5} - \frac{1}{7} + \cdots$$

converges very slowly. In other words taking $n$ terms of the series gives you an error which is *guaranteed* to be greater than $1/(2n)$. So, for example, it is impossible to get 50 digits of $\pi$ using the series directly.
Here is a way to speed up the convergence. Write the series as

$$(8.14) \qquad \sum_{n=1}^{\infty} \left( \frac{1}{4n-3} - \frac{1}{4n-1} \right).$$

Each summand can be written as

$$\frac{1}{4n-3} - \frac{1}{4n-1} = \frac{1}{4}\frac{1}{n}\left( \frac{1}{1 - \frac{3}{4n}} - \frac{1}{1 - \frac{1}{4n}} \right).$$

Now from the geometric series expansion

$$\frac{1}{1-r} = \sum_{k=0}^{\infty} r^k$$

one derives the expansion

$$\frac{1}{4}\left( \sum_{k=0}^{\infty} \frac{(3^k - 1)\, x^{k+1}}{4^k} \right).$$

Plugging this back into (8.14) gives

$$\frac{1}{4} \sum_{n=1}^{\infty} \sum_{k=1}^{\infty} \frac{3^k - 1}{4^k} \frac{1}{n^{k+1}} = \frac{1}{4} \sum_{k=1}^{\infty} \frac{3^k - 1}{4^k} \sum_{n=1}^{\infty} \frac{1}{n^{k+1}},$$

where the order of summation was interchange and the $k = 0$ term dropped since $3^0 - 1 = 0$. Now the summation over $n$ in the last equation is simply the Riemann-$\zeta$ function

$$\zeta(s) = \sum_{n=1}^{\infty} \frac{1}{n^s}.$$

So the resulting transformation of Gregory's series is

$$\pi = \sum_{k=1}^{\infty} \frac{3^k - 1}{4^k} \zeta(k+1) .$$

The benefit of this series is that $1 < \zeta(k) < 2$ for $k = 2, 3, \ldots$ so the error term for this series is around $(3/4)^k$ which is much better than before.

The method works in general for a general series of the form

$$\sum_{n=1}^{\infty} f(1/n)$$

where $f$ is a function with Taylor series

$$f(x) = \sum_{k=2}^{\infty} a_k x^k .$$

This can be seen by exchanging summation

$$(8.15) \qquad \sum_{n=1}^{\infty} f(1/n) = \sum_{n=1}^{\infty} \sum_{k=2}^{\infty} \frac{a_k}{n^k} = \sum_{k=2}^{\infty} a_k \, \zeta(k) .$$

One can further accelerate convergence by taking out the first $m$ terms from $\zeta(k)$. One can write

$$\zeta(k) = 1 + \frac{1}{2^k} + \cdots + \frac{1}{m^k}$$

$$+ \left( \zeta(k) - 1 - \frac{1}{2^k} - \cdots - \frac{1}{m^k} \right) .$$

and substituting this back into (8.15) gives

$$\sum_{n=1}^{\infty} f(1/n) = \sum_{k=2}^{\infty} \sum_{j=1}^{m} \frac{a_k}{j^k}$$

$$+ \sum_{k=2}^{\infty} a_k \left( \zeta(k) - 1 - 1/2^k - \cdots - 1/m^k \right)$$

$$= f(1) + f(1/2) + \cdots + f(1/m)$$

$$+ \sum_{k=2}^{\infty} a_k \left( \zeta(k) - 1 - 1/2^k - \cdots - 1/m^k \right)$$

and terms in the infinite sum go to zero at the rate $1/m^k$.

**Exercise 8.6** Use this method to accelerate the convergence of

$$\log 2 = 1 - \frac{1}{2} + \frac{1}{3} - \frac{1}{4} + \cdots$$

and Catalan's constant

$$1 - \frac{1}{9} + \frac{1}{25} - \frac{1}{49} + \cdots$$

**Exercise 8.7 (a) [P] [M]** *Mathematica*'s $\pi$ algorithm in V2.0 uses the following formula (with a corrected misprint) of D.V. Chudnovsky and G.V. Chudnovsky [17, p. 389] which gives 14 digits per term,

$$\frac{1}{\pi} \frac{640320^{3/2}}{6541681608}$$

$$= \sum_{n=0}^{\infty} \left( n + \frac{13591409}{545140134} \right) \frac{(6n)!}{(3n)!\,(n!)^3} \frac{(-1)^n}{640320^{3n}}.$$

Implement this in *Mathematica*.

**(b) [P] [M]** The following might be the least efficient $\pi$ algorithm possible. Explain how it works.

```
pi2[n_, m_]:=
Sqrt[N[6 m / Length[
        Select[Table[GCD[Random[Integer, {1,n}],
                    Random[Integer, {1,n}]], {m}],
            #==1&]]]]
```

## 8.3   The Euler-Maclaurin formula

The principle at work above seems somewhat mysterious, but it looks like what is going on is a convergent form of the Euler-MacLaurin formula. Indeed, the acceleration of the series is dependent on the evaluation of $\zeta(k)$, $k = 2, 3, \ldots$, and these are computed using the Euler-MacLaurin formula.

The content of this formula is that one can replace a sum of a function by an integral, one example is the integral test of undergraduate calculus, another is the well known estimate

$$\sum_{k=1}^{n} \frac{1}{n} \approx \log x .$$

There are various ways to write down the Euler-Maclaurin formula, but the one most useful for the purposes here is [49, page 466], which states that if $f(x)$ is a $2m + 4$–times differentiable function with $f^{(2m+2)}(x)$ and $f^{(2m+4)}(x)$ of one sign in the range $1 < x < \infty$ ($f^{(n)}(x)$ means the $n$th derivative of $f(x)$) then

$$\sum_{1 \le k < n} f(k) = \int_{1}^{n} f(x)dx + C - \frac{f(n)}{2}$$

$$+ \sum_{k=1}^{m} \frac{B_{2k}}{(2k)!} f^{(2k-1)}(n) + \alpha_{m,n} \frac{B_{2m+2}}{(2m+2)!} f^{(2m+1)}(n) ,$$

where $0 < \alpha_{m,n} < 1$, $C$ is a constant independent of $m$ and $n$, and $B_{2k}$ is the $2k$th Bernoulli number (given by `BernoulliB` in *Mathematica*).
    If the sum and integral

$$\sum_{k=1}^{\infty} f(k) \quad \text{and} \quad \int_{1}^{\infty} f(x)dx$$

converge, then one can evaluate $C$ in the above formula by letting $n \to \infty$, so that

$$C = \sum_{k=1}^{\infty} f(k) - \int_{1}^{\infty} f(x)dx .$$

This means that one can evaluate $\sum_{k=1}^{\infty} f(k)$ as

$$\sum_{k=1}^{\infty} f(k) = \sum_{k=1}^{n-1} f(k) + \int_{n}^{\infty} f(x)dx - \frac{f(n)}{2}$$

(8.16)
$$- \sum_{k=1}^{m} (-1)^{k-1} \frac{\zeta(2k)}{2^{2k-1}\pi^{2k}} f^{(2k-1)}(n)$$

$$- \alpha_{m,n} (-1)^{m} \frac{\zeta(2m+2)}{2^{2m+1}\pi^{2m+2}} f^{(2m+1)}(n) ,$$

where the substitution $B_{2k} \Rightarrow \zeta(2k)$ by Euler's famous identity (e.g., [49, p. 272])

$$\zeta(2k) = (-1)^{k-1} \frac{2^{2k-1} \pi^{2k} B_{2k}}{(2k)!}.$$

Note that Equation (8.16) has some similarity to formula (8.15).

## 8.3.1  Implementing the formula

The Euler-Maclaurin formula is implemented in *Mathematica* by `NSum` with the option `Method -> Integrate`. For example, one can easily evaluate

$$\zeta'(2) = -\sum_{n=1}^{\infty} \frac{\log n}{n^2}$$

to fourty places by

```
In[1]:=  -NSum[Log[k]/k^2, {k, 2, Infinity},
         PrecisionGoal -> 40,
         WorkingPrecision-> 43,
         NSumTerms-> prec,
         Method -> Integrate,
         VerifyConvergence->False]
```

```
Out[1]= -0.9375482543158437537025740945678649789786
```

which returns some extra digits (compare with [66, p. 659]). This program has to run in V2.0 since these options do not exist in V1.2. It is fairly simple to implement this in the specific case of $f(k) = -\log k/k^n$ since this function satisfies the condition of having its derivatives have one sign in the range $x > 2$. In fact the $m$th derivative of $-\log x/x^n$ is equal to

$$\alpha_m \frac{\log x}{x^{n+m}} + \beta_m \frac{1}{x^{n+m}},$$

where $\alpha_0 = 0$ and

$$\alpha_m = (-1)^{m-1} n(n+1)(n+2) \cdots (n+m-1),$$

and $\beta_m$ is given by the recurrence

$$\beta_0 = 0, \quad \beta_{m+1} = -(n+m)\beta_m + \alpha_m.$$

In particular, one can check that $|\alpha_m| > |\beta_m|$, so that $f^{(m)}(x)$ is of one sign for $2 \leq x < \infty$. One can therefore use formula (8.16) directly to evaluate $\zeta'(n)$.

First, one has that, for $n > 1$

$$\int \frac{\log x}{x^n} dx = \frac{-1}{(n-1)^2\, x^{n-1}} - \frac{\log x}{(n-1)\, x^{n-1}}$$

so that

$$\int_m^\infty \frac{\log x}{x^n} dx = -\frac{1}{(n-1)^2\, m^{n-1}} - \frac{\log m}{(n-1)\, m^{n-1}} \, .$$

Next, one has that the $k$th derivative of $-\log(x)/x^n$ is easily computed iteratively by D[Log[x]/x^n, x]. The program is therefore

```
ZetaPrime[n_, prec_]:=
 Block[{k = 1, term = 1,
        acc = N[10^(-prec)/2, prec+3],
        x, f = D[-Log[x]/x^n, x],
        sum = N[-Log[prec]/((n-1) prec^(n-1)) -
              1/((n-1)^2 prec^(n-1)) +
              Log[prec]/(2 prec^n) +
              Plus @@ (-Log[#]/#^n& /@ Range[prec]),
              prec+5]},
      While[Abs[term] > acc,
              term = N[BernoulliB[2 k]/(2 k)! f /.
                     x -> prec, prec+3];
              f = D[f, {x, 2}];
              sum -= term; k++];
        N[sum, prec]]
```

Exercise 8.8 [P] [M] Implement the general Euler-Maclaurin formula, e.g., as given in [49, p. 455]: For an $m$-times differentiable function $f(x)$ one has

$$\sum_{a \leq k < b} f(k) = \int_a^b f(x)dx + \sum_{k=1}^m \frac{B_k}{k!} f^{(k-1)}(x)\Big|_a^b + R_m \, ,$$

where $R_m$ is the error term given by

$$R_m = (-1)^{m+1} \int_a^b \frac{B_m(\{x\})}{m!} f^{(m)}(x)dx \,,$$

for integers $a \le b$, $m \ge 1$. Here $\{x\} = x - \lfloor x \rfloor$

**Caveat:** When implementing this formula, be careful about picking the length of the summation. If you let the upper limit be a power of ten, you can overlook some subtle errors [10].

## 8.4 Khinchin's constant

The method of this Chapter can also be used to evaluate some other constants that are harder to compute. For example, *Khinchin's constant*

$$K = \prod_{n=1}^{\infty} \left(1 + \frac{1}{n(n+2)}\right)^{\log n / \log 2} \,,$$

which occurs in the theory of continued fractions as follows [63]: Take a random real number $x$, $0 < x < 1$, and write down its continued fraction expansion $x = [a_1, a_2, \ldots]$. Then except for a set of measure zero, the geometric mean of the continued fraction coefficients approaches $K$, i.e.,

$$\lim_{n \to \infty} \sqrt[n]{a_1 a_2 \cdots a_n} = K \,.$$

One way to try to estimate $K$ is just to try doing this directly

```
Khinchin[n_, m_]:=
Plus @@
Table[Exp[(Plus @@
        Log[N[Rest[
          ContinuedFraction[
            N[Random[Integer, {1, 11^n}]/11^n], n]]
          ])/n],
      {m}]/m
```

where

```
ContinuedFraction[x_, n_]:=
Floor[NestList[1/(# - Floor[#]) &, x, n - 1]]
```

gives the continued fraction expansion of a real number.

Computing this 100 times gives

```
In[1]:= Khinchin[100, 100]

Out[1]= 2.69352
```

So one expects the values to be around 2.7. Actually R.W. Gosper has computed the first 1000 digits of Khinchin's constant using the Euler-Maclaurin formula directly. These are

2.68545200106530644530971483548179569382038229399446
2953051152345557218859537152002801141174931847697995153465905288090082897677716410963051792533483259
6683818523154213321194996260393285220448194096180686641664289308477880620360737053501033672633577289
0499042707027234517026252370235458106863185010323746558037750264425248528694682341899491573066189872
0799413723550005793573669893395087902124464207528974145914769301844905060179349938522547040420337798
5639831015709022233910000220772509651332460444439191691460859682348212832462282927101269069741823484
7767545734898625420339266235186208677813665096965831469952718374480540121953666660496482698908275481
1525472117733031967594738371939357810605923040189071134962467370684122179468107406089182766956671171
6683740590473936880953450489997047176390451343232377151032196515038246988883248709353994696082647818
1205663494671257843666457974097784836620497777486827656970871631929385128993141995186116737926546205
6350595138571376169712687229980532767327871051376 3 ...

In order to compute Khinchin's constant one first computes

$$(8.17) \qquad \log K = \frac{1}{\log 2} \sum_{n=1}^{\infty} \log n \, \log \left( 1 + \frac{1}{n(n+2)} \right)$$

and exponentiates. One can try a direct evaluation using NSum, i.e., implementing Euler-Maclaurin directly. Note that the integral

$$\int \log x \, \log \left( 1 + \frac{1}{x(x+2)} \right) dx$$

which will appear in the formula can be evaluated using the *dilogarithm* function

$$\text{Li}_2(x) = \sum_{n=1}^{\infty} \frac{x^n}{n^2}, \qquad |x| < 1$$

which is given by Polylog[2, x] in *Mathematica*. In fact one has

```
In[1]:= Integrate[Log[x] Log[1 + 1/(x(x+2))], x]

                 x
Out[1]= -2 Log[1 + -] Log[x]  -  2 Log[1 + x] +
                 2

>    2 Log[x] Log[1 + x] + 2 Log[2 + x] -

              1                                    1
>    x Log[1 + ---------] + x Log[x] Log[1 + ---------] +
             x (2 + x)                       x (2 + x)

                                  -x
>    2 PolyLog[2, -x] - 2 PolyLog[2, --]
                                   2
```

The dilogarithm is extended to $|x| > 1$ using functional equations [81] so one has to be careful to get the right branch. In this case one has to let $x \to 1/y$ in the integral.

The program is therefore

```
f[x_] := Log[x] Log[1 + 1/(x (x+2))]
```

```
Khinchin[prec_] :=
 Block[{k = 1, term = 1,
        acc = N[10^(-prec)/2, prec+3],
        x, sum, g},
        sum = N[(Integrate[f[1/x]/x^2, x] /.
                              x -> 1/prec) +
              f[prec]/2 +
              (Plus @@ (f /@ Range[2, prec-1])),
              prec+5];
        g = Expand[D[f[x], x]];
        While[Abs[term] > acc,
              term = N[BernoulliB[2 k]/(2 k)! g /.
                   x -> prec, prec+3];
              g = Expand[D[g, {x, 2}]];
              sum -= term; k++];
        Exp[N[sum/Log[2], prec]]]
```

It turns out that this method doesn't work too well, probably because the derivatives of

$$\log x \left(1 + \frac{1}{x(x+2)}\right)$$

become very complicated very quickly. For example, one can compute
the fourth derivative by

```
D[Log[x] Log(1 + 1/(x (x + 2))), {x, 4}]
```

to get

$$\frac{d^4}{dx^4} \log x \, \log\left(1 + \frac{1}{x(x+2)}\right)$$

$$= \frac{-8}{x^4(2+x)^6\left(1+\frac{1}{x(2+x)}\right)^3} - \frac{24}{x^5(2+x)^5\left(1+\frac{1}{x(2+x)}\right)^3} - \frac{24}{x^6(2+x)^4\left(1+\frac{1}{x(2+x)}\right)^3}$$

$$- \frac{8}{x^7(2+x)^3\left(1+\frac{1}{x(2+x)}\right)^3} + \frac{24}{x^3(2+x)^5\left(1+\frac{1}{x(2+x)}\right)^2} + \frac{54}{x^4(2+x)^4\left(1+\frac{1}{x(2+x)}\right)^2}$$

$$+ \frac{60}{x^5(2+x)^3\left(1+\frac{1}{x(2+x)}\right)^2} + \frac{30}{x^6(2+x)^2\left(1+\frac{1}{x(2+x)}\right)^2} - \frac{24}{x^2(2+x)^4\left(1+\frac{1}{x(2+x)}\right)}$$

$$- \frac{36}{x^3(2+x)^3\left(1+\frac{1}{x(2+x)}\right)} - \frac{44}{x^4(2+x)^2\left(1+\frac{1}{x(2+x)}\right)} - \frac{44}{x^5(2+x)\left(1+\frac{1}{x(2+x)}\right)}$$

$$- \frac{6\log(x)}{x^4(2+x)^8\left(1+\frac{1}{x(2+x)}\right)^4} - \frac{24\log(x)}{x^5(2+x)^7\left(1+\frac{1}{x(2+x)}\right)^4} - \frac{36\log(x)}{x^6(2+x)^6\left(1+\frac{1}{x(2+x)}\right)^4}$$

$$- \frac{24\log(x)}{x^7(2+x)^5\left(1+\frac{1}{x(2+x)}\right)^4} - \frac{6\log(x)}{x^8(2+x)^4\left(1+\frac{1}{x(2+x)}\right)^4} + \frac{24\log(x)}{x^3(2+x)^7\left(1+\frac{1}{x(2+x)}\right)^3}$$

$$+ \frac{72\log(x)}{x^4(2+x)^6\left(1+\frac{1}{x(2+x)}\right)^3} + \frac{96\log(x)}{x^5(2+x)^5\left(1+\frac{1}{x(2+x)}\right)^3} + \frac{72\log(x)}{x^6(2+x)^4\left(1+\frac{1}{x(2+x)}\right)^3}$$

$$+ \frac{24\log(x)}{x^7(2+x)^3\left(1+\frac{1}{x(2+x)}\right)^3} - \frac{36\log(x)}{x^2(2+x)^6\left(1+\frac{1}{x(2+x)}\right)^2} - \frac{72\log(x)}{x^3(2+x)^5\left(1+\frac{1}{x(2+x)}\right)^2}$$

$$- \frac{84\log(x)}{x^4(2+x)^4\left(1+\frac{1}{x(2+x)}\right)^2} - \frac{72\log(x)}{x^5(2+x)^3\left(1+\frac{1}{x(2+x)}\right)^2} - \frac{36\log(x)}{x^6(2+x)^2\left(1+\frac{1}{x(2+x)}\right)^2}$$

$$+ \frac{24\log(x)}{x(2+x)^5\left(1+\frac{1}{x(2+x)}\right)} + \frac{24\log(x)}{x^2(2+x)^4\left(1+\frac{1}{x(2+x)}\right)} + \frac{24\log(x)}{x^3(2+x)^3\left(1+\frac{1}{x(2+x)}\right)}$$

$$+ \frac{24\log(x)}{x^4(2+x)^2\left(1+\frac{1}{x(2+x)}\right)} + \frac{24\log(x)}{x^5(2+x)\left(1+\frac{1}{x(2+x)}\right)} - \frac{6\log\left(1+\frac{1}{x(2+x)}\right)}{x^4}$$

Instead, one can try to accelerate convergence using the methods of this Chapter, except that now, one assumes that a table of values of $\zeta'(k)$, $k = 2, 3, \ldots$, exists, and expresses Khinchin's constant in terms of them.

To do this you first have to express the sum in (8.17) as a sum of terms $f(1/n)$. Noting that

$$1 + \frac{1}{n(n+2)} = \frac{(1 + (1/n))^2}{1 + 2(1/n)}$$

each summand in (8.17) is of the form

$$\log n \log \left( \frac{(y+1)^2}{1+2y} \right) ,$$

where $y = 1/n$. Now one computes the Taylor series

$$\log \left( \frac{(x+1)^2}{1+2x} \right) = 2\log(1+x) - \log(1+2x) \sum_{k=0}^{\infty} a_k x^k ,$$

where $a_0 = 0$ and

$$a_k = (-1)^{k+1} \frac{2 - 2^k}{k} , \qquad k > 0 ,$$

in particular $a_1 = 0$.

Summing this over $n$ gives

$$\sum_{n=2}^{\infty} \log n \, \log \left( 1 + \frac{1}{n(n+2)} \right)$$

$$= 2 \sum_{n=2}^{\infty} \sum_{k=1}^{\infty} \frac{(-1)^{k+1}}{kn^k} - \sum_{n=2}^{\infty} \log n \sum_{k=1}^{\infty} \frac{(-1)^{k+1}2^k}{kn^k}$$

$$= 2 \sum_{k=2}^{\infty} \frac{(-1)^{k+1}}{k} \zeta'(k) - \sum_{k=2}^{\infty} \frac{(-1)^k 2^k}{k} \zeta'(k)$$

The terms in the first summand in of the last line of this equation go to zero like $\zeta'(k)/k \approx 2^{-k}/k$ so give an accelerated series. The terms of the second summand, on the other hand, only go to zero like $2^k \zeta'(k)/k \approx 1/k$, so this term must be accelerated using the trick of Section 8.2, i.e., removing the first couple of terms $\zeta'(k)$

$$\sum_{k=2}^{\infty} \frac{(-1)^k 2^k}{k} \zeta'(k) = \sum_{k=2}^{\infty} \frac{(-1)^k 2^k \left( \zeta'(k) + \frac{\log 2}{2^k} + \frac{\log 3}{3^k} \right)}{k}$$

$$+ \log 2 \sum_{k=2}^{\infty} \frac{(-1)^{k+1}}{k} + \log 3 \sum_{k=2}^{\infty} \frac{(-1)^{k+1}(2/3)^k}{k}$$

Using the expansion

$$\log(1+x) = \sum_{n=1}^{\infty} \frac{(-1)^{n+1} x^k}{k}$$

the last two terms are

$$\log 2 \sum_{k=2}^{\infty} \frac{(-1)^{k+1}}{k} = \log 2(1 - \log 2)$$

$$\log 3 \sum_{k=2}^{\infty} \frac{(-1)^{k+1}(2/3)^k}{k} = \log 3 \left(2/3 - \log(5/3)\right) .$$

Putting all this together gives

$$\log K = \frac{2}{\log 2} \sum_{k=2}^{\infty} \frac{(-1)^k}{k} \zeta'(k)$$

$$- \frac{1}{\log 2} \sum_{k=2}^{\infty} \frac{(-1)^k 2^k \left(\zeta'(k) + \frac{\log 2}{2^k} + \frac{\log 3}{3^k}\right)}{k}$$

$$+ \frac{\log 3}{\log 2} \left(\frac{2}{3} - \log(5/3)\right) + 1 - \log 2 .$$

You actually get convergence better than $1/2^k$ since for each $k$

$$\frac{(-1)^k 2\, \zeta'(k)}{k} - \frac{(-1)^k 2^k \left(\zeta'(k) + \frac{\log 2}{2^k} + \frac{\log 3}{3^k}\right)}{k}$$

$$= \frac{(-1)^k}{k} \left(-2 \frac{\log 2}{2^k} - \frac{\log 3}{3^k} - \cdots + 2^k \frac{\log 4}{4^k} + 2^k \frac{\log 5}{5^k} + \cdots \right)$$

$$= \frac{(-1)^k}{k} \left(-\frac{\log 3}{3^k} - \frac{\log 4}{4^k} - \cdots + 2^k \frac{\log 5}{5^k} + 2^k \frac{\log 6}{6^k} + \cdots \right) ,$$

and so, with respect to $k$, each term goes to zero at the rate $(2/5)^k$ instead of $1/2^k$.

The Khinchin program is therefore given by

```
Khinchin[prec_]:=
Block[{sum = 0, k = 2, ZetaPrime, term = 1,
        acc = N[10^(-prec-3)]},
        While[Abs[term] > acc,
            ZetaPrime = ZetaPrime[k, prec+5];
```

```
       term = N[(-1)^k 2 ZetaPrime/k -
               (-1)^k 2^k(ZetaPrime +
                          Log[2]/2^k + Log[3]/3^k)/k,
                 prec+5];
     sum += term; k++];
    sum /= N[Log[2], prec+5];
    sum +=N[Log[3]/Log[2] (2/3 - Log[5/3]) +
            1 -Log[2], prec + 5];
   N[Exp[sum], prec]]
```

where `ZetaPrime[n, prec]` evaluates $\zeta'(n)$ to precision `prec` using
`NSum`

```
ZetaPrime[n_, prec_]:=
  Block[{k},
        -NSum[Log[k]/k^n, {k, 2, Infinity},
        PrecisionGoal -> prec,
        WorkingPrecision-> prec + 3,
        NSumTerms-> prec,
        Method -> Integrate,
        VerifyConvergence->False]]
```

This program only runs in V2.0, however, and in any case one can do
better since the integral of $\log x/x$ can be computed explicitly instead
of relying on internal subroutines of `NSum`. A more efficient program for
the purposes of this section is

```
ZetaPrime[n_, prec_]:=
  Block[{k = 1, j = 4, s = N[-Log[4]/4^n, prec+5], term = 1,
        acc = N[10^(-prec-4) /2, prec+5],
        x, f,
        sum, m = Max[4, Ceiling[N[Log[10] prec/Log[n] ]]]},
        sum = N[-Log[2]/2^n - Log[3]/3^n, prec + 5];
        While[j < m,
              sum += s; j++;
              s = N[-Log[j]/j^n, prec + 5]];
        m = Min[j, m];
        term = N[-Log[m]/((n-1) m^(n-1)) -
```

```
                1/((n-1)^2 m^(n-1)) -
                Log[m]/(2 m^n), prec + 5];
        sum += term;
        f = D[-Log[x]/x^n, x];
        While[Abs[term] > acc,
                term = N[BernoulliB[2 k]/(2 k)! f /.
                        x -> m, prec+3];
                f = D[f, {x, 2}];
                sum -= term; k++];
        N[sum, prec]]
```

This program is able to obtain 200 digits of Khinchin's constant in about 3 hours on a IBM Risc workstation.

**Exercise 8.9 [P] [M]** (R.W. Gosper) Implement the arithmetic operations on real numbers using continued fraction representations.

**Exercise 8.10\* [HM]** (R.W. Gosper) Do the continued fraction coefficients of Khinchin's constant satisfy the condition of Khinchin's constant?

**Exercise 8.11 [P] [HM]** (P. Flajolet, I. Vardi [32]) Evaluate

$$\prod_{p \text{ prime}} \cos(1/p)$$

to 100 decimal places.

## 8.5 Notes

Some references about the theory of the Riemann zeta functions are [25] [61] [92] [94] [127].

References relating to the distribution of prime numbers [23] [24] [57] [60] [102]. The books of Davenport and Ingham use complex analytic methods, while Hardy and Wright's book and Diamond's article deal only with "elementary methods", i.e., methods which do not directly involve complex numbers.

An excellent informal treatment of these topics is given by G.H. Hardy in [56, Lecture II].

The two functions $Z(t)$ and $\vartheta(t)$ appear in Version 2.0 as
`RiemannSiegelZ[t]` and `RiemannSiegelTheta[t]`, respectively. The
following is an implementation of these functions in *Mathematica*

```
RiemannSiegelZ[t_Real]:=
 Re[Zeta[1/2 + I t] Exp[I RiemannSiegelTheta[t]]] /;
    t <= 1000

RiemannSiegelZ[t_Real]:=
 Block[{pi = N[Pi], theta, m, u, nu},
        u = Sqrt[t/(2 pi)];
        m = Floor[u];
        nu = 2(u - m) - 1;
        theta = RiemannSiegelTheta[t];
        r = N[Range[m]];
        2 (Cos[theta - t Log[r]] . (1/Sqrt[r]))+
        (-1)^(m-1) u^(-1/2) (
         (c[0] /. x -> nu) +
         (c[1] /. x -> nu)/u +
         (c[2] /. x -> nu)/u^2 +
         (c[3] /. x-> nu)/u^3)] /; t > 1000

(* The list of asymptotic coefficients  *)

psilist =
  NestList[D[#, x]&,
       N[Normal[Series[Cos[N[2 Pi, 30] x^2 +
                            N[(3 Pi/8), 30]]/
              Cos[2 Pi x], {x, 0, 40}]], 30],
              9]  /. x -> x/2

c[0] = N[psilist[[1]]]

c[1] = N[-psilist[[4]]]/(2^5 3 Pi^2)]

c[2] = N[psilist[[7]]]/(2^11 3^2 Pi^4) +
        psilist[[3]]/(2^6 Pi^2)]
```

```
c[3] = N[-psilist[[10]]/(2^16 3^4 Pi^6) -
          psilist[[6]]/(2^8 3 5 Pi^4) -
          psilist[[2]]/(2^6 Pi^2)]
```

The function $\vartheta(t)$ requires one to compute $\log(\Gamma(s))$ for large values of $s$. For these values it is inefficient to first compute $\Gamma(s)$ and then take logarithms, and a much better method is to compute this value directly from Stirling's formula

$$\log(\Gamma(s+1)) \sim s\log x - a + \frac{\log s}{2} + \frac{1}{2}\log(2\pi)$$

$$+ \sum_{k=1}^{\infty} \frac{B_{2k}}{(2k)(2k-1)s^{2k-1}},$$

where $B_n$ is the Bernoulli number given by `BernoulliB[n]` in *Mathematica*. This function is implemented as `LogGamma` in Version 2.0, but I have included the *Mathematica* code for it.

One therefore implements $\vartheta(t)$ by

```
RiemannSiegelTheta[t_Real] :=
  -Log[N[Pi]] t/2 + Im[Log[Gamma[1/4 + I t/2]]] /;
                                  t <= 10

RiemannSiegelTheta[t_Real] :=
  -Log[N[Pi]] t/2 + Im[LogGamma[1/4 + I t/2]] /;
                                  t > 10

LogGamma[s_] :=
    (s - 1/2) Log[s] - s + Log[N[2 Pi]]/2 +
        (LogGammaList . (s^(1- 2 Range[16])))

LogGammaList =  N[(BernoulliB /@ (2 Range[16]))/
                (4 Range[16]^2 - 2 Range[16])]
```

R.W. Gosper computed 1, 111 digits of Khinchin's constant in February of 1987.

The technique of [32] was developed when P. Sarnak asked me to compute the constant

$$\prod_{p \text{ prime}} \left\{ 1 - \left( 1 - \prod_{n=1}^{\infty} (1 - p^{-n}) \right)^2 \right\}$$

$$= .353236371854995984543516550432682011280164778566669\ldots$$

which represents the probability that two very large integer matrices have relatively prime determinants [54]. Note that this number is less than

$$\frac{6}{\pi^2} = .607927101854026628663276779258365833426152648033342\ldots$$

which is the probability that two large integers are relatively prime (see Exercise 8.4 (b)).

# 9

# The Running Time of TAK

# Chapter 9

# The Running Time of TAK

I. Takeuchi introduced a recursive function which has the property that it calls itself very often without having its values growing. The reason for defining a function with this property is to use it as a benchmark for testing the efficiency of Lisp implementations. Variations of this function were used by R.P. Gabriel [35] to compare various implementations of Lisp. In this Chapter I will analyze the running time of the original Takeuchi function as well as the version used by Gabriel. An exact lower bound will also be given on the running time of any Takeuchi type function.

First, one needs to define what is meant by a *Takeuchi function*

**Definition:** The Takeuchi function $TAK_h(x, y, z)$ defined by the function $h(x, y, z)$ for integers $x, y, z$ is given by

$$TAK_h(x, y, z) = h(x, y, z)$$

if $x \le y$ and, if $x > y$ then

$$TAK_h(x, y, z)$$

$$= TAK_h(TAK_h(x - 1, y, z), TAK_h(y - 1, z, x), TAK_h(z - 1, x, y))$$

The original function considered by Takeuchi had $h(x, y, z) = y$, and we denote this by $TAK_y$. R. Gabriel considered the function defined by J. McCarthy [35, p. 81] which had $h(x, y, z) = z$, and this function will be denoted by $TAK_z$. Note that $TAK_h$ may only be a partial function for some choices of $h$.

The relevance of this function as a benchmark is not limited to Lisp but applies to any language that uses recursion. In particular one can write a *Mathematica* implementation of the Takeuchi functions

```
Tak[h_, x_, y_, z_] := h[x, y, z]   /; x <= y

Tak[h_, x_, y_, z_] :=
     Tak[h, Tak[h, x-1, y, z],
             Tak[h, y-1, z, x],
             Tak[h, z-1, x, y]]

TakY[x_, y_, z_] := Tak[#2&, x, y, z]

TakZ[x_, y_, z_] := Tak[#3&, x, y, z]

$RecursionLimit = Infinity
```

(setting the recursion limit to infinity is crucial to the analysis of this highly recursive program).

**Exercise 9.1**

**(a) [M]** Show that $\text{TAK}_y(a, b, c)$ is the function

$$\text{TAK}_y(a, b, c) = \begin{cases} b & \text{if } a \leq b \\ a & \text{if } a > b \text{ and } b > c \\ c & \text{if } a > b \text{ and } b \leq c. \end{cases}$$

**(b) [M]** Show that $\text{TAK}_z(a, b, c)$ is the function

$$\text{TAK}_z(a, b, c) = \begin{cases} c & \text{if } a \leq b \\ b & \text{if } b \geq c \text{ and either } b = c \text{ or } a - b \text{ is odd} \\ c + 1 & \text{if } b \geq c \\ b & \text{if } c \leq a + 1 \text{ and either } c \leq a \text{ or } a > b + 1 \\ a & \text{if } c - a \text{ is even} \\ b + 1 & \text{otherwise} \end{cases}$$

where the value taken corresponds to the first of these conditions that holds.

**Exercise 9.2**

(a) [M] (D.E. Knuth [67]) Characterize the $0, 1$ valued functions $h(x, y, z)$ for which $TAK_h$ is a total function.

(b)* [M] For which set of functions $h$ is $TAK_h$ a total function?

# 9.1  The lower bound

This Section consists of showing that there is an absolute lower bound, independent of $h$, on the number of times $TAK_h(x, y, z)$ calls itself. This is done by considering the simplest Takeuchi function, namely the one with $h(x, y, z) \equiv 0$ (this will be denoted by $TAK_0$).

   To talk about the number of function calls in TAK you define the function $F_h(x, y, z)$ which returns the number of function calls to evaluate $TAK_h(x, y, z)$. Denoting this by `TakTime` one can write a quick and dirty program by using global constants

```
TakTimeGlobal[h_, x_, y_, z_]:=
Block[{},
      TakTimeConstant = 0;
      Tak[h, x, y, z];
      TakTimeConstant]

Tak[h_, x_, y_, z_]:=
Block[{},
      TakTimeConstant = TakTimeConstant + 1;
      h[x, y, z]]   /; x <= y

Tak[h_, x_, y_, z_]:=
Block[{},
      TakTimeConstant = TakTimeConstant + 1;
      Tak[h, Tak[h, x-1, y, z],
              Tak[h, y-1, z, x],
              Tak[h, z-1, x, y]]]
```

For example, writing $F_0$ for the running time of $TAK_0$, one computes $F_0(32, 12, 5)$ by

```
In[1]:= TakTimeGlobal[0&, 16, 13, 7]
```

```
Out[1]= 8217
```

A more elegant way to calculate the running time is to note that

$$F_h(x, y, z) = 1$$

if $x \le y$, and if $x > y$ then

$$F_h(x, y, z)$$

$$(9.1) \quad = 1 + F_h(x - 1, y, z) + F_h(y - 1, z, x) + F_h(z - 1, x, y)$$

$$\quad + F_h(\text{TAK}_h(x - 1, y, z), \text{TAK}_h(y - 1, z, x), \text{TAK}_h(z - 1, x, y))$$

In the case of $F_0$, the last term in the above is $F_0(0, 0, 0) = 1$ so (writing $a, b, c$ instead of $x, y, z$ in the analysis of special cases)

$$(9.2) \quad F_0(a, b, c) = 2 + F_0(a - 1, b, c) + F_0(b - 1, c, a) + F_0(c - 1, a, b)$$

when $a > b$. These recurrences can be implemented in *Mathematica* as

```
TakTime[h_, a_, b_, z_]:= 1  /; a <= b
```

```
TakTime[h_, a_, b_, z_]=
  1 + TakTime[h, a-1, b, c] + TakTime[h, b-1, c, a] +
      TakTime[h, c-1, a, b] +
      TakTime[h, Tak[h, a-1, b, c], Tak[h, b-1, c, a],
              Tak[h, c-1, a, b]]
```

```
TakTime0[a_, b_, c_]:= 1 /; a <= b
```

```
TakTime0[a_, b_, c_]:=
   2 + TakTime0[a-1, b, c] + TakTime0[b-1, c, a] +
       TakTime0[c-1, a, b]
```

Now (9.3) still looks like a mess, so it's time to actually think about what the function is doing. The first observation is that what matters in arguments $a, b, c$ is not their absolute size but their relative size, in other words for any integer $d$ one has

$$F_0(a + d, b + d, c + d) = F_0(a, b, c).$$

This simplifies the analysis a lot since it allows you to remove one of the variables $a, b, c$, i.e., it is sufficient to consider the running time of $\text{TAK}_0(a, b, 0)$ or the running time of $\text{TAK}_0(a, 0, b)$. Now the arguments $(a, b, 0)$ and $(b, 0, a)$ are cyclic shifts of each other, so the fact that the Takeuchi condition (9.1) is basically cyclic will give that $F_0(a, b, 0) = F_0(b, 0, a)$, for $a > b > 0$. To see this, substitute these values in the recurrence for $F_0$:

$$F_0(a, b, 0) = 2 + F_0(a - 1, b, 0) + F_0(b - 1, 0, a) + F_0(-1, a, b)$$
$$= 3 + F_0(a - 1, b, 0) + F_0(b - 1, 0, a)$$

and

$$F_0(b, 0, a) = 2 + F_0(a - 1, b, 0) + F_0(b - 1, 0, a) + F_0(-1, a, b)$$
$$= 3 + F_0(a - 1, b, 0) + F_0(b - 1, 0, a)$$

So the running time can be coded in by the function

$$F_0(a, b) = F_0(a, b, 0) = F_0(b, 0, a)$$

for $a > b > 0$, and

(9.4) $$F_0(a, a) = F_0(a, 0) = 1, \qquad a \geq 0,$$

(these values of $F_0(a, b)$ no longer correspond to $F_0(a, b, 0)$). The above implies that $F_0(a, b)$ satisfies the recurrence relation

(9.5) $$F_0(a, b) = 3 + F_0(a - 1, b) + F_0(a, b - 1),$$

with boundary conditions (9.4).

This recurrence can be converted into a more efficient *Mathematica* implementation of `TakTime0`:

```
TakTime0[a_, b_, c_]:= 1 /; a <= b
```

```
TakTime0[a_, b_, c_]:=
 TakTime0[a-c, b-c] /; b >= c

TakTime0[a_, b_, c_]:=
 TakTime0[c-b, a-b]  /; c > a

TakTime0[a_, b_, c_]:=
 4 (a - c + 1) + TakTime0[c, c-1]

TakTime0[a_, 0]:= 1

TakTime0[a_, a_]:= 1

TakTime0[a_, b_]:=
  3 + TakTime0[a-1, b] + TakTime0[a, b-1]
```

To solve (9.5) note that $F_0(a,b) \equiv -3$ is a particular solution to this inhomogeneous recurrence relation. So one looks at solutions of the homogeneous recurrence relation

$$(9.6) \qquad G(a,b) = G(a-1,b) + G(a,b-1)$$

with boundary conditions

$$(9.7) \qquad G(a,a) = G(a,0) = 1, \quad \text{if } a \geq 0.$$

To solve this recurrence it is helpful to introduce the notion of *lattice paths*, i.e., paths on a rectangular grid such that each step moves one step down or one step to the left. The point is that the recurrence (9.6) counts the number of lattice paths, while boundary conditions such as (9.7) restrict the kind of path considered, see Figure 9.1.

**Note:** The lattice point corresponding to $F_0(a,b)$ is denoted by $(b,a)$ in the figures so that the paths are always above the line $x = y$.

For example, the above recurrence with boundary conditions

$$G(0,0) = 1, \quad G(a,-1) = G(-1,a) = 0, \; a > 1$$

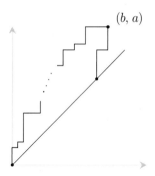

$(b, a)$

Figure 9.1: Paths from $(b, a)$ to $(0, 0)$, and to the line $x = y$.

counts all lattice paths from a point $(b, a)$ to the origin, and this number is easily seen to be

$$G(a, b) = \binom{a + b}{b}.$$

A more difficult question is

**Problem I:** *How many decreasing paths are there from $(b, a)$ to $(0, 0)$ which do not cross the line $x = y$?*

Letting $B(a, b)$ denote the number of such paths, this questions corresponds to the recurrence

$$B(a, b) = B(a - 1, b) + B(a, b - 1)$$

with boundary conditions

$$B(0, 0) = 1, \quad B(a, a) = 0, \; a > 0, \quad B(a, -1) = 0.$$

One can solve this by the reflection principle of D. André [19, page 22] to get the formula

$$B(a, b) = \frac{a - b}{a + b} \binom{a + b}{b}.$$

Note that Problem I has an equivalent formulation as the famous *ballot problem* [31, p. 67–97]

**Problem II:** *In an election with two candidates A and B, A wins with a votes and B loses with b votes. What is the probability that A was leading throughout the whole vote count?*

Since there are a total of $\binom{a+b}{b}$ paths, the formula for $B(a,b)$ implies that the answer to the Ballot Problem is

$$\frac{a-b}{a+b}.$$

One can therefore rephrase conditions (9.6) and (9.7) as

**Problem III:** *How many decreasing paths are there from $(b,a)$ which reach $(0,0)$ or stop first upon reaching the line $x = y$?*

This is clearly problem II summed over $(b,a), (b-1, a-1), \ldots, (1, a-b+1)$, i.e.,

$$(9.8) \qquad C(a,b) = \sum_{k=0}^{b} \frac{a-b}{a+b-2k} \binom{a+b-2k}{b-k}.$$

The numbers $C(a,b)$ satisfies the homogeneous problem (9.6) with boundary conditions $C(a,0) = C(a,a) = 1$, so $4\,C(a,b) - 3$ satisfies the inhomogeneous problem (9.5) with the correct boundary conditions and so you get

*The number of function calls $F_0(a,b)$ required to compute $\mathrm{TAK}_0(a,b,0)$, $a > b > 0$, is*

$$
\begin{aligned}
F_0(a,b) &= 4 \sum_{k=0}^{b} \frac{a-b}{a+b-2k} \binom{a+b-2k}{b-k} - 3 \\
&= 1 + 4 \sum_{k=0}^{b-1} \frac{a-b}{a+b-2k} \binom{a+b-2k}{b-k}
\end{aligned}
$$

(9.9)

This formula is very efficient for computing $F_0(a,b,0)$, for example a direct *Mathematica* implementation easily derived

$F_0(101, 100, 0)$

$= 4805672800953114008058898023404764734800915537848428631313$

The previous `TakTime0` program will take somewhat longer to evaluate this.

**Exercise 9.3 [M]** Show that if $b \geq a > 0$ then

$$F_0(b, 0, a) = 4(b - a + 1) + F_0(a, a - 1, 0).$$

**Exercise 9.4\* [P]** Is there a closed form for $F_0(a, b)$?

## 9.2 Asymptotics of the lower bound

To get a good lower bound on the running time $F_0(a, b, c)$ one can examine the slowest running time of $\text{TAK}_0(a, b, 0)$ where $a + b = m$ and $m$ is kept fixed. Since the value of $\binom{n}{k}$ for $n$ fixed increases with $k$ until $k = \lfloor n/2 \rfloor$ and then decreases (this is obvious from Pascal's triangle) maximum values of the summands

$$\frac{a - b}{a + b - 2k} \binom{a + b - 2k}{b - k}$$

in equation (9.9) occur when $a = n + 1$, $b = n$. In this case (9.9) becomes

$$F_0(n + 1, n) = 1 + 4 \sum_{k=0}^{n-1} \frac{1}{2n + 1 - 2k} \binom{2n + 1 - 2k}{n - k}$$

(9.10)

$$= 1 + 4 \sum_{k=1}^{n} \frac{1}{k + 1} \binom{2k}{k},$$

since

$$\frac{1}{2k + 1} \binom{2k + 1}{k} = \frac{1}{k + 1} \binom{2k}{k}.$$

These numbers are the famous *Catalan numbers* [26] [39, Chapter 20] [49] (see Exercise 9.8)

$$C(k) = \frac{1}{k + 1} \binom{2k}{k}.$$

Among their various properties is the asymptotic formula

$$C(k) \sim \frac{4^k}{\sqrt{\pi}\, k^{3/2}}$$

which follows from Stirling's formula [49, page 467]

$$\log k! \sim k \log k - k + \frac{\log(2\pi)}{2} + \frac{\log k}{2}$$

applied to the binomial coefficient $\binom{2k}{k} = (2k)!/(k!)^2$.

Plugging this into (9.10) gives

(9.11) $$F_0(n+1, n) \sim \frac{16}{3\sqrt{\pi}} \frac{4^n}{n^{3/2}},$$

which is proved by summing a geometric series (the details are left to the reader). This gives the following result about the running time of $\text{TAK}_0$

Let $\varepsilon > 0$, then there are values of $a, b$ for which $\text{TAK}_h(a, b, 0)$ makes at least

$$\frac{64(1 - \varepsilon)}{3\sqrt{2\pi}} \frac{2^{a+b}}{(a+b)^{3/2}}$$

function calls.

**Remark:** D.E. Knuth [67] has noted that if one stores the values of $\text{TAK}_0(a, b, 0)$, $a \geq b \geq 0$, then $F_0(a, b, 0) = O(a^2)$. To see this, note that, by the analysis of the previous section, the values needed to evaluate $\text{TAK}_0(a, b, 0)$ are $\text{TAK}_0(r, s, 0)$, $a \geq r \geq s \geq 0$, so at most $a^2$ values are ever computed.

## 9.3   The running time of $\text{TAK}_y$

As in the previous Section one writes $F_y(a, b, c)$ to represent the running time of $\text{TAK}_y(a, b, c)$. The first observation is that like the function $F_0(a, b, c)$, $\text{TAK}_y(a, b, c)$ essentially depends only on the relative values of $a, b, c$, i.e., for any integer $d$

$$\text{TAK}_y(a + d, b + d, c + d) = \text{TAK}_y(a, b, c) + d$$

and this once again this implies that

$$F_y(a + d, b + d, c + d) = F_y(a, b, c)$$

so one can restrict attention to $F_y(a, b, 0)$ and $F_y(b, 0, a)$ when $a > b > 0$. The conditions are more complicated in this case, so one has to do some more work. The first step is to use the evaluation of TAK$_y$ in Exercise 9.1 to get explicit recurrences for $F_y(a, b, 0)$ and $F_y(b, 0, a)$:

$$\text{TAK}_y(a - 1, b, 0) = a - 1$$

$$\text{TAK}_y(b - 1, 0, a) = \begin{cases} a & \text{if } b > 1 \\ 0 & \text{otherwise} \end{cases}$$

Thus the recurrence relation (9.1) for $F_h$ applied to $F_y(a, b, 0)$ gives

$$F_y(a, b, 0)$$
$$= 1 + F_y(a - 1, b, 0) + F_y(b - 1, 0, a) + F_y(-1, a, b)$$
$$\quad + F_y(\text{TAK}_y(a - 1, b, 0), \text{TAK}_y(b - 1, 0, a), \text{TAK}_y(-1, a, b))$$
$$= 2 + F_y(a - 1, b, 0) + F_y(b - 1, 0, a)$$
$$\quad + \begin{cases} F_y(a - 1, a, a) = 1 & \text{if } b \neq 1 \\ F_y(a - 1, 0, a) & \text{if } b = 1 \end{cases}$$

so

$$F_y(a, b, 0) = 3 + F_y(a, b, 0) + F_y(b - 1, 0, a), \quad b > 1$$
$$F_y(a, 1, 0) = 3 + F_y(a - 1, 1, 0) + F_y(a - 1, 0, a).$$

The computation for $F_y(b, 0, a)$ is simpler and gives

$$F_y(b, 0, a) = 3 + F_y(b - 1, 0, a) + F_y(a - 1, b, 0),$$

so that

$$F_y(a, b, 0) = F_y(b, 0, a) \qquad a > b > 1.$$

If $b = 1$ one has that

$$F_y(1, 0, a) = 4 + F_y(a - 1, 1, 0)$$
$$= 7 + F_y(a - 2, 1, 0) + F_y(a - 2, 0, a - 1)$$
$$= 3 + F_y(1, 0, a - 1) + F_y(a - 2, 0, a - 1).$$

Letting $F_y(a,b) = F_y(b,0,a)$, $a > b \geq 1$, one has the recurrence

(9.11)      $F_y(a,b) = 3 + F_y(a-1,b) + F_y(a,b-1)$,        $a > b > 1$,

with boundary conditions

(9.12)

$$F_y(1,0) = 5$$

$$F_y(2,1) = 5$$

$$F_y(a,1) = 3 + F_y(a-1,1) + F_y(a-1,a-2), \quad a > 2$$

$$F_y(a,b) = 1, \quad a \leq b.$$

This can be implemented as the program

```
TakTimeY[a_, b_] := 1 /; a <= b
```

```
TakTimeY[1,0] = 5
```

```
TakTimeY[2,1] = 5
```

```
TakTimeY[a_, 1] :=
3 + TakTimeY[a-1, 1] + TakTimeY[a-1, a-2] /; a > 2
```

```
TakTimeY[a_, b_] :=
3 + TakTimeY[a, b-1] + TakTimeY[a-1, b] /; a > b > 1
```

For example

```
In[1] := TakTimeY[8, 7]
```

```
Out[1]= 20885
```

```
In[2] := TakTime[9, 8]
```

```
Out[2]= 113749
```

Comparing this with the lower bound

```
In[3] := TakTime0[8, 7]
```

```
Out[3] := 2501
```

```
In[4] := TakTime0[9, 8]
```

```
Out[4] = 8221
```

leads one to suspect that $F_y$ grows much more quickly than the lower
bound $F_0$. In fact, it will be shown that $F_y(a, b, 0)$ grows faster than
any power of $b$.

The recurrence (9.11) with boundary conditions (9.12) comes down
to the following type of lattice path problem:

**Problem IV:** *How many lattice paths are there from* $(n-1, n)$ *to* $(0, 0)$
*which end at the line* $x = y$ *and when reaching* $(1, s)$*, are continued to*
$(s - 2, s - 1)$? *(See Figure 9.2.)*

**Remark:** One can think of the lattice paths of Problem IV as paths
beginning at $(n - 1, n)$ and at each $(1, s)$ generating a new lattice with
the path continuing at $(s - 2, s - 1)$ (see Figure 9.2).

Basically the recurrence (9.11) with boundary conditions (9.12) implies that TAK$_y(a, b, 0)$ runs optimally quickly until it runs into an
expression of the form

$$\text{TAK}_y(1, 0, n) \Rightarrow \text{TAK}_y(n - 1, n - 2, 0)$$

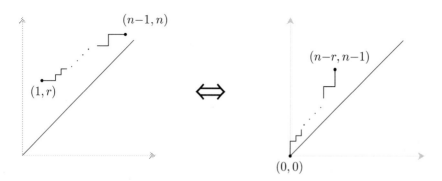

Figure 9.2: Lattice paths given by Problem IV.

which gives the worst possible canonical lower bound. In the language
of lattice, every path from $(b, a)$ to $(1, n)$ not crossing $x = y$ gives you a
term $F_y(n-1, n-2)$. Thus there is no loss of generality in restricting the
analysis to $F_y(n, n-1)$. Now every path from $(n-1, n)$ to $(1, r)$ which
doesn't cross $x = y$ corresponds to a path from $(0, 0)$ to $(n - r, n - 1)$
not crossing $x = y$ (see Figure 9.3), thus there are $B(n - 1, n - r)$ such
paths, where $B(a, b)$ is the function of the previous section.

These remarks show that the numbers $G(n)$ satisfying the recurrence

$$
G(n + 1)
$$

$$
= \binom{n}{0} G(n) + \frac{n - 1}{n + 1} \binom{n + 1}{1} G(n - 1)
$$

(9.13)

$$
+ \frac{n - 2}{n + 2} \binom{n + 2}{2} G(2) + \cdots
$$

$$
+ \frac{1}{2n - 1} \binom{2n - 1}{n - 1} G(1) + C(n, n - 1)
$$

will give upper and lower bounds for $F_y(n, n - 1)$ depending on the
initial conditions for $G(n)$.

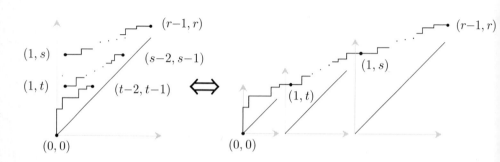

Figure 9.3: Equivalent paths

Looking at the second term on the right hand side of (9.13) one gets the inequality

$$G(n+1) \geq \frac{n-1}{n+1}\binom{n+1}{1} G(n-1) = (n-1)G(n-1).$$

This gives that

$$G(n) \geq (n-2)(n-4)\cdots(n-2[n/2]).$$

So Stirling's formula gives the lower asymptotic lower bound

$$F_y(n, n-1) \geq e^{(1/2-\varepsilon)\, n \log n}, \qquad \varepsilon > 0.$$

D.E. Knuth [67] has noted that by only keeping the $k$th term on the right side of the recurrence (9.13) one gets an asymptotic lower bound of the form

$$F_y(n, n-1) \geq e^{\left(\frac{k}{k+1}-\varepsilon\right) n \log n}, \qquad \varepsilon > 0.$$

In the other direction one can get an upper bound of $\alpha\, n!$, $\alpha$ a constant, for $G(n)$ in recurrence (9.13). Assume inductively that

$$G(k) \leq \alpha\, k!, \qquad k < n,$$

then replace $G(k)$ by $\alpha k!$ in (9.13) for all $k < n$ and prove that $G(n) \leq n!$. Expanding $B(n,k)$ out we get

$$G(n)$$
$$\leq \alpha\,(n-1)! + \alpha\,(n+1)(n-2)! + \cdots$$
$$= \alpha n! \left(\frac{1}{n} + \frac{n+1}{(n-1)n} + \cdots + \frac{(n+1)(n+2)\cdots(n+k-1)}{n(n-1)\cdots(n-k+1)\, k!} + \cdots\right)$$
$$\leq \alpha n!$$

The last step follows since the term in brackets on right hand side of the equation can easily checked to be less than one. Since one can always pick $\alpha$ large enough to start the induction, the upper bound therefore follows. By Stirling's formula and Exercise 9.5 one gets the inequalities

$$4\,e^{n\log n - n\log n\log n - n} < F_y(n+1, n) < \alpha\,e^{n\log n - n + \log n}\,.$$

Knuth has shown that second inequality holds with $\alpha = 4$.

**Exercise 9.5 [HM]** (D.E. Knuth [67]) Show that

$$F_y(n+1, n) > 4\,e^{n\log n - n\log n\log n - n}\,.$$

**Exercise 9.6\* [HM]** Consider the class of recurrences of the form

$$(9.14) \quad a_n = H(n, n-1)\,a_{n-1} + H(n, n-2)\,a_{n-2} + \cdots + H(n, 0)a_0\,.$$

Determine the behavior of the $a_n$ given that the $H(n, m)$ are known.

## 9.4 The running time of TAK$_z$

The analysis will be similar to the one for TAK$_y$. Let $F_z(a, b, c)$ be the running time of TAK$_z(a, b, c)$. As before, one has that

$$\text{TAK}_z(a + d, b + d, z + d) = \text{TAK}_z(a, b, c) + d$$

so we can restrict to the cases $\text{TAK}_z(a, b, 0)$ and $\text{TAK}_z(b, 0, a)$. Exercise 9.1 shows that for $a \geq b \geq 0$

$$\text{TAK}_z(a, b, 0) = \begin{cases} 0 & \text{if } a \leq b \\ b & \text{if } b = 0 \text{ or } a - b \text{ is odd} \\ 1 & \text{if } a - b \text{ is even}, a > b > 0 \end{cases}$$

$$\text{TAK}_z(b, 0, a) = \begin{cases} a & \text{if } b \leq 0 \\ 0 & \text{if } a \leq b + 1 \text{ and either } b > 1 \text{ or } b = a \\ a & \text{if } a - b \text{ is even} \\ 1 & \text{if } a - b \text{ is odd} \end{cases}$$

Substituting this into recurrence (9.1) applied to $F_z$ one gets

$$F_z(a, b, 0) = 1 + F_z(a - 1, b, 0) + F_z(b - 1, 0, a) + F_z(-1, a, b)$$
$$+ F_z(\text{TAK}_z(a - 1, b, 0), \text{TAK}_z(b - 1, 0, a), \text{TAK}_z(-1, a, b))$$
$$= 2 + F_z(a - 1, b, 0) + F_z(b - 1, 0, a)$$
$$+ \begin{cases} 1 & \text{if } a - b \text{ odd,} \\ F_z(b, 1, b) & \text{if } a - b \text{ even.} \end{cases}$$

$$F_z(b, 0, a) = 1 + F_z(b - 1, 0, a) + F_z(a - 1, b, 0) + F_z(-1, a, b)$$
$$+ F_z(\text{TAK}_z(b - 1, 0, a), \text{TAK}_z(-1, a, b), \text{TAK}_z(a - 1, b, 0))$$
$$= 3 + F_z(a - 1, b, 0) + F_z(b - 1, 0, a).$$

One therefore has that

$$F_z(a, b, 0) = F_z(b, 0, a)$$

when $a - b$ is odd, and if $a - b$ is even then

$$F_z(a, b, 0) = 2 + F_z(a - 1, b, 0) + F_z(b - 1, 0, a)$$
$$+ F_z(b - 1, 0, b - 1)$$
$$= 6 + F_z(a - 1, b, 0) + F_z(a, b - 1, 0)$$
$$+ F_z(b - 1, b - 2, 0)$$

since $F_z(b - 1, 0, a) = F_z(a, b - 1, 0)$ and

$$F_z(b, 1, b) = F_z(b - 1, 0, b - 1) = 2 + F_z(b - 1, 0, b)$$
$$= 4 + F_z(b - 1, b - 2, 0)$$

for $b > 3$. One concludes that

$$F_z(a, b, 0) = 3 + F_z(b, 0, a) + F_z(b - 1, b - 2, 0)$$

when $a - b$ is even.

To get bounds on $F_y(a, b, 0)$, note that the above discussion implies the recurrence

$$F_y(a, b, 0) = 3 + F_z(a - 1, b, 0) + F_z(a, b - 1, 0)$$

(9.15)  $$F_y(a, b, 0) = 6 + F_z(a - 1, b, 0) + F_z(a, b - 1, 0)$$
$$+ F_z(b - 1, b - 2, 0)$$

where the first equality holds if $a - b$ is odd and the second if $a - b$ is even. (9.15) implies the recurrence inequalities

$$F_y(a, b, 0) \leq 2 + F_y(a - 1, b, 0) + F_y(a, b - 1, 0) + F_y(a - 1, b - 1, 0)$$
$$\leq 2\left(F_y(a - 1, b, 0) + F_y(a, b - 1, 0) + F_y(a - 1, b - 1, 0)\right).$$

since the term $F_y(b - 1, b - 2, 0)$ of (9.15) is generated by the term $F_y(a - 1, b - 1, 0)$ (i.e., a lattice path starting at $(b - 1, a - 1)$ passes through $(b - 2, b - 1)$) so

$$F_y(b - 1, b - 2, 0) \leq F_y(a - 1, b - 1, 0).$$

Therefore, if one looks at the homogeneous recurrence relation

(9.16)    $$D(a, b) = D(a - 1, b) + D(a, b - 1, 0) + D(a - 1, b - 1)$$

with boundary condition

$$D(0, 0) = 1,$$

one gets an upper bound

$$\alpha D(a, b) > F_y(a, b, 0)$$

for a suitable constant $\alpha$ which depends only on the boundary conditions for $F_y$ and the constant term in (9.15).

It turns out that the numbers $D(a, b)$ have been studied and are called *Delannoy numbers* [19, p. 81]. These numbers count the number of lattice paths in the following problem

**Problem V**

*How many lattice paths are there from $(b, a)$ to $(0, 0)$ where a diagonal step $(x, y) \Rightarrow (x - 1, y - 1)$ is also allowed?*

(If the usual lattice problems are thought of representing the number of ways a rook can move from one square of a chessboard to another, this problem represents the number of *king* walks on a chessboard[1] [89].) The special case $D(n, n)$ has been evaluated [89] as

$$D(n, n) = P_n(3)$$

where $P_n(t)$ is the *Legendre polynomial* defined by

$$\sum_{k=0}^{\infty} P_k(t)x^k = \frac{1}{\sqrt{1 - 2tx + x^2}}.$$

Now it is known (e.g., [6, p. 231]) that

$$P_n(t) \sim (2\pi n)^{-1/2} \left(t^2 - 1\right)^{-1/4} \left(t + \sqrt{t^2 - 1}\right)^{n+1/2}, \qquad n \to \infty; \, t > 1.$$

Therefore one gets that

$$P_n(3) \sim \beta \frac{(3 + \sqrt{8})^n}{\sqrt{n}}, \qquad \text{where } \beta = \sqrt{\frac{3 + \sqrt{8}}{2\sqrt{8}\,\pi}}.$$

So one gets

The running time $F_z(n, n-1, 0)$ of TAK$_z(n, n-1, 0)$ satisfies the upper bound

$$F_z(n, n - 1, 0) < \gamma \frac{(3 + \sqrt{8})^n}{\sqrt{n}},$$

for some constant $\gamma$.

From Section 9.2 one has the lower bound

$$F_z(n, n - 1, 0) > \frac{4^n}{n^{3/2}}.$$

Since $3 + \sqrt{8} = 5.828\ldots > 4$ there is a gap between the upper and lower bounds.

**Exercise 9.7\* [HM]** Find the true order of growth of $F_z(n, n - 1, 0)$.

---

[1]This answers the trivia question: What is the relation between chess and Legendre polynomials?

**Exercise 9.8 [HM]** ([49, Exercise 7.56]) Express the coefficient of $z^n$ in $(1 + z + z^2)^n$ in closed form.

**Exercise 9.9 [HM]** (J. Justeson, I. Vardi)  Actually, solutions to recursion (9.15) can be also be bounded above by considering the recursion (9.16) with boundary conditions

$$D(a, a) = 0, \qquad a > 0,$$

in other words, lattice paths of Problem IV restricted to paths that do not touch the line $x = y$. These numbers have been studied by Schröder [112] as the number of ways to bracket certain expressions [19, page 56] (see (ii) below) but also occur in many different contexts [119, Sequence 1163]. In fact these numbers are very similar to Catalan numbers so I will call them *super Catalan numbers* and write them as $S(n)$. One can define these numbers via the recurrence [19, page 57]

$$(n - 1) S(n + 1) = 2(2n - 1) S(n) - (n - 2) S(n - 1)$$

with initial conditions $S(1) = 1$, $S(2) = 1$, so that the first few values are

| | |
|---|---|
| 1 | 1 |
| 2 | 1 |
| 3 | 3 |
| 4 | 11 |
| 5 | 45 |
| 6 | 197 |
| 7 | 903 |
| 8 | 4279 |
| 9 | 20793 |
| 10 | 103049 |

Analogies with Catalan numbers are:

(i) Catalan numbers count the number of lattice paths from $(n, n)$ to $(0, 0)$ which do not cross $x = y$. The super Catalan numbers count the number of lattice paths with diagonal steps from $(n, n)$ to $(0, 0)$ which do not cross $x = y$.

(ii) Catalan numbers count the number of ways of bracketing an expression $X_1 X_2 \ldots X_n$ such that only 2 adjacent non-bracketed factors are allowed. The super Catalan numbers count the number of bracketings where you can have an arbitrary number of adjacent non bracketed terms in a factor [112].

(iii) Catalan numbers count the number of ways to "triangulate" a regular polygon, i.e, join vertices of the polygons with non-intersecting straight lines so that the polygon is completely divided into triangles. The super Catalan numbers count the number of such partial divisions, i.e., how many ways can you join vertices of the polygon with non-intersecting straight lines [90, pages 357–59] [49, Exercise 7.50].

**(a) [M]** There are at least 40 such properties of Catalan numbers [26] [39, Chapter 20] ([44] contains over 400 references). Find analogues for super Catalan numbers.

**(b) [HM]** Show that the $S(n)$ can be expressed in terms of Legendre polynomials by

$$S(n) = \frac{1}{4n}(3P_{n-1}(3) - P_{n-2}(3)) \quad n > 1.$$

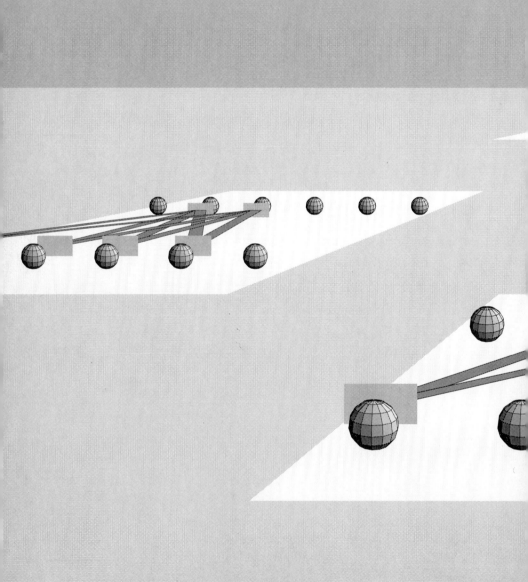

# 10

# The Condom Problem

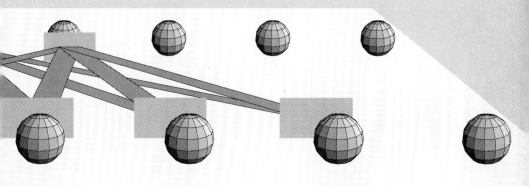

# Chapter 10

# The Condom Problem

A well known puzzle among combinatorialists is the following: $m$ men and $n$ women, each with a different sexually transmitted disease, want to engage in all $mn$ sexual encounters with no one catching anyone else's disease and with the minimal number of condoms being used. You are allowed to nest condoms and to turn them inside out, but once a surface becomes infected by a disease it stays infected for all time. This problem first appeared in print in the euphemistic form of doctors, patients, and surgical gloves in Martin Gardner's column in *Isaac Asimov's Science Fiction Magazine* [36, Gar1] (also[37]). The paper of Hajnal and Lovász [55] (see Section 10.1) uses the terminology of rabbits, radioactive plates, and membranes while the paper of Orlitzky and Shepp [93] (see Exercise 10.2) talks about computers and interfaces.

The cases of $m = n = 2$ and $m = 2k + 1$, $n = 1$ were the original formulations of the problem (the case $m = 3$, $n = 1$ appeared in [37, page 134]), and these examples will be described before moving on to the general case. First, one needs to set up notation to formulate the problem in mathematical terms.

**Notation:** The men will be denoted by $M_i, M'_j$, and the women by $W_i, W'_j$. The condoms will be denoted by $C_i$ with $\overrightarrow{C_i}$ or $\overleftarrow{C_i}$ in order to distinguish the direction used ($C_i$ if no confusion is possible). An encounter will therefore be of the form

$$M_a \, \overrightarrow{C_i} \, \overrightarrow{C_j} \, \cdots \, \overleftarrow{C_k} \, W_b \,,$$

or if the diseases will are denoted by $D_i$

$$D_a \overrightarrow{C_i} \, \overrightarrow{C_j} \cdots \overleftarrow{C_k} \, D_b \,,$$

since the diseases uniquely identify the $M_i$'s and $W_j$'s. If there is no confusion the $\overrightarrow{C}$'s may be dropped.

**The case** $m = n = 2$: Two condoms is the answer. Let $M_1, M_2$ be the men and $W_1, W_2$ be the women, and $C_1, C_2$ be the condoms. The solution consists of the sequence of encounters

(1) $\qquad\qquad\qquad\qquad M_1 \overrightarrow{C_1} \, \overrightarrow{C_2} \, W_1$

(2) $\qquad\qquad\qquad\qquad M_1 \overrightarrow{C_1} \, W_2$

(3) $\qquad\qquad\qquad\qquad M_2 \overrightarrow{C_2} \, W_1$

(4) $\qquad\qquad\qquad\qquad M_2 \overrightarrow{C_2} \, \overrightarrow{C_1} \, W_2$

To see that two is the minimum possible note that each condom provides two clean surfaces, and there are four people involved.

**The case** $m = 2k + 1$, $n = 1$: $k + 1$ condoms is the answer. Label the men $M_1, M_2, ..., M_k, M_1', M_2', \ldots, M_k'$ and $M$. The woman will be denoted by $W$, and the condoms by $C_1, C_2, \ldots, C_k$, and $C$.

The solution consists of the sequence

(1) $\qquad\qquad\qquad\qquad M_1 \overrightarrow{C_1} \, \overrightarrow{C} \, W$

(2) $\qquad\qquad\qquad\qquad M_2 \overrightarrow{C_2} \, \overrightarrow{C} \, W$

$$\vdots$$

$(k)$ $\qquad\qquad\qquad\qquad M_k \overrightarrow{C_k} \, \overrightarrow{C} \, W$

$(k+1)$ $\qquad\qquad\qquad\qquad M \overrightarrow{C} \, W$

$(k+2)$ $\qquad\qquad\qquad\qquad M_1' \overleftarrow{C_1} \, \overrightarrow{C} \, W$

$(k+3)$ $\qquad\qquad\qquad\qquad M_2' \overleftarrow{C_2} \, \overrightarrow{C} \, W$

$$\vdots$$

$(2k+2)$ $\qquad\qquad\qquad\qquad M_k' \overleftarrow{C_k} \, \overrightarrow{C} \, W$

As before it can be seen that $k + 1$ is optimal since this number is exactly equal to half the number of participants.

In their paper, A. Hajnal and L. Lovász [55] considered the condom problem (in an equivalent formulation) and they gave an elegant solution by providing upper and lower bounds that differed by an additive constant of one. I complete this analysis by presenting an algorithm that is optimal for all $m$ and $n$. I will show

**Theorem.** *Assume there are $m$ men and $n$ women with $m \geq n$ (if $n > m$ then the proof is identical but with the role of men and women interchanged). Then there is an algorithm that uses*

$$(10.1) \qquad \left\lceil \frac{m}{2} + \frac{2n}{3} \right\rceil$$

*condoms, where $\lceil x \rceil$ represents the smallest integer greater than or equal to $x$. (10.1) is optimal except for the case $m = n = 2$ when 2 condoms suffice, and the case $n = 1$, $m = 2k + 1$ when $(m + 1)/2$ condoms suffice (these are also optimal).*

(Hajnal and Lovász provided a lower bound of $\lceil m/2 + 2n/3 - 1/3 \rceil$ for all $m, n$ and an upper bound of $\lceil m/2 + 2n/3 \rceil + 1$ in the case of $m = n = 6k$.)

# 10.1   The work of Hajnal and Lovász

## 10.1.1   The algorithm

The Hajnal and Lovász algorithm works for $m = 2k$ men and and $n = 3\ell$ women, where $n \geq m$, and uses $n/2 + 2m/3 + 1$ condoms. The method is identical to one with 2 men and 3 women and 4 condoms so this will be used to illustrate the algorithm, see Figure 10.1

**Note on the figures:**

• denotes a person not protected by a condom.

—•  denotes a person protected by a condom with a clean other side.

$\stackrel{\perp}{\bullet}$ denotes a person protected by a condom with an infected other side.

* denotes a person who has finished all encounters.

Labeling the men $M_1, M_2$ and the women $W_1, W_2, W_3$, and the condoms $C_1, C_2, C_3, J$ one has the algorithm (following Figure 10.1)

**Algorithm for two men, three women, four condoms:**

**(a)** $M_1$ will use $C_1$, $W_1$ will use $C_2$, $W_2$ will use $C_3$. $J$ will be the *master condom* which always has a clean side and is used as an accessory to protect $C_i$'s that need to stay clean.

**(b)** The encounters $M_1C_1C_2W_1$, $M_1C_1C_3W_2$.

**(c)** $W_2$ gives up $C_2$ which is turned inside out and will be used by $W_3$ for all time.

**(d)** Encounter $M_1C_1 \overrightarrow{J} C_2W_3$.

**(e)** $M_1$ has completed all encounters and so gives up $C_1$ which is turned inside out and will be used by $M_2$ for all time.

**(f)** Encounters $M_2C_1 \overleftarrow{J} C_2W_1$, $M_1C_1C_2W_3$.

**(g)** $W_1$ has completed all encounters, and $C_2$ is turned inside out and used by $W_2$.

**(h)** Encounter $M_2C_1C_2W_2$.

The method for $m = 2k$ men, $n = 3\ell$ women, and $k + 2\ell + 1 = m/2 + 2n/3 + 1$ condoms, where $m \geq n$, is very similar to the above algorithm. Label the men $M_1, \ldots, M_m$, and the women $W_1, \ldots, W_n$, and the condoms $C_1, \ldots, C_k$, $C'_1, \ldots, C'_{2\ell}$. Then the algorithm is as above but replacing all encounters of the form $M_i \Leftrightarrow W_j$ in the above with $M_{2a+i} \Leftrightarrow W_{3b+j}$, $a = 1, \ldots, k$, $b = 1, \ldots, \ell$.

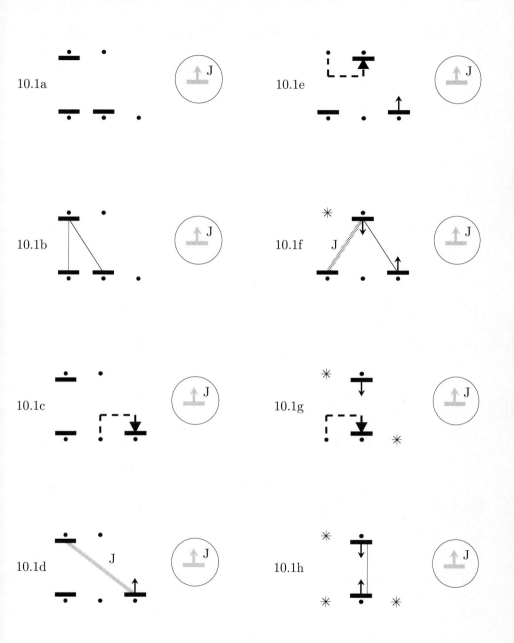

Figure 10.1: Two men, three women, four condoms.

**Algorithm for $n$ men, $m$ women, $n/2 + 2m/3 + 1$ condoms:**

(a) $M_{2i-1}$ will use condom $C_i$, $i = 1, \ldots, k$. $W_{3j-2}$ will use $C'_{2j-1}$, $W_{3j-1}$ will use $C'_{2j}$, $j = 1, \ldots, \ell$. $J$ will be the *master condom* which always has a clean side and is used as an accessory to protect $C_i$'s that need to stay clean.

(b) All encounters $M_{2i-1}C_iC'_{2j-1}W_{3j-2}$, $M_{2i-1}C_iC'_{2j}W_{3j-1}$.

(c) Each $C'_{2j}$ is turned inside out and will be used by $W_{3j}$ for all time.

(d) All encounters $M_{2i-1}C_i \overrightarrow{J} C'_{2j}W_{3j}$.

(e) Each $M_{2i-1}$ has completed all encounters and so each $C_i$ is turned inside out and will be used by $M_{2i}$ for all time.

(f) All encounters $M_{2i}C_i \overleftarrow{J} C'_{2j-1}W_{3j-2}$, $M_{2i}C_iC'_{2j}W_{3j}$.

(g) Each $W_{3j-2}$ has completed all encounters so gives up $C'_{2j-1}$ which is turned inside out and used by $W_{2j-1}$.

(h) All encounters $M_{2i}C_iC'_{2j-1}W_{2j-1}$.

**Remark:** This gives that $6n$ men and $6n$ women only need $7n + 1$ condoms.

## 10.1.2   The lower bound

As above, let $M_1, M_2, \ldots, M_m$ be the men and $W_1, W_2, \ldots, W_n$ be the women. Following [55] these will be the vertices of a graph. The condoms will be edges of this graph.

A surface of a condom $C$ becomes *infected* by a disease if the surface was clean and then came into contact with this disease only.

This is how the graph is connected:

1. If a side of a condom $C$ becomes infected first with the disease corresponding to person $D_1$ and then the other side becomes infected with the disease corresponding to person $D_2$ then we draw a directed edge $\overrightarrow{D_1 D_2}$ connecting person $D_1$ to $D_2$.

2. If the infection occurred simultaneously then an arbitrary direction is chosen. If a side of condom becomes infected by two diseases simultaneously then we connect this side to an arbitrary vertex, likewise if the side remains clean throughout.

For example the reader can check that the solution for $m = n = 2$ given in the introduction has the graph

and the solution for $n = 1$, $m = 2k + 1$ has the graph

The Hajnal and Lovász algorithm given above has the graph

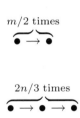

The next step is to find a lower bound, but first here is a general observation about the optimal way to use condoms. The idea is to turn a condom inside out and pass it to someone after you've used it. For example the most efficient way is for one person $D_1$ to use a condom for all interactions, then turn it inside out and give it to person $D_2$ who then uses it for all interactions. This gives the connected two-component

$$(10.2) \qquad\qquad D_1 \to D_2 \, .$$

The next most efficient method is for three people to use two condoms

$$D_1 \to D_2 \to D_3 \, ,$$

where $D_2$ passes to $D_3$ and then $D_1$ passes to $D_2$, and so forth. The Hajnal-Lovász algorithm chooses to use 2-components for either the men or the women, depending, on which are more numerous, and then uses 3-components for the others.

The next observation is that in (10.2), $D_i$ must accomplish all encounters before passing to $D_j$ and so $D_j$ must wait for this before beginning. This immediately implies:

(i) two connected components of the form

$$M_i \longleftrightarrow M_j \qquad W_k \longleftrightarrow W_\ell$$

cannot occur. In other words, only the men or only the women can contain a 2-component.

(ii) If two connected components

$$M_i \longleftrightarrow W_j \qquad M_k \longleftrightarrow W_\ell$$

exist, then one must point toward the woman and the other toward the man.

Now using the observation that no vertex in the graph is isolated and the restrictions of (i) and (ii) it follows that an optimal solution must look something like

$$\overbrace{\bullet \to \bullet}^{(m-2)/2 \text{ times}}$$

$$\bullet \quad \bullet$$
$$\uparrow \quad \downarrow$$
$$\bullet \quad \bullet$$

$$\overbrace{\bullet \to \bullet \cdots \to \bullet}^{\text{rest of women}}$$

where the "rest of the women" part of the graph does not contain a 2-component. It follows there must be at least

$$(10.3) \qquad \frac{m-2}{2} + 2 + \frac{2}{3}(n-2) = \frac{m}{2} + \frac{2n}{3} - \frac{1}{3}$$

edges and so at least $\lceil m/2 + 2n/3 - 1/3 \rceil$ condoms.

**Remark:** In the case $6n$ men and $6n$ women, one sees that the lower bound gives $7n$ condoms, so the upper and lower bounds of Hajnal and Lovász differ by one. This upper bound will be reduced in the next section.

## 10.2 The algorithm

Before doing the general case, I'll describe the algorithm for 4 men, 6 women, and 6 condoms since this case already contains all the ingredients of the general case. The key idea is to fabricate the master condom from the ones used by the men and women, instead of just adding an extra one as in the Hajnal-Lovász algorithm.

As before, label the men $M_1, \ldots, M_4$, and the women $W_1, \ldots, W_6$. Here is a description of the algorithm

**Algorithm for four men, six women, six condoms:**

(a) $M_2$ will use condom $C_1$, $M_3$ will use $C_2$, $W_1$ will use $C_3$, and $W_3, W_4, W_5$ will use $C_4, C_5, C_6$ respectively.

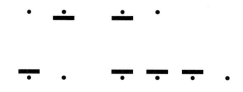

(b) All encounters $M_2C_1$ and $M_3C_2$ with $C_3W_1$, $C_4W_3$, $C_5W_4$, and $C_6W_5$.

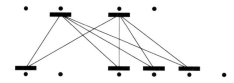

(c) $W_4$ gives up $C_5$ which will then be used as a master condom, and so will be denoted by $J$ for the rest of the algorithm. $W_5$ passes $C_6$ to $W_6$.

(d) Encounters $M_2 C_1 \overrightarrow{J} C_6 W_6$ and $M_3 C_2 \overrightarrow{J} C_6 W_6$.

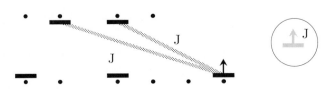

(e) $M_2$ has completed all encounters except $W_2$, so will no longer need $C_1$. One therefore has the encounter $M_2 C_1 W_2$.

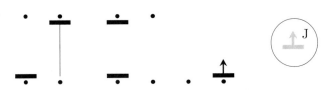

(f) $M_2$ now passes $C_1$ to $W_2$.

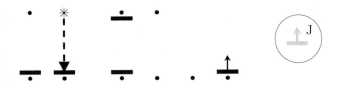

(g) Encounter $M_3 C_2 \overrightarrow{J} C_1 W_2$.

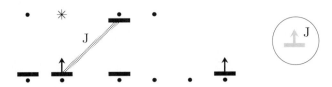

**(h)** $M_3$ has completed all encounters so passes $C_2$ to $M_4$.

**(i)** Encounter $M_4 C_2 \overleftarrow{J} C_3 W_1$

**(j)** $W_1$ has completed all encounters except with $M_1$ so that one has the encounter $M_1 C_3 W_1$.

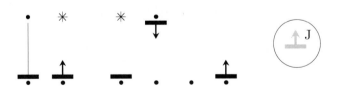

**(k)** $W_1$ passes $C_3$ to $M_1$.

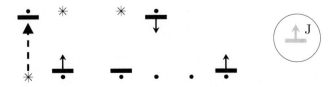

**(l)** Encounters $M_1C_3$ and $M_4C_2$ with $C_1W_2$ and $C_6W_6$.

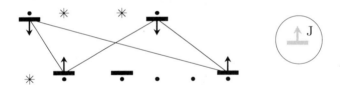

**(m)** Encounters $M_1C_3$ and $M_4C_2$ with $\overleftarrow{J}\,C_4W_3$.

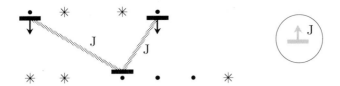

**(n)** $W_3$ has finished so passes $C_4$ to $W_4$. $W_5$ uses $J$ from now on.

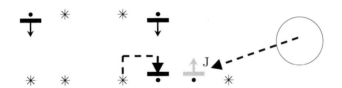

**(o)** Encounters $M_1C_3$ and $M_4C_2$ with $C_4W_4$ and $JW_5$.

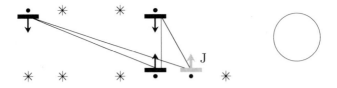

The point of this much more complicated method is that the master condom was generated by using a four-component in a nontrivial way. Note that this method needs to use two connected components that go from a man to a woman and from a woman to a man.

We now proceed to the general case of $m = 2k+2$ men and $n = 3\ell+6$ women, $m/2 + 2n/3 = k + 2\ell + 5$ condoms, where $m \geq n$. This is very similar to the previous algorithm. One labels the men $M_1$, $M_2$, and $M'_i$, $i = 1, 2, \ldots, 2k$, and labels the women $W_1, W_2, W_3, W_4, W_5, W_6$, and $W'_j$, $j = 1, \ldots 3\ell$. Also label the condoms $C_1, C_2, C_3, C_4, C_5, C'_i$, $i = 1, \ldots, k$, $C''_j$, $j = 1, \ldots, 2\ell$. The steps of the algorithm are:

**Algorithm for $m$ men, $n$ women, $m/2 + 2n/3$ condoms:**

(a)  $M_2$ will use condom $C_1$, $M'_{2i-1}$ will use $C'_i$, $i = 1, \ldots, k$. $W_1$ will
     use $C_2$, and $W_3, W_4, W_5$ will use $C_3, C_4, C_5$ respectively. $W'_{3j-2}$
     will use $C'''_{2j-1}$, $j = 1, \ldots, \ell$ and $W'_{3j-1}$ will use $C'''_{2j}$, $j = 1, \ldots, \ell$.

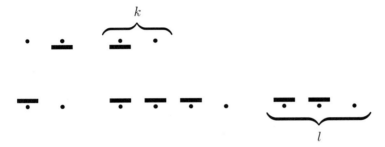

(b)  All encounters $M_2C_1$ and $M'_{2i-1}C'_i$ with $C_2W_1, C_3W_3, C_4W_4, C_5W_5$,
     $C''_{2j-1}W'_{3j-2}$, $C''_{2j}W'_{3j-1}$.

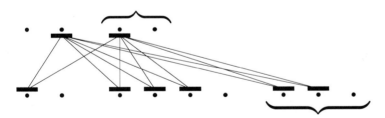

(c)  $W_4$ gives up $C_4$ which will then be used as a master condom, and
     so will be denoted by $J$ for the rest of the algorithm. $W_5$ passes
     $C_5$ to $W_6$. Each $W'_{3j-1}$ passes $C''_{2j}$ to $W'_{2j}$.

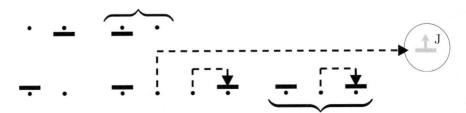

**(d)** Encounter $M_2C_1 \overrightarrow{J} C_5W_6$, all encounters $M_2C_1 \overrightarrow{J} C''_{2j}W'_{3j}$. All encounters $M'_{2i-1}C'_i \overrightarrow{J} C_5W_6$ and all encounters $M'_{2i-1}C'_i \overrightarrow{J} C''_{2j}W'_{3j}$.

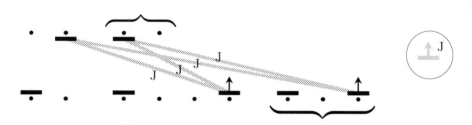

**(e)** $M_2$ has completed all encounters except $W_2$, so will no longer need $C_1$. One therefore has the encounter $M_2C_1W_2$.

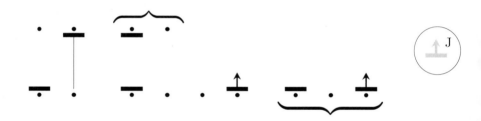

**(f)** $M_2$ now passes $C_1$ to $W_2$.

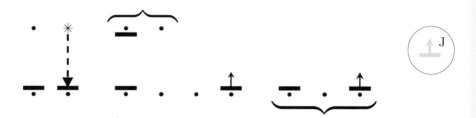

**(g)** All encounters $M'_{2i-1} C'_i \overrightarrow{J} C_1 W_2$.

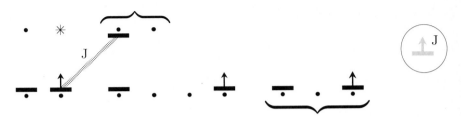

**(h)** Each $M'_{2i-1}$ has completed all encounters so passes $C'_i$ to $M'_{2i}$.

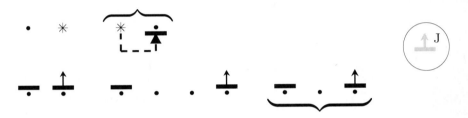

**(i)** All encounters $M'_{2i} C'_i \overleftarrow{J} C_2 W_1$

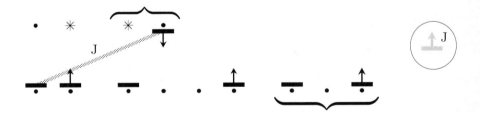

**(j)** $W_1$ has completed all encounters except with $M_1$ so that one has the encounter $M_1 C_2 W_1$.

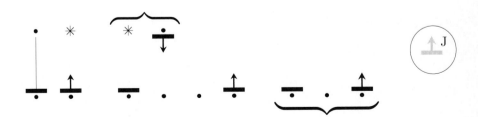

**(k)** $W_1$ passes $C_2$ to $M_1$.

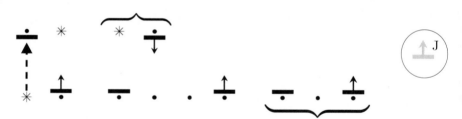

**(l)** Encounters $M_1C_2$ and $M'_{2i}C'_i$ with $C_1W_2$, $C_5W_6$, and all $C''_{2j}W_{3j}$.

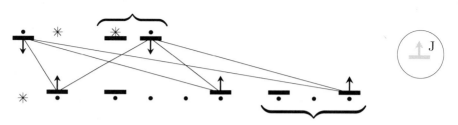

**(m)** Encounters $M_1C_2$ and $M'_{2i}C'_i$ with $\overleftarrow{J}\,C_3W_3$ and all $C''_{2j-1}W'_{3j-2}$.

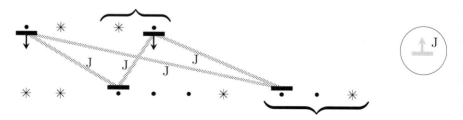

**(n)** $W_3$ has finished so passes $C_3$ to $W_4$. $W_5$ uses $J$ from now on. Each $W'_{3j-2}$ has finished and passes $C''_{2j-1}$ to $W'_{3j-1}$.

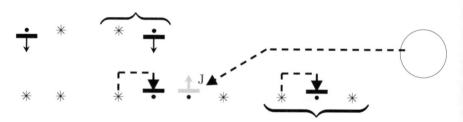

**(o)** All remaining encounters $M_1 C_2$ and $M'_{2i} C'_i$ with $C_3 W_4$, $J W_5$, and all $C''_{2j-1} W'_{3j-1}$.

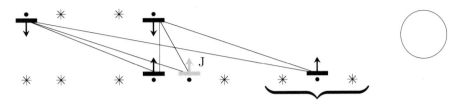

**Remark:** In the case of $6n$ men and $6n$ women this algorithm needs $6n/2 + 2 \cdot 6n/3 = 7n$ condoms. By the lower bound of Section 10.1.2, this algorithm is optimal.

Here is a graph of the algorithm

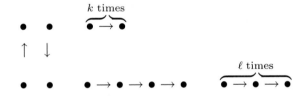

## 10.3   The general case

The algorithm of the last section can be modified to treat all the cases for $m, n \geq 6$. We only present the generic cases since the others can be handled similarly.

(a) $m \equiv 1 \pmod 2$ and $n \equiv 2 \pmod 3$

(b) $m \equiv 0 \pmod 2$ and $n \equiv 2 \pmod 3$

(a) We have an algorithm similar to the above based on the graph

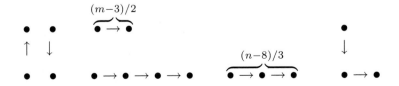

(b) This case uses a different algorithm (similar to the Hajnal-Lovász method) using the graph

$J = $ master condom

where $J$ serves as a "master condom," i.e., one side is always clean and the other always unclean, as before, but it never comes in contact *directly* with a $M_i$ or $W_j$.

As in [55] I leave the case of $n < 6$ to the reader. Note, however, that the cases $m = n = 2$ and $n = 1$, $m = 2k + 1$, are the only ones for which (10.1) can be improved.

## 10.4    Lower bounds

To show that (10.1) is optimal, we must improve the lower bound of (10.3).

**Lemma 1.** *If $m \geq n \geq 6$, then (10.1) is optimal.*

(As before, I leave the case $n < 6$ to the reader.)

**Proof:** The only case when the lower bound of (1) doesn't follow directly from (10.3) is if

$$\left\lceil \frac{m}{2} + \frac{2n}{3} \right\rceil \neq \left\lceil \frac{m}{2} + \frac{2n}{3} - \frac{1}{3} \right\rceil$$

which happens when

(a) $m \equiv 0 \pmod 2$ and $n \equiv 2 \pmod 3$

(b) $m \equiv 1 \pmod 2$ and $n \equiv 1 \pmod 3$

We will prove the Lemma for (a). The proof for (b) is similar.

**Proof for (a):** By the comments at the end of §2 the graph of an algorithm taking $m/2 + 2n/3 - 1/3$ condoms must look like

(10.4)

$$(m-2)/2$$

$$\bullet \to \bullet$$

$$\bullet \quad \bullet$$
$$\uparrow \quad \downarrow$$
$$\bullet \quad \bullet$$

$$(n-2)/3$$

$$\bullet \leftrightarrow \bullet \leftrightarrow \bullet$$

I leave the proof for $n = 2$ to the reader. For $n > 2$ I will need the fact that the 3-components in (10.4) must all be of the form $\bullet \to \bullet \to \bullet$. As a matter of fact, the following stronger statement is true:

**Lemma 2.** *For any algorithm, if the men have a 2-component, then the 3-components of the women must be of the form* $\bullet \to \bullet \to \bullet$.

For the moment assume that Lemma 2 is true, then the graph (10.4) looks like

$$(m-2)/2$$

$$\bullet \to \bullet$$

$$\bullet \quad \bullet$$
$$\uparrow \quad \downarrow$$
$$\bullet \quad \bullet$$

$$(n-2)/3$$

$$\bullet \to \bullet \to \bullet$$

Now consider the last $W_{3i+5}M_3$ for $0 \le i \le (n-5)/3$, say it is $W_{3j+5}M_3$. $M_3$ has to be protected, but I will show that no intermediate condoms can be used: It is fairly clear that $\overrightarrow{W_1 M_1}$ and $\overrightarrow{M_2 W_2}$ can't be used. None of the $\overrightarrow{W_{3i+3}W_{3i+4}}$ can be used since one side is reserved for $W_{3i+3}M_4$ and the other is reserved for $W_{3i+4}M_4$. Finally, by assumption all other $\overrightarrow{W_{3i+4}W_{3i+4}}$ are unclean on both sides. Therefore $W_{3j+5}M_3$ is impossible.

**Proof of Lemma 2:** Let $M_1 \to M_2$ be a 2-component of the men, and $W_1 \leftrightarrow W_2 \leftrightarrow W_3$ be a 3-component of the women. The possibilities for the 3-component that have to be ruled out are:

(i) $\bullet \leftarrow \bullet \to \bullet$

(ii) $\bullet \to \bullet \leftarrow \bullet$

We consider the case of (i) (the (ii) case is handled similarly).

We try to figure out in which order $W_1, W_2, W_3$ will have sex with $M_2$. Without loss of generality, one can assume that $\overrightarrow{W_2 W_3}$ will be used for $W_2 M_2$. Now by definition of the directed graph $\overrightarrow{M_1 M_2}$ is unclean on both sides. Furthermore, since $M_1$ has completed all its encounters, $\overrightarrow{W_2 W_1}$ and $\overrightarrow{W_2 W_3}$ are unclean on both sides (this follows from the shape of the component).

(a) $W_2$ cannot be first since this would mean that the $W_3$ side of $\overrightarrow{W_2 W_3}$ would have to be protected, which is impossible, since a new condom would become infected by $W_3$, and $W_3$ only has one edge incident to it.

(b) $W_3$ cannot be first since the $W_2$ side of $\overrightarrow{W_2 W_3}$ would have to be protected. From the assumption about the 3-component, this means that $\overrightarrow{W_2 W_1}$ would have to be put over $\overrightarrow{W_2 W_3}$. But the $W_1$ side of $\overrightarrow{W_2 W_1}$ would have to be protected, which is impossible as before.

(c) Using the same argument as in (b) it is seen that $W_1$ cannot be first.

This means that none of $W_1, W_2, W_3$ can be first and the lemma follows by contradiction.

**Exercise 10.1** Show that a formula similar to (10.1) holds for the case where all pairs of individuals have a sexual encounter.

**Exercise 10.2** [M] (A. Orlitzky and L. Shepp [93]) Analyze the condom problem with $m$ men, $n$ women, $m \geq n$ where all men are bisexual.

**Exercise 10.3\*** [M] In general consider the condom problem where a *preference graph* is given and two people have a sexual encounter if and only if they are joined by an edge (thus the original problem corresponds to the complete bipartite graph).

# Appendix A

# Answers to Exercises

## A.0 Preface

**0.1** The following programs will work

```
ContinuedFraction[x_Real, n_Integer?Positive] :=
   Floor[NestList[ 1/(# - Floor[#]) &, x, n - 1]]

FromContinuedFraction[a_List] :=
   Fold[1/ #1 + #2&, 1, Reverse[a]]
```

**0.2** `MysteryOne` and `MysteryTwo` implement the functions `ToCycles` and `FromCycles`, e.g., [135, p. 524], [120, p. 20], which respectively give the cycle decomposition of a permutation, and the permutation corresponding to a cycle decomposition. (A permutation in *Mathematica* is denoted by a list, for example $\{3, 2, 1\}$ means the permutation $1 \rightarrow 3, 2 \rightarrow 2, 3 \rightarrow 1$.)

MysteryOne is one of the most obscure *Mathematica* programs ever written. The function can be implemented in linear time using procedural programming but the functional program `MysteryOne` takes quadratic time. It is unclear whether a short functional implementation that takes linear time exists.

**0.3**

```
SquareFreeQ1[n_] := Times @@ Last /@ FactorInteger[n] == 1
```

For example

```
In[1]:= FactorInteger[60]

Out[1]=  {{2, 2}, {3, 1}, {5, 1}}

In[2]:=  Last /@ %

Out[2]=  {2, 1, 1}

In[3]:=  Times @@ %

Out[3]=  2

In[4]:= % == 1

Out[4]= False
```

A more simple program is

```
SquareFreeQ2[n_]:= MoebiusMu[n] != 0
```

where the built-in function `MoebiusMu[n]` implements $\mu(n)$ defined in Exercise 1.1.

# A.1 Elegant programs in *Mathematica*

### 1.1

**(a)** This can be implemented directly as

```
Moebius[f_, n_]:=
  Plus @@ (f[n/#] MoebiusMu[#]& /@ Divisors[n])
```

It is interesting to implement this using the methods of this Section. The idea is to do a symbolic implementation of the formula

$$\sum_{d|n} \mu(d)f(d) = \prod_{p|n} (1 - f(p))$$

which holds if $f(ab) = f(a)f(b)$ when $a$ and $b$ have no common factors.

```
Moebius[f_, n_] := Moebius[f, Plus, Times, n]
```

where

```
Moebius[f_, plus_, times_, n_] :=
Block[{list =
        n/Distribute[{1, -#[[1]]}& /@
          FactorInteger[n], List, List, List, Times]},
Inner[times[f[#1], #2]&, Abs[list], Sign[list], plus]]
```

The formula for $\Phi_n(x)$ replaces Plus with Times and Times with Power so the program is

```
MyCyclotomicPolynomial[n_, x_] :=
  Simplify[Moebius[1 - x^# &, Times, Power, n]]
```

which uses Simplify otherwise one get a sum of rational functions.

One can also implement CyclotomicPolynomial by noting that the logarithm of the formula

$$\Phi_n(x) = \prod_{d|n} (1 - x^{n/d})^{\mu(d)}$$

is just the ordinary Möbius inversion formula.

**1.2** The answer is interesting since it is the shortest solution as well as the most efficient solution (you only get one Sqrt[p] term per intermediate polynomial).

```
SwinnertonDyer[n_, x_] :=
  Fold[Expand[(#1 /. x-> x + #2) (#1 /. x-> x - #2)]&,
       x, Sqrt[Prime[Range[n]]]]
```

This is the only example of Fold in this book that actually makes nontrivial use of the second argument.

Another way of doing this is to use the methods of Section 1.1 (this will be much slower)

```
SwinnertonDyer2[n_, x_]:=
    Expand[Distribute[x/n + {-1, 1} #& /@
            Sqrt[Prime[Range[n]]],
            List, List, Times, Plus]]
```

### 1.3

**(a), (b)** The following is weird, but true. You can compute $a \uparrow\uparrow k$ $(\bmod\, n)$ in polynomial time (modulo factorization of $n$). This has been rediscovered by several authors (including this one); it is not too difficult to establish this result [9] [83] [116] [115].

This problem can be treated using the *Carmichael function* $\lambda(n)$ [14] which is the least common multiple of the orders of all numbers $(m, n) = 1$, i.e., $\lambda(n)$ is the smallest number $d$ such that

$$m^d \equiv 1 \pmod{n} \qquad \text{for all } (m, n) = 1.$$

I have not used $\lambda(n)$ below, so the programs could be improved by implementing this.

So denoting $a \uparrow\uparrow k$ $(\bmod\, n)$ by `SuperPowerMod[a, k, n]` this program will evaluate

```
In[1]:= SuperPowerMod[2, 4, 137]
```

```
Out[1]= 50
```

which can be checked by a direct computation

```
In[2]:= Mod[2^(2^(2^2)), 137]
```

```
Out[2]= 50
```

The answer to example of part (a) is

```
In[3]:= SuperPowerMod[2354246773200,
                235235356676221244402348,
                3235462343]
```

```
Out[3]= 1598361768
```

which returns in a couple of seconds.

Working up the Ackerman hierarchy: e.g., let `SuperSuperPowerMod`
`[a, k, n]` be the next one (a stack of $k - 1$ superexponentials) the
program below will evaluate such examples as

```
In[4]:= SuperSuperPowerMod[1351341, 1351235125, 564654271]
```

```
Out[4]= 326588196
```

returns in less than a minute. You can also implement Ackerman's
function (given that a standard definition exists) but this is left to the
reader.

The idea is that (essentially)

```
SuperPowerMod[a, k, n]
```

is evaluated by using Euler's theorem (1.2), i.e., as

```
PowerMod[a, SuperPowerMod[a, k-1, EulerPhi[n]], n].
```

This will also give that all $k > \log_2 n$ return the same value (so all the
higher functions are essentially reducible to `SuperPowerMod`).

The following code implements this. Note the use of $\log^*(a, n)$, the
inverse of $a \uparrow\uparrow n$.

```
SuperPowerMod[a_, k_, n_]:= 0  /;
   Mod[a, n]  == 0
```

```
SuperPowerMod[a_, k_, n_]:=
   Mod[a, n]  /; k == 1
```

```
SuperPowerMod[a_, k_, n_]:=
   PowerMod[a, a, n]  /;  k==2
```

```
SuperPowerMod[a_, k_, n_]:= Mod[2, a]  /;
   n == 2
```

```
SuperPowerMod[a_, k_, n_]:=
SuperPowerMod[a, k, n]=
Block[{fi = FactorInteger[n], m = Mod[a, n],
      i, rprimem, gcdn},
    rprimem = m;
    gcdlist =
    Block[{i=0},
          While[Mod[rprimem, #[[1]]]==0,
                rprimem /= #[[1]]; i++];
          {#[[1]], #[[2]], i}& /@
          Select[fi, Mod[m, #[[1]]] == 0&];
  If[gcdlist == {},
  PowerMod[m,
          SuperPowerMod[a, k - 1, EulerPhi[n]],
          n],
  gcdn = Times @@ (#[[1]]^#[[2]] & /@ gcdlist);
  If[LogStar[a, Max[#[[2]] - #[[3]]&
            /@ gcdlist]] > k-1,
    PowerMod[m, SuperPower[a, k-1], n],
    If[gcdn == n, 0,
      Mod[gcdn PowerMod[gcdn, -1, n/gcdn]
        PowerMod[m/rprimem,
          SuperPowerMod[a, k-1,EulerPhi[n/gcdn]],
                                        n/gcdn]
          PowerMod[rprimem,
          SuperPowerMod[a, k-1, EulerPhi[n]], n],
                                        n]]]]]

LogStar[a_, n_]:= 0 /; n < a

LogStar[a_, n_]:= LogStar[a, Log[a, N[n]]] + 1

LogStarStar[a_, n_]:= 0 /; n < a

LogStarStar[a_, n_]:=
 LogStarStar[a, LogStar[a, n]] + 1
```

```
SuperSuperPowerMod[a_, k_, n_] := Mod[a, n] /;
   k == 1

SuperSuperPowerMod[a_, k_, n_] :=
  SuperPowerMod[a, a, n]    /; k == 2

SuperSuperPowerMod[a_, k_, n_] :=
  SuperPowerMod[a, SuperSuperPower[a, k-1], n] /;
            LogStarStar[Log[2, n]] > k

SuperSuperPowerMod[a_, k_, n_] :=
  SuperPowerMod[a, n, n]

SuperPower[a_, 1] := a

SuperPower[a_, k_] := a^SuperPower[a, k-1]

SuperSuperPower[a_, 1] := 1

SuperSuperPower[a_, k_] :=
  SuperPower[a, SuperSuperPower[a, k-1]]
```

**(c)** The fast evaluation of $a^n = a \uparrow n$ is the method `MyPower` of this section. This method is itself the analogue of the "schoolboy" multiplication method, which multiplies two numbers by expanding them in binary, and then uses repeated doubling (see Section 5.2). Analysis of this method reveals that one needs commutativity of addition to do schoolboy multiplication (repeated addition) and commutativity of multiplication is need for `MyPower` (repeated multiplication). This method therefore fails for repeated exponentiation, since it is not a commutative operation, i.e., $a^b \neq b^a$ in general.

**(d) (i)** One can define $A^A$ for matrices by $e^{A \log A}$ where

$$e^A = \sum_{k=0}^{\infty} \frac{A^k}{k!}$$

and

$$\log(I + A) = \sum_{k=1}^{\infty} (-1)^{k-1} \frac{A^k}{k}, \qquad \|A\| < 1.$$

An analogue of Eisenstein's result should hold.

**(d) (ii)** This problem has been essentially solved completely by D.B. Shapiro and S.D. Shapiro who have shown the following [115]:

*n is a positive integer:* In this case the sequence

$$n, \; n^n, \; n^{n^n}, \; n^{n^{n^n}}, \dots$$

has a well-defined limit $\beta_p(n)$ in the ring of $p$-adic integers. With the appropriate definition of $f(x) = n^x$ for a $p$-adic variable $x$ this limit $\beta_p(n)$ is the unique fixed point of $f(x)$.

Furthermore the map $\beta_p$ is an injective map from the positive integers to the $p$-adics. It turns out that if $n > 1$ and $n$ is not divisible by $p$ then $\beta_p(n)$ is a transcendental $p$-adic number.

*Arbitrary $a \in \mathbf{Z}_p$:* Generalizing this to arbitrary $a \in \mathbf{Z}_p$ is nontrivial since one cannot always define $a^a$. The method of [115] is to work in the ring $\mathbf{Z}^{\wedge}$, the inverse limit of $\mathbf{Z}/n\,\mathbf{Z}$, taken over all natural numbers $n$. Then $\mathbf{Z}^{\wedge}$ is isomorphic to the direct product of all the $p$-adic rings $\mathbf{Z}_p$ (as an additive group this is just $\mathbf{Q}/\mathbf{Z}$, the rationals mod the integers). In this ring the function $a^x$ is nicely defined for any $a, x$ in $\mathbf{Z}^{\wedge}$, so the analogue of Eisenstein's result should hold.

**(e) (i)** Actually one can show that

$$\sum_{n < x} \frac{1}{f(n)} \approx \log^*(n),$$

where $\log^*(n)$ is the number of times one needs to iterate log to get less than or equal to $e$ ($\log^*(n)$ is essentially the inverse of $e \uparrow\uparrow n$). To see this, let $\alpha = e \uparrow\uparrow r$ and $\beta = e \uparrow\uparrow (r + 1)$. Then for $\alpha < n < \beta$ one has that

$$f(n) = n \log n \; \log \log n \cdots \log_r(n)$$

and so

$$\sum_{\alpha < n < \beta} \frac{1}{f(n)} = \sum_{\alpha < n < \beta} \frac{1}{n \log n \log \log n \cdots \log_r(n)}$$

$$\approx \int_\alpha^\beta \frac{1}{x \log x \log \log x \cdots \log_r(x)} \, dx$$

$$= \log_{r+1}(\beta) - \log_{r+1}(\alpha) = 1 - 0 \, .$$

So each time $\log^*(x)$ increases by 1, the sum increases by about 1. Note that the choice of the base of logarithms in this example is critical since taking logarithms in base $b$ introduces a factor of $(\log b)^r$ in each term of this sum so divergence is insured for $b > e$ and convergence is insured for $b < e$.

**Remark:** This says that in some vague sense one can think of $f(n)$ as being the "derivative" of $\log^*(n)$.

**(ii)** You can always define an infinite series which diverges as slowly as you want so the question makes sense only if you restrict yourself to classes of functions. In other words, one wants a function $g(n)$ defined by iterated logarithms such that

$$\sum \frac{1}{g(n)}$$

diverges but

$$\sum \frac{1}{g(n)h(n)}$$

converges for any functions $h(n)$ restricted in a certain class of nondecreasing functions going to infinity.

One can build up slower and slower divergent series as follows: Let $f_1(n) = f(n)$ and consider

$$f_2(n) = f_1(n)f_1(\log^*(n))f_1(\log^*(\log^*(n))) \cdots f_1(\log_r^*(n))$$

where $\log_r^*(n)$ is the $r$ fold iterate of $\log^*$ such that $\log_r^*(n) \leq 1$. This $r$ is defined to be the function $\log^{**}(n)$. At this point one could define a *downarrow notation* with

$$e \downarrow n = \log n, \quad e \downdownarrows n = \log^*(n), \quad e \downdowndownarrows n = \log^{**}(n),$$

and so forth. In any case, as before, one has

$$\sum_{n<x} \frac{1}{f_2(n)} \approx \log^{**}(n).$$

Continuing with $\log^{***}(n)$ etc., let $\alpha(n)$ be the number of $*$'s needed to get $\log^{*\cdots*}(n)$ down to one and defining $f_\alpha(n)$ to be $f_{\alpha(n)}(n)$ one can show that

$$\sum_{n<x} \frac{1}{f_\alpha(n)} \approx \alpha(n).$$

Here $\alpha(n)$ is simply the inverse of the Ackerman function which appears in the analysis of many algorithms as R. Tarjan has shown [124]. Now the theory of Ackerman's function [106] shows that

$$\sum \frac{1}{f_\alpha(n)h(n)}$$

converges for any *primitive recursive* function $h(n)$ that is increasing to infinity. Once again one can think of $f_\alpha(n)$ as being the "derivative" of the inverse of Ackerman.

One can similarly define $\alpha^*(n)$ to be the number of iterations of $\alpha$ so that you get to 1, $\alpha^{**}(n)$ the number of iterations of $\alpha^*$ and so forth, and finally getting $\alpha_1(n)$ the number of $*$'s needed to get to one. $\alpha_2(n)$ is derived similarly from $\alpha_1(n)$ and one can define $\beta(n)$ and the number of subscripts needed to get to one. Associated to $\beta(n)$ is the function $f_\beta(n)$ in the denominator and $f_\beta$ has the property that

$$\sum \frac{1}{f_\beta(n)h(n)}$$

converges for any $h(n)$ defined by first order arithmetic (see [106] [121]). In this way one gets a hierarchy of slow growing functions corresponding to Ackerman type hierarchies (see [106] [121]). One would like to construct a natural function $f_{\text{rec}}(n)$ consisting of iterated logarithms as above with the property that

$$\sum \frac{1}{f_{\text{rec}}(n)}$$

diverges but

$$\sum \frac{1}{f_{rec}(n)\, h(n)}$$

converges for any total recursive function $h(n)$ increasing to infinity. Such a function seems analogous to Chaitin's function in [15]. A direct application of the above method will never achieve this, but one can probably use a diagonalization argument on the set of recursive functions.

**1.4** The following search method will work

```
SignSearch[accuracy_]:=
Block[{cf = CoefficientList[polynomial, x],
  lambda2 =
  1.3037320846025763839006800405119185232225652686 1420},
  Select[Range[0, 71],
        Block[{u= cf}, u[[# + 1]] *= -1;
              Abs[((x^Range[0,71]) . u) /. x->lambda2]] <
              accuracy &
             ]
     ]
]
```

**1.5** The sequence is given by

$$\{1, 2, 2, 1, 1, 2, 1, 2, 2, 1, 2, 2, 1, 1, 2, 1, 1, 2, 2, 1, \ldots\}$$

and is not periodic, see [68].

# A.2. Digital Computing

**2.1** The answer is that 43 is the largest non-McNugget number.

(a) 43 is not a McNugget number. If it were, then 20 would have to be a summand for otherwise 43 would be a sum of 6's and 9's and so divisible by 3, a contradiction. If 20 were a summand then 23 would also be a McNugget number, and clearly it would also be a sum of 6's and 9's and so divisible by 3, a contradiction

(b) Now all the numbers 44 to 49 are McNugget numbers

$$44 = 6 + 2 \times 9 + 20$$
$$45 = 5 \times 9$$
$$46 = 6 + 2 \times 20$$
$$47 = 3 \times 9 + 20$$
$$48 = 8 \times 6$$
$$49 = 9 + 2 \times 20$$

so all integers $> 43$ are McNugget numbers since you can just add the necessary multiple of 6 to one of the numbers $\{44, \ldots, 49\}$.

Since 6,9,20 have no common factor, a general theorem in number theory says that every sufficiently large number $n$ can be written as a sum

$$n = 6a + 9b + 20c, \qquad a, b, c > 0.$$

Actually, the theorem affirms that is true for any $n \geq \mathrm{lcm}\,(6, 9, 20) = 180$. Finding the smallest number is a harder problem.

**2.2** This question was posted to the electronic newsgroup `rec.puzzles` by B. Ambati [1]. There were a number of responses to this. The analysis presented here was also found by D. Hickerson [59].

The following is a complete list of numbers less than $10^{42}$ with this property

```
1
4
9
49
144
441
1444
11449
44944
991494144
4914991449
```

149991994944
9141411449911441
199499144494999441
9914419419914449449
444411911999914911441
41999499914914994414914994419149444441

The last number was discovered by D. Applegate and G. Jacobson [4] using a C program which ran for 5 minutes on a DEC 3100. They used a combined most significant/least significant digit attack which takes $O(3^{n/(4-2\log_{10}(3))}) = O(3^{.66n/2})$ steps to check all numbers up to $10^n$, as opposed to the $O(3^{n/2})$ algorithm below.

The *Mathematica* program below was able to find the other numbers by doing a search of all numbers less than $10^{30}$ using the following algorithm which does on the order of $3^{n/2}$ operations to check all numbers $< 10^n$, i.e, the running time is

$$x^{\log 3/(2\log 10)} = x^{0.238561}$$

to check the conjecture for $< x$.

Assume $n$ is odd for convenience, ($n$ even is similar). Construct all numbers with $(n+1)/2$ leading digits 1,4,9, whose $(n-1)/2$ lower digits are zero. Now take $\lceil\sqrt{x}\rceil$ for each of these numbers. Squaring this gives you the unique square with those leading digits. One just has to check whether the lower $(n-1)/2$ digits of the result are of the form 1,4,9.

Note that the probability of success (assuming this behaves randomly) is about $3^{(n-1)/2}/10^{(n-1)/2}$ for each choice of the first $(n-1)/2$ leading digits, so one would expect about

$$\sum_{n=1}^{\infty} 3^{(n+1)/2} \frac{3^{(n-1)/2}}{10^{(n-1)/2}} < \sum_{n=1}^{\infty} \frac{9^{(n+1)/2}}{10^{(n-1)/2}}$$

$$< 3\sqrt{10} \sum_{n=0}^{\infty} \left(\frac{9}{10}\right)^{n/2}$$

$$= 3\sqrt{10}\, \frac{1}{1-\sqrt{9/10}} < \infty$$

solutions, i.e., only a finite number. This heuristic was also noted by
D. Hickerson [59] and G. Kuperberg [70].

In any case this gives a method that only needs to check $O(3^{n/2})$
numbers to find all examples less than $10^n$.

Here is a *Mathematica* program that implements this algorithm:

```
LeadingCheck[n_Integer?OddQ] :=
  Block[{k = (n+1)/2, m, leading, lower, lowersqrt,
         mzeroes, answer},
         m = n - k;
         mzeroes = 10^Quotient[m, 2];
          lowersqrt = LowerSqrtDigits[3];
          leading = LeadingDigits[k];
          lower = LowerDigits[5];
  answer =
  Select[
   Select[
    Select[Union[Ceiling[mzeroes *
            Sqrt[N[If[EvenQ[m], leading, 10 leading]]]]],
              MemberQ[lowersqrt, Mod[#, 1000]]&]^2,
              MemberQ[lower, Mod[#, 100000]]&],
          Union[Digits[#, 10]] == {1,4,9}&];
    Share[];
    m = m - 1; mzeroes = 10^Quotient[m, 2];
    Union[answer,
      Select[
   Select[
    Select[Union[Ceiling[mzeroes *
            Sqrt[N[If[EvenQ[m], leading, 10 leading]]]]],
              MemberQ[lowersqrt, Mod[#, 1000]]&]^2,
            MemberQ[lower, Mod[#, 100000]]&],
          Union[Digits[#, 10]] == {1,4,9}&]
      ]]


LowerDigits[1] := {1,4,9}
```

```
LowerDigits[2]= {41, 44, 49}

LowerDigits[3]= {144, 441, 444, 449, 944}

LowerDigits[4]=
{1441, 1444, 1449, 4144, 4441, 4449,
   4944, 9441, 9444, 9449}

LowerDigits[n_]:=
   Block[{t = LowerDigits[n-1]},
         Join[9 10^(n-1)+t,
             4 10^(n-1)+t,
             10^(n-1)+t]]  /; n > 4

LowerSqrtDigits[n_]:=
   Select[Range[10^n],
         MemberQ[LowerDigits[n], Mod[#^2, 10^n]]&]

LeadingDigits[1] = {1, 4, 9}

LeadingDigits[n_]:=
   Block[{t = LeadingDigits[n-1]},
         Join[9 10^(n-1)+t,
             4 10^(n-1)+t,
             10^(n-1)+t]]  /; n > 1
```

**2.5** The similar question for numbers divisible by the number of their divisors has been solved by C. Spiro [122]

# A.3 The Calendar

**3.1** Probably the shortest algorithm for computing the day of the week for the Gregorian calendar was discovered by the Reverend Zeller (see [129, pages 206–211]). It is convenient to denote the day of the week as a number 0–6, with 0=Sunday,..., 6=Saturday.  Reverend Zeller's formula is given by

$$d + \lfloor 2.6\,m - 0.2 \rfloor + \lfloor y/4 \rfloor + \lfloor c/4 \rfloor - 2c \bmod 7\,,$$

where $d$ is the day of the month, $m$ the month, $y$ is the year of century, $c$ is the century, and furthermore, *the year is assumed to begin on March first.* Thus January and February are assumed to be months 11 and 12 of the previous year.

A *Mathematica* program can be given by

```
DayOfWeek[year_Integer, month_Integer, day_Integer]:=
  Block[{y = year, m = month - 2},
        If [m < 3, {m, y} = {m + 12, y - 1}];
        {
        "Sunday", "Monday", "Tuesday", "Wednesday",
        "Thursday", "Friday", "Saturday"
        }
        [[1 +
          Mod[day + Floor[2.6 m - 0.2] + Mod[y, 100] +
              Quotient[Mod[y, 100], 4] +
              Quotient[Quotient[y, 100], 4] -
              2 Quotient[y, 100],
              7]
        ]]]
```

**3.2** The answer seems to be

```
ShortDigits[n_, b_]:=
  Reverse[Mod[Floor[n b^-Range[0, Log[b, n]]], b]]
```

**3.3 (a)** See [49, page 281].

**3.4 (b)** In order to catch up to the seasons Julius Caesar added 90 days to the year 46 B.C. (between November and February).  To get a 365 day year he rearranged the number of days in each month.  January, March, May, July, September, and November were all to have 31 days.

All months except February would contain 30 days. February would have 29 days in common years and 30 in leap years.

After Caesar's death the number of days in each month was rearranged to their present form. Around 10 B.C. it was discovered that the priests who were in charge of the calendar had added the leap year every *three years* rather than every fourth year. To correct this no leap years were added until 8 A.D.

In order to compute exactly when March 15, 44 B.C., occurred one must therefore get hold of the complete table of the years 44 B.C. to 8 A.D. It is unclear where this information can be found.

**Exercise 3.5** The French revolutionary calendar is very similar to the Gregorian calendar. The only significant change is that the 5 Sans Culottides are coded in as a thirteenth month of five days.

```
NumberToDate[n_, French]:=
Prepend[Drop[#, 4],
        DigitsToNumber[Take[#-1, 4], {4, 25, 4}] + 1]& @
        MyDigits[n, FrenchCalendar, {}]

DateToNumber[date_, French]:=
Block[{d = Join[MyDigits[First[date]-1, {4, 25, 4}],
               Rest[date]-1]},
       d = Join[Table[0, {6 - Length[d]}], d];
       DigitsToNumber[d, FrenchCalendar, d]]

CalendarChange[Gregorian, French] =
   DateToNumber[{1792, 9, 21}, Gregorian]

FrenchCalendar =
  {FrenchFourCenturies, FrenchCentury, FrenchFourYears,
   FrenchYears, FrenchMonths}

FrenchFourCenturies[_]:= {146097}

FrenchCentury[_]:= {36524, 36524, 36524, 36525}

FrenchFourYears[path_]:=
```

```
Append[Table[1461, {24}],
       1460 + Quotient[path[[2]], 4]]

FrenchYears[path_]:=
  {365, 365, 365, 366 -
   (1-Quotient[path[[2]], 4]) Quotient[path[[3]], 25]}

FrenchMonths[path_]:=
  Append[Table[30, {12}], 5 + Quotient[path[[4]], 4] -
    (1 - Quotient[path[[2]], 4]) Quotient[path[[3]], 25]]

CalendarChange[Gregorian, French] =
 -DateToNumber[{1792, 9, 21}, Gregorian]

CalendarChange[French, Gregorian] =
 -CalendarChange[Gregorian, French]
```

**3.7 (a)** The Jewish calendar is much more difficult to implement since it keeps track of both the lunar cycle and the solar cycle. For example, knowing the day of the month in this calendar tells you what the phase of the moon is.

A Lisp implementation has been given by [99] in GNU Emacs Lisp and can be gotten by anonymous ftp from a.cs.uiuc.edu in the directory pub/calendar.

A simple formula for computing Rosh Hashana, the Jewish new year, is given in [7, page 800].

# A.4 Searching for Numbers

### 4.1

**(a)** The following is basically the proof in [72] (the case $2^n + 1$ is similar). Let $d$ be the smallest number such that $2^d \equiv 1 \pmod{p}$, so that $2^n \equiv 1 \pmod{p}$ and $2^{p-1} \equiv 1 \pmod{p}$ imply that $d|n$ and $d|(p-1)$.
(i) $2^n \not\equiv 1 \pmod{p^2} \Rightarrow 2^{p-1} \not\equiv 1 \pmod{p^2}$:

Since $d|n$ one has that $2^n \not\equiv 1 \pmod{p^2}$ implies that $2^d \not\equiv 1 \pmod{p^2}$. One can then write $2^d = 1 + kp$, $(k,p) = 1$, and since $p - 1 = dm$, where $(m,p) = 1$, one has

$$2^{p-1} = 2^{dm} \equiv (1 + pk)^m \equiv 1 + pkm \not\equiv 1 \pmod{p^2}.$$

(ii) $2^n \equiv 1 \pmod{p^2} \Rightarrow 2^{p-1} \equiv 1 \pmod{p^2}$:

Since $d|(p-1)$ this will follow if one can show that $2^d \equiv 1 \pmod{p^2}$. Assuming that this were false, then as in (i) one would have $2^d = 1 + kp$, $(k,p) = 1$. By assumption one has that $n = dm$, where $(m,p) = 1$ and so

$$2^n = 2^{dm} \equiv (1 + pk)^m \equiv 1 + pkm \not\equiv 1 \pmod{p^2},$$

which contradicts the assumption.

**(b)** Follows immediately by noting that the conjecture implies that one of $2^n - 1, 2^n, 2^n + 1$ must be divisible by a prime but not by the square of that prime. Note that this also gives the $\log x$ lower bound of part (c).

**(c)** Let $a = -2^n$, $b = 1$, $c = 2^n - 1$, then the *abc* conjecture implies that for every sufficiently large $n$, $c$ is divisible by a prime but not by the square of that prime. This gives a $\log x$ lower bound on the number of non Wieferich primes.

**4.3** See Exercise 8.3 for an outline of the proof.

**4.5** It follows from Lucas' theorem that $\binom{2n}{n} \not\equiv 0 \pmod{p}$ if and only if all the digits of $n$ are $\leq p/2$. These numbers form an infinite set of density zero, so cannot be periodic.

**4.6** The answer is that this holds if and only if $n + 1$ is a power of two. To see this, assume that all $\binom{n}{k}$, $k = 0, 1, \ldots, n$ are odd, then the binomial theorem gives

$$(1-x)^n = \sum_{k=0}^{n} (-1)^k \binom{n}{k} x^k \equiv 1 + x + x^2 + \cdots x^n = \frac{1 - x^{n+1} - 1}{1 - x} \pmod 2$$

(recall that $1 \equiv -1 \pmod 2$). The condition is therefore equivalent to

$$(1 - x)^{n+1} \equiv 1 - x^{n+1} \pmod 2.$$

Clearly this holds if $n + 1 = 2^m$, for some $m$ (e.g., use induction). Conversely, if $n + 1 = q\,2^m$, $q > 1$ odd, then

$$(1 - x)^{n+1} = (1 - x)^{q\,2^m} \equiv (1 - x^{2^m})^q = 1 - qx^{2^m} + \cdots + x^{n+1} \pmod{2},$$

which gives a contradiction since $q \equiv 1 \pmod 2$ and and $2^m < n$.

**4.7** Clearly one will compute factorials using the prime decomposition of $n!$. However, it is seen that one can speed up the evaluation of $(p - 1)! \pmod{p^2}$ by a factor of two using formula (4.7)

$$(A.4.1) \qquad (p - 1)! \equiv \left\{ \left( \frac{p - 1}{2} \right)! \right\}^2 (-1)^{(p-1)/2} 4^{p-1} \pmod{p^2}.$$

Now it turn out that for $p \equiv 1 \pmod 4$ one can do better since it is a theorem of Chowla, Dwork, and Evans [16] that if

$$(A.4.2) \qquad p = a^2 + b^2, \qquad a \equiv 1 \pmod 4$$

(this specifies $a$ uniquely) then

$$(A.4.3) \qquad \binom{(p - 1)/2}{(p - 1)/4} \equiv \left( 1 + \frac{2^{p-1} - 1}{2} \right) \left( 2a - \frac{p}{2a} \right) \pmod{p^2}.$$

Substituting this into (A.4.1) gives

$$(p - 1)! \equiv \left\{ \left( \frac{p - 1}{4} \right)! \right\}^4 \left( 1 + \frac{2^{p-1} - 1}{2} \right)^2$$

$$\times \left( 2a - \frac{p}{2a} \right)^2 (-1)^{(p-1)/2} \, 4^{p-1} \pmod{p^2}.$$

The point of this is that the value of $a$ given by (A.4.2) can be computed very quickly using an algorithm of Cornacchia [131] (actually, this function is built in to V2.0, see below). Equation (A.4.3) is a refinement of a famous equation of Gauss

$$(A.4.4) \qquad \binom{(p - 1)/2}{(p - 1)/4} \equiv 2a \pmod{p^2}.$$

Wagon's article states that (A.4.4) is not useful for computing $a$, which is true. But the point is that every identity has two directions, so one uses (A.4.4) to get values of binomials $\bmod\, p$ from values of $a$.

Results of Kit Ming Yeung [136] allow even more speed up for primes of the form $p = 6k + 1$ by expressing $(p - 1)! \pmod{p^2}$ in terms of $((p - 1)/6)! \pmod{p^2}$.

A *Mathematica* program to generate the representation $p = a^2 + b^2$, for $p \equiv 1 \pmod 4$ using Cornacchia's algorithm can given by

```
SumOfTwoSquares[p_Integer] :=
Block[{r1 = p, r2 = 2},
       While[JacobiSymbol[r2, p] == 1, r2++];
       r2 = PowerMod[r2, (p-1)/4, p];
       While[r1^2 > p, {r1, r2} = {r2, Mod[r1, r2]}];
       {r1, r2}]  /; PrimeQ[p] && Mod[p, 4] == 1
```

This algorithm has been built into V2.0 and is used to factor primes of the form $4k+1$ over the ring of Gaussian integers $\{m+in \mid m, n \text{ integers}\}$. The program is

```
SumOfTwoSquares[p_] :=
  {Re[#], Im[#]}& @
  FactorInteger[p, GaussianIntegers -> True][[-1,1]] /;
     PrimeQ[p] && Mod[p, 4] == 1
```

# A.5  How Not to Use *Mathematica*

**5.4** Obviously no one can tell what Euclid could or could not have understood, but it is an interesting exercise to try to write up classical theorems in the style of Euclid.

The fact that primes have zero density was first proved explicitly by Legendre [77] along the following lines:

Let $p_1, p_2, \ldots, p_n$ be the primes less than or equal to $x$, and let $N = p_1 p_2 \cdots p_n$. One has that

$$\phi(N) = N \prod_{p \leq x} \left(1 - \frac{1}{p}\right)$$

and the number of primes less than or equal to $Nk$ is less than

$$n + \phi(N) k = \prod_{p \leq x} \left(1 - \frac{1}{p}\right) Nk + n,$$

where $k = 1, 2, \ldots$ and $n$ remains constant. This part of the argument should not be too difficult to write in the "Euclidean" style since it only depends on the principle of inclusion-exclusion, a fairly elementary technique. The key to the argument is that

$$\prod_{p \leq x} \left(1 - \frac{1}{p}\right) \to 0 \qquad \text{as } x \to \infty.$$

This is easy to show by using the Euler product idea of Chapter 8

$$(\text{A.5.1}) \qquad \prod_{p \leq x} \left(1 - \frac{1}{p}\right)^{-1} \geq \sum_{n \leq x} \frac{1}{n}.$$

It is straightforward to argue that

$$\sum_{n \leq x} \frac{1}{n} \geq C \log x$$

for some constant $C$, and inequality (A.5.1) can be translated to Euclid's level without too much difficulty.

It would be interesting to find a simple proof of the theorem independent of these ideas. It is probably harder to find different methods for upper bounds on the number of primes (as opposed to the many lower bound proofs) since the proof requires one to show that the primes are regularly distributed (see Remark). Moreover, there is not as much "room" above, i.e., the number of primes $x/\log x$ is quite close to $x$ (Legendre's argument gives $x/\log \log x$). The only "elementary" arguments (in the sense of not very technical) seem to be Legendre's method and Chebyshev's estimate of Exercise 4.3.

**Remark:** Legendre's method shows that the divergence of

$$\sum_{p \text{ prime}} \frac{1}{p}$$

implies that the primes have zero density. However, even the fact that

$$\sum_{\substack{p \text{ prime} \\ p < x}} \frac{1}{p} \approx \log \log x$$

does not *directly* imply that the primes have zero density!

**5.5** F. Morain easily found the factorization

`{{31401519357481261, 1}, {77366930214021991992277, 1}}`

using the Multiple Polynomial Quadratic Sieve implemented in LeLisp.

**5.8** This is just a recursive implementation of `PowerMod`

```
(defun PowerMod (a b c)
 (cond
   ((zerop b) 1)
   ((evenp b) (mod (expt
           (PowerMod a (ash b -1) c) 2) c))
   (T (mod (* (PowerMod a (1- b) c) a) c)))))
```

**5.9** Most of the time taken for $2^{n-1} \bmod n^2$ is spent computing squares $\bmod n^2$. Writing a number mod $n^2$ as

$$m = an + b, \qquad 0 \le a, b < n,$$

then

$$m^2 \bmod n^2 = ((2ab + \text{quotient}\,(b^2, n)) \bmod n)\, n + (b^2 \bmod n).$$

This also implies that one can compute $2^{n-1} \bmod n$ as a subroutine of $2^{n-1} \bmod n^2$ using some extra storage and a few extra operations. One can implement the `PowerMod` algorithm such that the expressions

$$(2ab + \text{quotient}\,(b^2, n)) \bmod n$$

are only evaluated when it is seen that $2^{n-1} \equiv 1 \pmod{n}$.

For numbers of order $10^{10}$ extra function calls can be almost as costly as multiplications or mod operations. Just using a bignum package with assembly language multiplication such as [113] can give up to a factor of five speedup so these methods themselves will not win very much.

# A.6 The *n*-Queens Problem

**6.1**

```
QueensSolutions[n_]:=
Block[{r = Range[n]},
      Select[Permutations[r],
             Length /@
             {Union[# + r], Union[# - r]} ==
             {n, n}&]]
```

**6.2** The Gray code has the following recursive property:

```
Gray[0] = {{}}
```

```
Gray[n]:= Gray[n] =
  Join[Gray[n-1],
       Append[#, n]& /@ Reverse[Gray[n-1]]]
```

A slightly more efficient program is the procedural version

```
Gray2[n_]:=
Block[{s = {{}}, i},
      Do[s = Join[s,
             Append[#, i]&/@ Reverse[s]], {i, n}];
      s]
```

It is unclear how to implement `Gray` elegantly using functional programming.

**6.3** Let $(0, f(0), (1, f(1)), \ldots, (n-1, f(n-1)))$ represent the coordinates of a solution then

$$i \mapsto f(i) \pmod n$$

is a one to one map. One therefore has that

$$\sum_{i=0}^{n-1}(f(i) - i) \equiv \sum_{i=0}^{n-1} i = \frac{n(n-1)}{2} \pmod n.$$

On the other hand

$$\sum_{i=0}^{n-1}(f(i) - i) = \sum_{i=0}^{n-1} f(i) - \sum_{i=0}^{n-1} i \equiv \sum_{i=0}^{n-1} i - \sum_{i=0}^{n-1} i = 0 \pmod{n}.$$

One therefore has that

$$\frac{n(n-1)}{2} \equiv 0 \pmod{n}$$

which is impossible if $n$ is even.

This argument, due to G. Pólya [96] can also be sued to show that there are no toroidal queen solutions if $n$ is divisible by 2 or 3.

**6.4 (b)** Ryser's formula give that

$$\operatorname{perm} \operatorname{circ}(y_0, \ldots, y_{n-1}) = \sum_{s \subseteq \{1,\ldots,n\}} (-1)^{|s|} \prod_{i=0}^{n-1} \sum_{j \in s} y_{i-j \bmod n}$$

but by (6.1), the coefficient of the squarefree term in

$$\prod_{i=0}^{n-1} \sum_{j \in s} y_{i-j \bmod n}$$

is

$$\operatorname{perm} \operatorname{circ}(\varepsilon_s(j)), \qquad \varepsilon_s(j) = \begin{cases} 0 & \text{if } j \in s, \\ 1 & \text{otherwise,} \end{cases}$$

and the result follows.

**6.6 (a)** The explicit definition of the permanent is

$$\operatorname{perm}(a_{ij}) = \sum_{\sigma \in S_n} \prod_{i=1}^{n} a_{i\sigma(i)},$$

where $S_n$ is the set of all permutations of $\{1, \ldots, n\}$. Applying this to $\operatorname{Sc}(n)$ gives

$$\operatorname{perm} \operatorname{Sc}(n) = \sum_{\sigma \in S_n} \prod_{i=1}^{n} \xi^{i\sigma(i)} = \sum_{\sigma \in S_n} \xi^{\sum_{i=1}^{n} i\sigma(i)}.$$

Now one splits this sum up according to the value of $\sigma(0)$, i.e., let $S_n^r = \{\sigma \in S_n \mid \sigma(0) = r\}$, the above is equal to

(A.6.1)
$$\sum_{r=1}^{n} \sum_{\sigma \in S_n^r} \xi^{\sum_{i=1}^{n} i\sigma(i)} .$$

Now if $\sigma'$ is a cyclic left shift of $\sigma$ by $r$ places, i.e., $\sigma'(i) = \sigma(i-r \bmod n)$ then

$$\sum_{i=1}^{n} i\sigma'(i) = \sum_{i=1}^{n} i\sigma(i - r \bmod n)$$

$$\equiv \sum_{i=1}^{n} (i+r)\sigma(i) \; (\bmod\, n)$$

$$= \sum_{i=1}^{n} i\sigma(i) + \sigma_{i=1}^{n} r\sigma(i)$$

$$\equiv \sum_{i=1}^{n} i\sigma(i) \; (\bmod\, n) ,$$

since

$$\sum_{i=1}^{n} \sigma(i) \equiv \sum_{i=1}^{n} i \equiv 0 \; (\bmod\, n) .$$

This implies that

$$\xi^{\sum_{i=1}^{n} i\sigma(i)} = \xi^{\sum_{i=1}^{n} i\sigma'(i)}$$

and so one has that all the inner sums in (A.6.1) are equal, since the $\sigma \leftrightarrow \sigma'$ gives a correspondence between all the $\Sigma_n^r$. In particular one has that

$$\sum_{\sigma \in S_n \, , \, \sigma(0)=0} \xi^{\Sigma i\sigma(i)} = \frac{1}{n} \operatorname{perm} \operatorname{Sc}(n) ,$$

but since $\xi^{0\sigma(0)} = 1$, the left side of this equation is $\operatorname{perm} \operatorname{Sc}'(n)$.

# A.8 The Riemann Zeta Function

**8.1** Good luck!

## 8.2 (a)

```
Lambda[n_]:=
Log[Times @@ Select[n^(1/Range[Log[2, n]]), PrimeQ]]
```

**(b)** The first version just uses part (a)

```
Psi[x_]:= Plus @@ Lambda /@ Range[2, x]
```

There is a much shorter program based on the identity

$$\psi(x) = \log \operatorname{lcm}(1, 2, 3, \ldots, \lfloor x \rfloor)$$

but it runs much more slowly

```
Psi2[x_]:= Log[LCM @@ Range[x]]
```

**8.3** This is essentially Chebyshev's method of Exercise 4.2. The first step, by Principle II, is to substitute $\pi^*(x)$ with $\psi^*(x)$ where

$$\psi^*(x) = \sum_{k=1}^{\lfloor x/2 \rfloor} \sum_{x/(2k)<p^n \le x/(2k-1)} \log p .$$

By the partial summation method of Section 8.2, the assertion of the exercise follows from

(A.8.1) $$\psi^*(x) = \log 2\, x + O(\sqrt{x}\log^2 x) .$$

On the other hand, by equation (4.8) of Section 4.3, $\psi^*(x)$ is just $\log \left( \begin{smallmatrix} \lfloor x \rfloor \\ \lfloor x \rfloor/2 \end{smallmatrix} \right)$, so (A.8.1) follows from Stirling's formula, which gives that

(A.8.2) $$\log \left( \frac{\lfloor x \rfloor}{\lfloor x \rfloor/2} \right) = x \log 2 - \frac{\log x}{2} + O(1) ,$$

which is even better than (A.8.1).

The following seems to explain what is going on: Note first that by part (c) of the previous exercise one has that

(A.8.3) $$\psi^*(x) = \psi(x) - \psi(x/2) + \psi(x/3) - \cdots \pm \psi(x/\lfloor x \rfloor)$$

(Note that Chebyshev's estimate follows from the fact that this implies

$$\psi(x) > \psi^*(x) > \psi(x) - \psi(x/2).)$$

Combining (A.8.3) with formula (8.4) which is

(A.8.4)                    $$\psi(x) = \frac{1}{2\pi i} \int_{2-i\infty}^{2+i\infty} -\frac{\zeta'(s)}{\zeta(s)} \frac{x^s}{s} \, ds$$

one has that

$$\psi^*(x)$$

(A.8.5)
$$= \frac{1}{2\pi i} \int_{2-i\infty}^{2+i\infty} -\frac{\zeta'(s)}{\zeta(s)} \left(1 - \frac{1}{2^s} + \frac{1}{3^s} - \cdots \pm \frac{1}{\lfloor x \rfloor^s}\right) \frac{x^s}{s} \, ds \, .$$

This integral picks off the first $\lfloor x \rfloor$ terms of any Dirichlet series inside it [23, 104], so extending the Dirichlet series past $\lfloor x \rfloor$ inside the brackets does not affect its value. Because of the identity

$$\zeta(s) \left(1 - \frac{1}{2^{1-s}}\right) = 1 - \frac{1}{2^s} + \frac{1}{3^s} - \frac{1}{4^s} + \cdots$$

it follows that the term in the brackets cancels the $\zeta(s)$ in the denominator of (A.8.5). In effect going from $\psi$ to $\psi^*$ has canceled all the poles due to $1/\zeta(s)$ from the integral formula for $\psi(x)$ (the poles are what determine the asymptotics in (A.8.4) and (A.8.5)).

The conclusion is that (A.8.2) and therefore Chebyshev's estimate, are what can be deduced if you ignore the zeroes of the Riemann zeta function!

**8.4** The Farey sequence has many interesting properties [49, Section 4.5] and I will present two entirely different solutions to the problem.

**First method**

The theory of Farey fractions shows that if $a/b$, $a'/b'$, and $a''/b''$ are three successive terms of the sequence then

$$\frac{a'}{b'} = \frac{a + a''}{b + b''}$$

(Bart Simpson's dream).  This process doesn't use the fact that the elements of the sequence are fractions, and one should avoid using division until the last moment since the *Mathematica* function a/b uses the Euclidean algorithm to reduce the fraction in lowest terms but all the fractions involved in the algorithm are already known to be in lowest terms, by the theory of Farey fractions. So

```
FareyList[{{0,1}, {1,1}}, n]
```

will generate the list of numerators and denominators of the elements of the $n$th Farey sequence where FareyList is given by the simple recursive program

```
FareyList[{a_, b_}, n_]:=
  If[a[[2]] + b[[2]] <= n,
     Join[FareyList[{a, a+b}, n],
          Rest[FareyList[{a+b, b}, n]]],
     {a, b}]
```

The actual Farey sequence can be now be gotten by

```
Farey[n_]:= Divide @@ # & /@
            FareyList[{{0,1}, {1,1}}, n]
```

It seems that this program is optimal in the sense that the number of recursion calls is equal to the number of elements in $\mathcal{F}_n$. One can write a slightly more efficient program by using the central symmetry of the Farey sequence, i.e., the sequence is symmetric with respect to the map $x \mapsto 1 - x$.

```
FareyFaster[n_]:=
  Block[{list = FareyList[{{0,1}, {1,2}}, n]},
        Divide @@ #& /@
        Join[list,
             {#[[2]] - #[[1]], #[[2]]}& /@
             -Rest[Reverse[list]]]]
```

An interesting question is whether there are further symmetries in the Farey sequence which speed up the computation further. Note that the Farey sequence in the text can be considered a reduced form of a larger version of the Farey sequence $\mathcal{F}'_n$ which includes *all* fractions in order where both numerator and denominator are $\leq n$. For example

$$\mathcal{F}'_5 = \Big\{ 0, \frac{1}{5}, \frac{1}{4}, \frac{1}{3}, \frac{2}{5}, \frac{1}{2}, \frac{3}{5}, \frac{2}{3}, \frac{3}{4}, \frac{4}{5}, \frac{1}{1},$$
$$\frac{5}{4}, \frac{4}{3}, \frac{3}{2}, \frac{5}{3}, \frac{2}{1}, \frac{5}{2}, \frac{3}{1}, \frac{4}{1}, \frac{5}{1} \Big\} \, .$$

$\mathcal{F}'_n$ is symmetric with respect to the map $x \mapsto 1/x$. The question at hand therefore asks whether $x \mapsto 1/x$ and $x \mapsto 1 - x$ are the only symmetries to be found in this sequence.

**Remark:** The recursion in `FareyList` does a traversal of part of a binary tree called the *Stern-Brocot tree* [49, page 116].

## Second method

Given an element $a/b$ in $\mathcal{F}_n$, the theory of Farey fractions gives an algorithm for computing its successor as follows [57, Section 3.4]: since $a$ and $b$ are relatively prime one can find $x_0, y_0$ satisfying

$$x_0 b - y_0 a = 1 \, .$$

This is implemented by the built-in *Mathematica* function `ExtendedGCD`. The successor to $a/b$ is then given by

$$\frac{x_0 + ra}{y_0 + rb} \, ,$$

where $r$ is such that $n - b < y_0 + rb \leq n$. This says that, for minimal $y_0 > 0$ (which holds for `ExtendedGCD[b, -a]`), $r$ can be given by the quotient of $n - y_0$ and $b$. Once again one avoids using fractions and a program can therefore be given by

```
FareySuccessor[{a_, b_}, n_]:=
        Divide @@
        (# + Quotient[n - #[[2]], b] {a, b})& @
        Last[ExtendedGCD[b, -a]]
```

This function can be used to generate the Farey sequence, but a more efficient method along these lines relies on the fact that that the successor of a pair of Farey terms is easy to compute [49, p. 150]. Namely, if $p/q, p'/q', p''/q''$ are three consecutive elements of $\mathcal{F}_n$ then

$$p'' = \left\lfloor \frac{q+n}{q'} \right\rfloor p' - p$$

$$q'' = \left\lfloor \frac{q+n}{q'} \right\rfloor q' - q$$

and one gets

```
Farey2[n_]:=
 Block[{a = {0, 1}, b = {1, n}, list},
       list = {a, b};
       While[b != {1, 2},
             {a, b} = {b, Quotient[a[[2]] + n,
                                    b[[2]]] b - a};
             AppendTo[list, b]];
       Divide @@ #& /@
       Join[list, {#[[2]] - #[[1]], #[[2]]}& /@
             - Rest[Reverse[list]]]]
```

This method will be slower than the first method since one uses the more expensive operation `Quotient`.

**(b) (i)** This is a well known result, for example [49, pages 448–449].

**(ii)** This is a less well known result and is due to Schanuel [109] (see [71, Chapter 3, Section 5]). The answer is that this number is asymptotic to

$$\frac{N^n}{\zeta(n)}$$

(note that $\zeta(2) = \pi^2/6$). Schanuel actually proved much more, generalizing this to sequences of algebraic integers and also providing very good error terms.

**(c) (i)** Weyl's criterion requires one to find nontrivial bounds on sums

$$\text{(A.8.6)} \qquad \sum_{\substack{0<a<b\leq N \\ (a,b)=1}} e^{2\pi i m a/b}\,,$$

for $m = 1, 2, \ldots$, where "nontrivial" means that this sum divided by $\Phi(N) \approx 3N^2/\pi^2$ goes to zero as $N \to \infty$ (the sum is of lower "order" than $\Phi(N)$).

The sum in (A.8.6) can be rewritten as

$$\text{(A.8.7)} \qquad \sum_{0<b\leq N} c_b(m)\,,$$

where

$$c_b(m) = \sum_{\substack{0<a<b \\ (a,b)=1}} e^{2\pi i m a/b}$$

is the *Ramanujan sum* studied by S. Ramanujan. Now a straightforward application of the Möbius inversion formula of Exercise 1.1 gives the evaluation

$$c_b(1) = \mu(b)$$

so (A.8.7) for $m = 1$ is

$$M(N) = \sum_{b\leq N} \mu(b)\,.$$

Since $|\mu(n)| = 1$ or $0$, this implies the bound $|M(N)| \leq N$ which is of smaller order than $3N^2/\pi^2$.

One can also evaluate $c_b(m)$ as

$$c_b(m) = \mu(b/(b,m)) \frac{\phi(b)}{\phi(b/(b,m))}$$

(see [57, page 238]) which implies that

$$\sum_{b<N} c_b(m) = O(N^{1+\varepsilon})\,, \qquad \varepsilon > 0\,.$$

An analytic proof of this is indicated below, but I leave an elementary argument to the reader.

These arguments show that (A.8.6) is of order less than $\Phi(N)$. This almost completes the proof of equidistribution but there is an extra problem since the sequence

$$\left\{0, 1, \frac{1}{2}, \frac{1}{3}, \frac{2}{3}, \ldots\right\}$$

doesn't have to end at exactly a Farey sequence. In that case, the sequence ends at most $\phi(N)/2$ terms away from an exact Farey sequence, so the extra error introduced is less than $N/2$, and this is again of smaller order than $\Phi(N)$. This completes the proof of (i).

(ii) To get better error terms would require, in particular, getting better bounds on $M(N)$. It is well known that $M(N)/N \to 0$ is "equivalent" to the prime number theorem [74] [24, page 564] in the sense that it is much easier to prove either result from the other than find an independent proof. The discrepancy in the equidistribution of the Farey sequence is therefore related to the error term in the prime number theorem. It turns out that it is equivalent to this since the Ramanujan sum satisfies the series identity [98, page 185]

$$\sum_{n=1}^{\infty} \frac{c_n(m)}{n^s} = \frac{\sigma_{1-s}(m)}{\zeta(s)},$$

where

$$\sigma_s(n) = \sum_{d|n} d^s.$$

By standard techniques of analytic number theory [23] (A.8.7) can be written as

$$\frac{1}{2\pi i} \int_{2-i\infty}^{2+i\infty} \frac{\sigma_{1-s}(m)}{\zeta(s)} \frac{N^s}{s} \, ds$$

so the asymptotics of (A.8.7) are determined by the poles of

$$\frac{\sigma_{1-s}(m)}{\zeta(s)},$$

i.e., by the zeroes of the Riemann zeta function (the $\sigma_{1-s}(m)$ term doesn't cancel any poles). So, modulo standard techniques, cancellation in (A.8.7) is equivalent to bounding the zeroes of $\zeta(s)$ away from $\text{Re}(s) = 1$, i.e., the Riemann hypothesis.

**Remark:** Just finding the correct order of growth of $M(x)$ is equivalent to the Riemann hypothesis, so the following weaker statement of J. Franel [33] (see [75, pages 167–169]) is already equivalent to the Riemann hypothesis

$$\sum_{k=1}^{\Phi(n)} \left| \mathcal{F}_n(k) - \frac{k}{\Phi(n)} \right| = O(n^{1/2+\varepsilon}) \qquad \text{all } \varepsilon > 0.$$

Here $\Phi(n)$ is the number of elements in $\mathcal{F}_n$ (note that the ordering of the Farey sequence has simplified this statement).

**(iii)** The following generalization to elliptic curves is fairly straightforward: One can think of the unit circle as being parametrized by $t \in [0,1]$, and the fraction $a/b$ corresponds to a *division point*, which is a solution to $bx \equiv 0 \pmod 1$, i.e., $x^b = 1$ on the circle. Part (i) above states that the set of $n$ division points, $n \le N$ are equidistributed as $N$ goes to infinity. The analogue on an elliptic curve $E$ is to look at division points on the elliptic curve, i.e., points $P$ on $E$ that satisfy $nP = O$, where $O$ is the identity. The generalized problem is whether the $n$ division points are equidistributed (see below) as $N$ goes to infinity.

As usual one can parametrize an elliptic curve over the complex numbers by points in $[0,1] \times [0,1]$ (for example, [117, Chapter 6]). Equidistribution is generalized by saying that the probability of a sequence $x_1, x_2, \ldots, x_i \in [0,1] \times [0,1]$, being in $[\alpha, \beta] \times [\gamma, \delta]$ approaches $(\beta - \alpha)(\delta - \gamma)$.

The $n$ division points correspond to $(a/b, c/d)$, $b|n$, $d|n$, $a < b$, $c < d$. Weyl's criterion can be generalized to two dimensions [69] so that equidistribution of a sequence $(x_1, y_1), (x_2, y_2), \ldots$, of points in $[0,1] \times [0,1]$ is equivalent to

$$\lim_{N \to \infty} \frac{1}{N} \sum_{n=1}^{N} e^{2\pi i(mx_n + ky_n)} = 0$$

for each $m, k = 1, 2, \ldots$. In this case, one needs bounds for

$$(A.8.8) \qquad \sum_{\substack{0 < a < b \le N,\ 0 < c \le N \\ (a,b)=1,\ (c,d)=1}} e^{2\pi i\left(m\frac{a}{b} + k\frac{c}{d}\right)} = \sum_{0 < bd \le N} c_b(m) c_d(k).$$

Multiplying Ramanujan's identity for $m$ and $k$ gives

$$\frac{\sigma_{1-s}(m)\,\sigma_{1-s}(k)}{(\zeta(s))^2} = \sum_{n=1}^{\infty} \frac{1}{n^s} \sum_{bd=n} c_b(m)c_d(k).$$

Exactly as before, the asymptotics of (A.8.8) can be recovered from the zeroes of $\zeta(s)$, i.e., a nontrivial bound follows directly, while the best bound is equivalent to the Riemann hypothesis.

**(d)** Under the canonical parametrization, the smaller limbs of the Mandelbrot set occur at $p/q$ for relatively prime $p, q$, and the size of the limb is proportional to $q$. If this size were monotonic in $q$ then since producing the picture requires throwing out limbs smaller than a certain size, the limbs that you see would correspond to the Farey sequence.

**8.7 (a)** One must be very careful about using rational arithmetic on very large fractions, requiring a GCD operation at every step. One way is to use faster GCD algorithms [78]. Another is to try to use the factorization of $\binom{n}{k}$ and to do cancellation by keeping track of the factors. The following implementation avoids rational arithmetic altogether by keeping numerators and denominators separate and doing one large floating point division at the end.

```
pi[n_]:=
Block[{i = Ceiling[1.05 n / 14], num = 0, den = 1},
   While[i > 0,
        num = (num + (-1)^i den *
              (13591409 + 545140134 i)) *
              ((6 i -1) (2 i -1) (6 i -5));
        den *= 10939058860032000 i^3;
        i--];
   num += 13591409 den; den *= 426880;
   N[(N[den, n + 3] N[1/num, n + 3]) *
     N[Sqrt[10005], n + 3], n]]
```

**(b)** Exercise 8.4 (b) (i) states that the probability that two large random numbers are relatively prime is about $6/\pi^2$.

**8.9** See [45] [66, Exercise 4.5.3.15].

**Exercise 8.10** Gosper has noted that this is less than Khinchin's constant for the first two thousands digits. [47]

**8.11** Since each term $\cos(1/p)$ in the product is of the order $1 - 1/(2p^2)$ evaluating the product by expanding term by term will only yield about $2N$ digits for $N$ terms. Thus evaluating 100 places will need about $10^{50}$ terms, so a better method is required.

The idea in general is to evaluate

$$E(f) = \prod_p f(1/p)$$

where

$$f(x) = 1 + \sum_{n=2}^{\infty} a_n x^n$$

by factoring $f(x)$ formally as

(A.8.9) $$f(x) = \prod_{n=2}^{\infty} (1 - x^n)^{-b_n} .$$

One then has that

$$E(f) = \prod_{n=2}^{\infty} \zeta(n)^{b_n} .$$

Now since

$$\zeta(s) = 1 + \frac{1}{2^s} + R(s), \qquad \text{where } |R(s)| < \frac{4}{3^s} ,$$

where a necessary criterion for the product on the right hand side of (A.8.9) to converge is that that $\lim_{n \to \infty} b_n/2^n = 0$.

One can implement this method directly by developing the $b_n$ from the factorization of the Taylor series for $f(x)$ as above. A more efficient method consists of the following ideas based on the Möbius inversion formula of Exercise 1.1: Taking logarithms in the product (A.8.9) one has

(A.8.10) $$\log f(x) = \sum_{n \geq 2} \log(1 - x^n)^{-b_n} .$$

Set $L(x) = \log f(x)$ and assume that $L(x)$ has a Taylor series expansion

$$L(x) = \sum_{n \geq 1} \ell_n x^n \,.$$

From (A.8.10) one has

$$L(x) = -\sum_{n \geq 2} a_n \sum_{k \geq 1} \frac{x^{nk}}{k} = -\sum_{k \geq 1} \frac{1}{k} B(x^k) \,,$$

where $B(x) = \sum_n b_n x^n$ is the generating function of the $b_n$. By the Möbius inversion formula one can solve for $B(x)$:

$$B(x) = -\sum_{d \geq 1} \frac{\mu(d)}{d} L(x^d)$$

so the coefficients of $x^n$ in the power series for $B(x)$ is

$$b_n = -\sum_{d \mid n} \frac{\mu(d)}{d} \ell_{n/d}.$$

Note that this implies that the order of growth of the $b_n$ is determined by the order of growth of the $\ell_n$, i.e., by the closest singularity of $\log f(x)$, which occurs either at the closest zero of $f(x)$ to the origin. Since one needs to have $b_n/2^n \to 0$, one get

**Theorem.** *The rate of convergence of this method is determined by the closest zero or singularity of $f(x)$ to the origin. In particular the method works if $f(x)$ has no zeroes or singularities in $|z| \leq 1/2$.*

The procedure for computing $b_2, \ldots, b_n$ therefore consists of

(i) Computing the first $n$ coefficients of $L(x)$. This can be done directly by `Series[L[x], {x, 0, n}]` or can be implemented using the identity

$$\log f(x) = \int \frac{f'(x)}{f(x)}\, dx$$

which produces a simple recurrence formula for the $\ell_n$ in terms of the $a_n$.
(ii) One uses `Moebius[f, n]` of Exercise 1.1 to do Möbius inversion on the $\ell_n$ in order to obtain the $b_n$.

(iii) One computes a table of $\zeta(k)$ values where the length of the table depends on the asymptotic properties of $b_n$. Finally, one exponentiates these values by the $b_n$ and multiplies everything together to get the result.

An implementation of this in *Mathematica* is

```
EulerProduct[f_, n_]:=
Block[{coeff = N[Rest[CoefficientList[
                   Normal[Series[Log[f],
                        {x, 0,4 n}]], x]],
              n+5], y},
       N[Times @@ ((N[Zeta[#], n+5]& /@ Range[2,4 n])^
              ((Moebius[Function[y, y coeff[[y]]], #]& /@
              Range[2,4 n])/Range[2,4 n])), n]]
```

The special case $f(x) = \cos x$ can be done more efficiently since the Taylor series for $\log \cos x$ is known. The Taylor series for $\tan x$ is

$$\sum_{n=1}^{\infty} \frac{2^{2k}(2^{2k}-1)}{(2k)!} |B_{2k}| x^{2k-1},$$

where $B_k$ is the $k$th Bernoulli number. Since

$$\int \tan x \, dx = -\log \cos x$$

(e.g., [48, page 35]) you have the Taylor series

$$\log \cos x = -\sum_{n=1}^{\infty} \frac{2^{2k}(2^{2k}-1)}{2k(2k)!} |B_{2k}| x^{2k}.$$

(It is amusing to note that expressing $B_{2k}/(2k)!$ in terms of $\zeta(2k)$ as in (8.16) will mean that the answer will consist of terms of the form $\zeta(a)^{\zeta(b)}$.) A program to implement to implement this is

```
EulerProductCos[n_]:=
  Block[{coeff =
    -If[EvenQ[#],
       N[2^(#) (2^(#) -1) Abs[BernoulliB[#]]/(# #!), n+5],
```

```
      0]& /@ Range[1, 4 n]},
  N[Times @@ ((N[Zeta[#], n+5]& /@ Range[2, 4 n])^
    ((Moebius[Function[y, y coeff[[y]]], #]& /@
      Range[2,4 n])/Range[2,4 n])), n]]
```

This gives the evaluation

```
In[1]:= EulerProductCos[120]

Out[1]= 0.79219404524681376352874575946877142780880
>          774014981787335102541141879394501693838
>          468179121743916306015590813735533956199 1
```

The computation took under an hour on an IBM Risc machine.

# A.9 The Running Time of TAK

**9.2 (a)** The $0, 1$ valued function $h(x, y, z)$ always defines a total function $\mathrm{TAK}_h$ unless one of the following holds

(i) $h(0, 0, 0) = 1$ and $h(-1, 0, 1) = h(-1, 1, 0) = 0$;

(ii) $h(0, 0, 1) = h(0, 1, 0) = 1$ and $h(-1, 1, 1) = 0$;

(iii) $h(0, 0, 0) = h(0, 0, 1) = h(-1, 1, 0) = 1$ and
    $h(-1, 0, 1) = h(-1, 1, 1) = 0$.

**9.2 (b)** Knuth [67] has obtained partial results.

**9.4** D. Zeilberger and H. Wilf [133] have developed algorithms to convert definite summation of binomial coefficients into a recurrence relation (this extends a method of R.W. Gosper [46] for indefinite summation implemented in the package Gosper.m). Zeilberger has implemented these algorithms as a Maple package. Moreover, M. Petkovsek [95, Pet] has developed a method which can be used to determine from recurrence relations whether a closed form exists. Petkovsek has implemented this in the *Mathematica* package RSolve.m.

**9.6** It seems that this is a new class of recurrence relations. Note that one can "solve" (9.14) for the $a_n$ as

$$a_n = \sum_{n=i_1>i_2>...i_k>0} \prod_{j=1}^{k-1} H(i_j, i_{j+1})$$

but it is unclear what kind of generating function, for example, would take advantage of such a formula.

**Exercise 9.8** By [49, page 550] these can be written as the coefficients of $z^n$ in the power series of

$$\frac{1}{\sqrt{1 - 2z - 3z^2}}.$$

From the definition of Legendre polynomials, it is seen that this coefficient is

$$3^{n/2} \, i^{-n} P_n(i/\sqrt{3}).$$

**Exercise 9.9 (b)** The recurrence relation for $S(n)$ implies [19, pages 56–57] that the ordinary generating function for the $S(n)$ has the form

$$\sum_{n=1}^{\infty} S(n)z^n = \frac{1}{4}(1 + z) - \frac{1}{4}\sqrt{1 - 6z + z^2}.$$

Since

$$\sum_{n=0}^{\infty} P_n(3)z^n = \frac{1}{\sqrt{1 - 6z + z^2}}$$

the result follows by integrating this term by term.

## A.10  The Condom Problem

**10.3** Note that the analysis is complicated by the following consideration: If the graph consists of two populations which do not interact and which are of the same size then an optimal algorithm exists by giving everyone in the first population a condom, and after all encounters are completed each person passes to someone in the other population. The problem is therefore related to matching properties of the preference graph.

# Appendix B

# Glossary of Functions

`BinomialMod` Evaluates $\binom{2n}{n} \bmod m$, efficiently. Pages 66, 67, 70, 71.

`BinomialSearch` Searches for composite solutions of

$$\binom{n-1}{(n-1)/2} \equiv (-1)^{(n-1)/2} \pmod{n}.$$

The function `BinomialSearchTest` checks to see if this holds. Pages 72, 73.

`CalendarChange` Converts date from one calendar to another. Pages 36, 51–53, 55, 240.

`CheckRangeNine` Checks to see if all $\binom{2^{k+1}}{2^k}$, $k \le 2 \cdot 3^{n-1}$ are divisible by 9. Pages 26, 27.

`CheckRangeTwo` Checks to see if all $2^k$, $k \le 2 \cdot 3^{n-1}$, have a 2 in their base 3 expansion. Page 23.

`ChineseRemainderTheorem` On input

$$(a_1, p_1), (a_2, p_2), \ldots, (a_n, p_n),$$

where $p_1, \ldots, p_n$ are primes, computes the unique $0 \le a < p_1 p_2 \cdots p_n$ satisfying

$$a \equiv a_1 \pmod{p_1}, a \equiv a_2 \pmod{p_2}, \ldots, a \equiv a_n \pmod{p_n}.$$

The program uses input from a file generated by a C program. Page 94.

**Collatz** Give the list of iterates of the Collatz function $T(x) = x/2$ if $x$ is even and $(3x + 1)/2$ if $x$ is odd (up to the known cycles). Pages 132–135.

**CollatzIterate** Gives a list of every tenth iterate of **Collatz** when $n > 2^{11}$. Page 135.

**CollatzT** Collatz function $T(x) = x/2$ if $x$ is even and $(3x + 1)/2$ if $x$ is odd. Pages 133, 135.

**CollatzTable** Gives a table of $2^k$ rational numbers representing the Collatz function $T(x)$ iterated $k$ times. The algorithm in the book uses $k = 10$ and **CollatzTable[10]** is denoted by the constant **CollatzTable10**. Pages 133–137.

**ContinuedFraction** Gives the continued fraction expansion of a real number. Pages xiii, 163, 223.

**ConwaySequence** Gives the iterates of a special sequence defined by J.H. Conway. Page 12.

**DateToNumber** Gives the $n$th day of a calendar corresponding to a given date. Pages 35, 36, 49, 51–53, 240.

**DayOfWeek** Gives the day of the week for a given day in a given calendar. Pages 36, 52, 238.

**DaysBetween** Gives the number of days between two dates. Page 36.

**DaysPlus** Gives the date $n$ days away from a given date. Page 36.

**DetCirculant** Evaluates the determinant of a circulant matrix efficiently. Page 124.

**DigitsToNumber** Converts a digit list (ordinary, mixed radix, or tree radix) back to the number. Pages 38, 40, 43, 48, 49, 51, 53, 241.

**EuclidSearch** Searches for square factors of Euclid numbers $e(n)$ using a modified Pollard $\rho$ algorithm. Page 84.

**EulerProduct** Numerically evaluates an Euler product. Page 262.

**EulerProductCos** Numerically evaluates $\prod \cos(1/p)$. Page 260–261.

**FactorialExponent** Gives the exact power of a prime dividing $n!$. Page 68.

**Farey** Generates the $n$th Farey sequence. **FareyFaster** generates the $n$th Farey sequence twice as fast as **Farey**. **FareyList** generates the Farey sequence as order pairs instead of fractions since this is a more efficient representation. Page 251.

**FareySuccessor** Gives the successor of $a/b$ in the $n$th Farey sequence. Page 252.

**FastBinomial** An efficient evaluation of $\binom{n}{k}$ based on its prime factorization. Pages 69.

**Fold** Implementation of built-in V2.0 function which gives the last element produced by `FoldList[f, x, {a, b,...}]`. Pages xii, 9–10, 12, 38, 41, 43, 49, 223, 225.

**FoldList** Implementation of built-in V2.0 function which creates the list $\{$x, f[x, a], f[f[x, a], b],...$\}$ on input `FoldList[f, x, {a, b,...}]`. Pages xii, 9.

**FromContinuedFraction** Converts a list of continued fraction coefficients to a regular fraction. Pages xiii, 223.

**GolygonNumber** Computes the number of Golygons of length $n$, where all initial directions are considered different. Pages 92, 94.

**GolygonNumberC** Computes **GolygonNumber** only using basic constructs of C programming. A model program for the C implementation of `GolygonNumber` mod $p$, $p$ prime. Page 95.

**Gray** Gives the subsets of $\{1,\ldots,n\}$ in Gray code order, i.e., by inserting or deleting one element at a time. Pages 112, 246.

**GrayInsert** Gives the element and whether it is added or deleted on the $n$th step of the Gray code. Pages 112, 122, 125.

`Khinchin` Evaluates Khinchin's constant numerically. Pages 163, 164, 166, 169.

`Lambda` Evaluates the von Mangoldt function $\Lambda(n)$. Page 249.

`LeadingCheck` Searches for squares with $n$ or $n-1$ digits, all of which are $1, 4, 9$ ($n$ is odd). The algorithm uses the leading $(n+1)/2$ digits to do the search. Page 236.

`LogGamma` Evaluates `Log[Gamma[]]` using Stirling's formula directly (this is built in to V2.0). Pages xii, 173.

`LogStar` The number of times you iterate $\log_b$'s to become less than $b$. Pages 227, 229.

`LogStarStar` The number of times you iterate `LogStar[b, ]` to become less than $b$. Page 229.

`Moebius` Implements the Möbius inversion formula. Pages 8, 225, 259–260.

`MyCyclotomicPolynomial` Implements the `CyclotomicPolynomial` built-in function using the Möbius inversion formula. Page 225.

`MyDigits` Generalizes `Digits` to mixed radix and tree radix bases. Pages 37–40, 42–43, 48–49, 51, 53, 72, 239.

`MyMod` Generalizes `Mod` to lists. Pages 41, 43, 49.

`MyPower` A top level implementation of `Power`. Pages 9, 229.

`MyPowerMod` A more efficient implementation of `PowerMod` for very large arguments. Pages 10, 88, 98–99.

`MyQuotient` Generalizes `Quotient` to lists. Pages 41, 43, 49.

`NumberToDate` Gives the date of the $n$th day of a calendar. Pages 35–36, 49, 51, 53, 239.

`Permanent` Evaluates the permanent of a matrix. Pages 109, 112, 125.

**PollardRho** Factors integers using the Pollard-$\rho$ algorithm. This is included in V2.0's `FactorInteger`. Pages xii, 102, 103.

**PrimeList** Generates a file consisting of the first $n$ primes. Page 94.

**PrimePi** Gives $\pi(x)$, the number of primes $\leq x$ (this is a built-in function in V2.0). Pages xii, 68–71, 73–74, 76.

**Psi** Evaluates $\psi(x)$ in the theory of distribution of prime numbers. Page 249.

**Queens** Generates the number of $n$-queens solutions on an $n \times n$ chess board. Pages 109, 110.

**QueensSolutions** Generates all queens solutions on an $n \times n$ chessboard. Page 246.

**RiemannR** Evaluates $R(x)$ in prime number theory. Pages 75–76.

**RiemannSiegelTheta** Evaluates $\vartheta$ in the theory of the Riemann-$\zeta$ function. Pages xii, 172–173.

**RiemannSiegelZ** Evaluates the function $Z(t)$ in the theory of the Riemann-$\zeta$ function. Pages xii, 172.

**RunEncode** Given a list returns a list of pairs indicating contiguous runs of identical elements. Pages 3, 5, 12–14.

**Schur** Evaluates the permanent of the Schur matrix efficiently. Page 122.

**SquareFreeQ** Test if an integer is divisible by a perfect square. Pages xiii, 223–224.

**Subsets** Generates all the subsets of a set. Pages 3, 7, 111.

**SumOfTwoSquares** On input $p$, $p$ a prime of the form $4n + 1$, generates $a, b$ such that $p = a^2 + b^2$. Built into V2.0 as the option `GaussianIntegers -> True`. Pages xii, 243.

**SuperPower** Evaluates the tower of power $a^{a^{\cdot^{\cdot^{a}}}} \Big\}^{k}$ . Page 229.

**SuperPowerMod** Evaluates the tower of power $a^{a^{\cdot^{\cdot^{a}}}} \small{k}$ mod $n$. Pages 226–227, 229.

**SuperSuperPower** Evaluates $a \uparrow\uparrow\uparrow k$. Page 229.

**SuperSuperPowerMod** Evaluates $a \uparrow\uparrow\uparrow k$ mod $n$ efficiently. Pages 227, 229.

**SwinnertonDyer** Finds the minimal polynomial of the square roots of the first $n$ primes. Is included in V2.0 as the package `SwinnertonDyer.m`. Pages 11, 225.

**Tak** Computes the value of the generalized Takeuchi function TAK$(h, x, y, z)$. Pages 180–182.

**TakTime** Computes the running time of the generalized Takeuchi function TAK$(h, x, y, z)$ without using stored values. Includes the functions `TakTime0` which computes the running time of the fastest TAK function, `TakTimeY` which gives the running time of Takeuchi original function, and `TakTimeZ` which gives the running time of McCarthy's version. Pages 181–184, 187, 190.

**ToroidalQueens** Gives the number of toroidal queens on an $n \times n$ chessboard. Page 113.

**ToroidalSemiQueens** Gives the number of toroidal semiqueens on an $n \times n$ chessboard. Page 114.

**TotalStoppingTime** Give the number of iterations of the Collatz function (see `Collatz`) needed to get to one of the known cycles. Pages 135–137.

**wieferich** A Lisp program to search for Wieferich primes in a given range. Pages 99–102.

**ZetaPrime** Evaluates the derivative of the Riemann-$\zeta$ function at positive integers. Pages 162, 169–170.

# Bibliography

[1] B. Ambati, Message to `rec.puzzles`, January 26, 1990.

[2] A.O.L. Atkin, Personal communication, March 1990.

[3] A.O.L. Atkin and B.J. Birch editors, *Computers in Number Theory*, Academic Press 1971.

[4] D. Applegate and G. Jacobson, Message to `rec.puzzles`, February 14, 1990.

[5] M. Beeler, R.W. Gosper, and R. Schroeppel, *HAKMEM*, A.I. Lab Memo # 239, M.I.T. 1972.

[6] C.M. Bender and S.A. Orszag, *Advanced mathematical methods for scientists and engineers*, McGraw-Hill, New York, 1978.

[7] E.R. Berlekamp, J.H. Conway, and R.K. Guy, *Winning Ways*, Volume 2, Academic Press 1982.

[8] E.J. Bickerman, *The Chronology of the Ancient World*, Revised Edition, Thames and Hudson, London 1980.

[9] G.R. Blakley and I. Borosh, *Modular arithmetic of iterated powers*, Comp. and Maths. with Appl. **9** (1983), 567–581.

[10] J.M. Borwein, P.B. Borwein, and K. Dilcher, *Pi, Euler Numbers, and Asymptotic Expansions*, American Math. Monthly **96** (1989), 681–687.

[11] R. Brent, *An improved Monte Carlo Factorization Algorithm*, Nordisk Tidskrift for Informationsbehandling (BIT) **20** (1980), 176–184.

[12] D. Bressoud, *Factorization and Primality Testing*, Springer-Verlag 1989.

[13] J. Brillhart, J. Tonascia, and P. Weinberger, *On the Fermat Quotient*, in "Computers and Number Theory," A.O.L Atkin and B.J. Birch editors, Academic Press 1971, pages 213–222.

[14] R.D. Carmichael, *Note on a new number theory function*, Bull. Amer. Math. Soc. **16** (1910), 232–238.

[15] G. Chaitin, *Algorithmic Information Theory*, Cambridge University Press 1987.

[16] S. Chowla, B Dwork, and R. Evans, *On the $p^2$ determination of* $\binom{(p-1)/2}{(p-1)/4}$, J. Number Theory **24** (1986), 188–196.

[17] D.V. Chudnovsky and G.V. Chudnovsky, *Approximations and complex multiplication according to Ramanujan*, in "Ramanujan Revisited," Academic Press 1987, p. 375–472.

[18] H. Cohen and A.K. Lenstra, *Implementation of a new primality test*, Mathematics of Computation **48** (1987), 103–121.

[19] L. Comtet, *Advanced combinatorics* (translation of *Analyse combinatoire*, 2 vols., 1970), D. Reidel, Dordrecht, 1974.

[20] J.H. Conway, *The Weird and Wonderful Chemistry of Audioactive Decay*, in T.M. Cover and B. Gopinath, "Open Problems in Communications and Computation," Springer Verlag 1987.

[21] C.N. Cooper and R.E. Kennedy, *Chebyshev's inequality and natural density*, American Math. Monthly **96** (1989), 118–124.

[22] R. Crandall, *On the "3x + 1" problem*, Math. Comp. **32** (1978), 1281–1292.

[23] H. Davenport, *Multiplicative Number Theory*, Second Edition, Springer Verlag, New York 1980.

[24] H. Diamond, *Elementary methods in the study of the distribution of prime numbers*, Bulletin of the A.M.S. **7** (1982), 553–589.

[25] H.M. Edwards, *Riemann's Zeta Function*, Academic Press, New York 1974.

[26] R.B. Eggleton and R.K. Guy, *Catalan strikes again! How likely is a function to be convex?* Math. Magazine **61** (1988), 211–219.

[27] G. Eisenstein, *Entwicklung von $\alpha^{\alpha^{\alpha}}$*, J. Für die Reine und Andgew. Math. **28** (1844), 49–52.

[28] P. Erdös and R.L. Graham, *Old and New Problems and Results in Combinatorial Number Theory*, L'Enseignement Mathématique Université de Genève **28**, 1980.

[29] Euclid, *The Elements*, Translated by T.L. Heath, Second Edition, Dover 1956.

[30] C. Everett, *Iteration of the number theoretic function $f(2n) = n$, $f(2n + 1) = f(3n + 2)$*, Adv. Math. **25** (1977), 42–45.

[31] W. Feller, *An introduction to probability theory and its applications, Vol. 1*, Wiley, New York 1968.

[32] P. Flajolet and I. Vardi, *Numerical evaluation of Euler products*, Preprint 1990.

[33] J. Franel, *Les suites de Farey et le problème des nombre premiers*, Göttinger Nachrichten (1924), 198–201.

[34] H. Furstenburg, *Intersection of Cantor sets and transversality of semigroups*, in "Problems in Analysis," a symposium in honor of S. Bochner, R.C. Gunning editor, Princeton University Press 1970.

[35] R.P. Gabriel, *Performance and implementation of Lisp systems*, MIT Press 1985.

[36] M. Gardner, "Science Fiction Puzzle Tales," Clarkson Potter, 1981, p.5, 67, 104–105.

[37] M. Gardner, *aha! Insight*, Scientific American, Inc./W.H. Freeman and Company, New York 1978.

[38] M. Gardner, *Knotted Doughnuts and Other Mathematical Entertainments*, Freeman 1986.

[39] M. Gardner, *Time Travel and Other Mathematical Bewilderments*, Freeman 1988.

[40] M. Gardner, *from Penrose Tiles to Trapdoor ciphers*, Freeman 1988.

[41] M. Gardner, *Hexaflexagons and Other Mathematical Diversions*, University of Chicago Press 1988.

[42] M. Gardner, R.K. Guy, and D.E. Knuth, *Serial Isogons of 90 Degrees*, Math. Magazine, to appear.

[43] P. Goetgheluck, *Prime divisors of binomial coefficients*, Math. Comp. **51** (1988), 325–329.

[44] H.W. Gould, *Research bibliography of two special number sequences (Catalan and Bell numbers)*, Math. Monongliae, 12, Morgantown WV 1971, 6th edition, 1985.

[45] R.W. Gosper, *Continued Fraction Arithmetic*, Preprint.

[46] R.W. Gosper, *Decision procedure for indefinite hypergeometric summation*, Proc. Nat. Acad. Sci. USA **75** (1978), 40–42.

[47] R.W. Gosper, Personal communication.

[48] I.S. Gradshteyn and I.M. Ryzhik, *Table of Integrals, Series, and Products*, Academic Press 1980.

[49] R.L. Graham, D.E. Knuth, and O. Patashnik, *Concrete Mathematics*, Addison Wesley 1989.

[50] R.L. Graham and D.H. Lehmer, *On the permanent of Schur's matrix*, J. Austr. Math. Soc. **21** (Series A) (1976), 487–497.

[51] A. Granville, *Power numbers and Fermat's last theorem*, C.R. Math. Rep. Acad. Sci. Canada **8** (1986), 215–218.

[52] A. Granville and M. Monagan, *The first case of Fermat's last theorem is true for all prime exponents up to* $714, 591, 416, 091, 389$, Trans. Amer. Math. Soc. **306** (1988), 329–359.

[53] R.K. Guy, *Unsolved Problems in Number Theory*, Springer Verlag, New York 1981.

[54] J.L. Hafner, P. Sarnak, and K. McCurley, *Relatively prime values of polynomials*, Preprint 1990.

[55] A. Hajnal and L. Lovász, *An algorithm to prevent the propagation of certain diseases at minimum cost*, in "Interfaces between computer science and operations research," edited by J.K. Lenstra, A.H.G. Rinnooy Kan, and P. Van Emde Boas, Matematisch Centrum, Amsterdam 1978.

[56] G.H. Hardy, *Ramanujan*, Third Edition, Chelsea, New York 1978.

[57] G.H. Hardy and E.M. Wright, *An Introduction to the Theory of Numbers*, Fifth Edition, Clarendon Press, Oxford 1979.

[58] P. Harvey, *The Oxford Companion to English Literature*, 4th ed., Oxford, 1967, Appendix III, The Calendar.

[59] D. Hickerson, Messages to `rec.puzzles`, February 2–5, 1990.

[60] A.E. Ingham, *The Distribution of Prime Numbers*, Cambridge 1990.

[61] A. Ivić, *The Riemann Zeta-Function*, Wiley-Interscience 1985.

[62] W. Johnson, *On the non-vanishing of Fermat's quotient*, J. für die Reine und Angew. Math. **293** (1977), 196–200.

[63] A.Ya. Khintchine, *Continued Fractions*, P. Noordhoff, Groningen; The Netherlands 1963.

[64] K. Knopp, *Theory and Application of Infinite Series*, Dover 1990.

[65] D.E. Knuth, *Mathematics and Computer Science: Coping with Finiteness*, Science **194** (1976), 1235–1242.

[66] D.E. Knuth, *Seminumerical Algorithms*, Second Edition, Addison Wesley 1981.

[67] D.E. Knuth, *Textbook examples of recursion*, Preprint 1990.

[68] W. Kolakoski, *Problem 5304*, American Math. Monthly **72** (1965), page 674; solution by Necdet Üçoluk, American Math. Monthly **73** (1966), 681–682.

[69] L. Kuipers and H. Niederreiter, *Uniform Distribution of Sequences*, Wiley, New York 1974.

[70] G. Kuperberg, Message to `rec.puzzles`, February 4, 1990.

[71] S. Lang, *Fundamentals of Diophantine Geometry*, Springer-Verlag 1983.

[72] S. Lang, *Old and new conjectured Diophantine inequalities*, Bulletin of the A.M.S. **23** (1990), 37–75.

[73] J.C. Lagarias, *The $3x + 1$ problem and its generalizations*, American Math. Monthly **92** (1985), 3–23.

[74] E. Landau, *Handbuch der Lehre von der Verteilung der Primzahlen*, Teubner, Leipzig 1909; reprinted Chelsea, New York 1953.

[75] E. Landau, *Vorlesungen über Zahlentheorie*, Vol. 2, Hirzel, Leipzig 1927; reprinted Chelsea, New York 1947.

[76] E. Landau, *Elementary Number Theory*, Chelsea, New York 1958.

[77] A.M. Legendre, *Théorie des nombres*, Didot, Paris 1830.

[78] D.H. Lehmer, *Euclid's algorithm for large numbers*, American Math. Monthly **45** (1938), 227–233.

[79] D.H. Lehmer, *The Economics of Number Theoretic Computation*, in "Computers and Number Theory," A.O.L Atkin and B.J. Birch editors, Academic Press 1971, pages 1–9.

[80] D.H. Lehmer, *On Fermat's quotient, base two*, Math. of Computation **36** (1981), 289–290.

[81] L. Lewin, *Polylogarithms and associated functions*, North Holland, New York 1981.

[82] E. Lucas, *Théorie des Nombres*, Paris 1891, 491–495.

[83] H. Maurer, *Ueber die Funktion $x^{x^{x^{\cdot^{\cdot^{\cdot}}}}}$ fuer ganzzahliges Argument (Abundanzen)*, Mitt. der Math. Gessellschaft Hamburg **4** (1901), 33-50.

[84] M. Metropolis, M.L. Stein, and P.R. Stein, *Permanents of cyclic $(0,1)$ matrices*, J. Combinatorial Theory **7** (1969), 291–321.

[85] H. Minc, *Permanents*, Addison-Wesley 1978.

[86] D. Mirimanoff, *Sur le dernier théorème de Fermat et le critérium de Wieferich*, Enseignement Math. **11** (1909), 455–459.

[87] R.A. Mollin and P.G. Walsh, *On powerful numbers*, Intern. J. Math. and Math. Sci. **9** (1986), 801–806.

[88] J. Monaco, *The French Revolutionary Perpetual Calendar*, Zoetrope, New York 1982.

[89] L. Moser, *King paths on a chessboard*, Mathematical Gazette **39** (1955) p.54.

[90] T. Motzkin, *Relations between hypersurface cross ratios, and a combinatorial formula for partitions of a polygon, for permanent preponderance, and for non-associative products*, Bull. of the A.M.S. **54** (1948), 352–60.

[91] A. Nijenhuis and H. Wilf, *Combinatorial Algorithms*, Academic Press 1975.

[92] A. Odlyzko, *The $10^{20}$th Zero of the Riemann Zeta Function and 70 Million of its Neighbors*, Preprint 1989.

[93] A. Orlitzky and L. Shepp, *On curbing virus propagation*, Technical Memorandum, Bell Labs 1989.

[94] S.J. Patterson, *An Introduction to the Theory of the Riemann Zeta-function*, Cambridge 1988.

[95] M. Petkovsek, Ph.D. thesis, Carnegie Mellon 1990.

[96] G. Pólya, *Über die "doppelt-periodischen" Lösungen des n-Damenproblems*, Collected Works, Vol. 5 , p. 237–247, originally in: *Mathematische Unterhaltung und Spiele*, Dr. W. Ahrens, Zweiter Band, B.G. Teubner, Leipzig 1918, p. 363–374.

[97] G. Pólya and G. Szegö, *Problems and Theorems in Analysis I*, Springer-Verlag 1972.

[98] S. Ramanujan, *On certain trigonometrical sums and their applications in the theory of numbers*, Trans. Cambridge Phil. Soc. **22** (1918), 259–276; In "Collected Papers of Srinivasa Ramanujan," Chelsea, New York 1962, 179–199.

[99] E.M. Reingold and N. Dershowitz, *Calendrical Calculations*, Technical Report UIUCCDCS–R–89–1541 (1989), Dept. of Computer Science, Univ. of Ill. at Urbana-Champaign.

[100] P. Ribenboim, *13 Lectures on Fermat's Last Theorem*, Springer-Verlag 1979.

[101] P. Ribenboim, *The Book of Prime Number Records*, Second Edition, Springer Verlag, New York 1989.

[102] H. Riesel, *Prime Numbers and Computer Methods in Factorization*, Birkhäuser 1985.

[103] J. Riordan, *An Introduction to Combinatorial Analysis*, Princeton University Press 1978.

[104] I. Rivin and R. Zabih, *An Algebraic Approach to Constraint Satisfaction Problems*, in "Proceedings of the International Joint Conference on Artificial Intelligence" (IJCAI–89).

[105] I. Rivin, I. Vardi, and P. Zimmerman, *The n-Queens Problem*, Preprint 1989.

[106] H.E. Rose, *Subrecursion, Functions, and Hierarchies*, Clarendon Press, Oxford 1984.

[107] H.E. Rose, *A Course in Number Theory*, Clarendon Press, Oxford 1988.

[108] A. Sárközy, *On divisors of binomial coefficients, I*, J. Number Theory **20** (1985), 70–80.

[109] S. Schanuel, *Heights in number fields*, Bull. Soc. Math. France **107** (1979), 433–449.

[110] W.A. Schocken, *The Calculated Confusion of the Calendar*, Vantage Press, New York 1976.

[111] E. Schmidt, *Über die Anzahl der Primzahlen unter gegebener Grenze*, Math. Annalen **57** (1903), 195–204.

[112] E. Schröder, *Vier combinatorische Probleme*, Z. für M. Phys. **15** (1870), 361–376.

[113] B. Serpette, J. Vuillemin, and J.C. Hervé, *BIGNUM: A portable and Efficient Package for Arbitrary-Precision Arithmetic*, Digital Equipment Corporation and INRIA, 1989.

[114] D. Shanks, *Solved and Unsolved Problems in Number Theory*, Third Edition, Chelsea, New York 1985.

[115] D.B. Shapiro and S.D. Shapiro, *Iterated exponents in Number Theory*, Preprint.

[116] W. Sierpinski, *Sur la periodicité* mod *m de certaines suites infinies d'entiers*, Ann. Soc. Polon. Math. **23** (1950), 252-258.

[117] J. Silverman, *The Arithmetic of Elliptic Curves*, Springer-Verlag 1986.

[118] J. Silverman, *Wieferich's criterion and the abc conjecture*, J. of Number Theory **30** (1988), 226–237.

[119] N.J. Sloane, *A Handbook of Integer Sequences*, Academic Press, New York 1973.

[120] S. Skiena, *Implementing Discrete Mathematics*, Addison Wesley, 1990.

[121] R. Sommer, *Transfinite Induction and Hierarchies Generated by Transfinite Recursion within Peano Arithmetic*, Ph.D. Thesis, U.C. Berkeley 1990.

[122] C. Spiro, *How often does the number of divisors of an integer divide $n$ divide $n$?* J. of Number Theory **21** (1985), 81–100.

[123] R.P. Stanley, *Enumerative Combinatorics, Volume I*, Wadsworth & Brooks/Cole, Monterey CA 1986.

[124] R.E. Tarjan, *Data Structures and Network Algorithms*, SIAM, Philadelphia 1983.

[125] R. Terras, *A stopping time problem on the positive integers*, Acta. Arith. **30** (1976), 241–252.

[126] R. Terras, *On the existence of a density*, Acta. Arith. **35** (1979), 101–102.

[127] E.C. Titchmarsh, *The Theory of the Riemann Zeta-function*, Second Edition revised by D.R. Heath-Brown, Oxford 1986.

[128] J. Touchard, *Sur un problème de permutations*, C.R. Acad. Sci. Paris **198** (1934), 631–633.

[129] J.V. Uspensky and M.A. Heaslet, *Elementary Number Theory*, McGraw-Hill 1939.

[130] L. Valiant, *The complexity of computing the permanent*, Theoretical Comp. Sci. **8** (1979), 189–201.

[131] S. Wagon, *The Euclidean algorithm strikes again*, American Math. Monthly **97** (1990), 125–124.

[132] A. Wieferich, *Zum letzten Fermat'schen Theorem*, J. für die reine und andgew. Math. **136** (1909), 293–302.

[133] H. Wilf and D. Zeilberger, *Towards computerized proofs of identities*, Bulletin of the A.M.S. **23** (1990), 77–83.

[134] D. Wilson, Message to `rec.puzzles`, March 20, 1990.

[135] S. Wolfram, *Mathematica: A System for Doing Mathematics by Computer*, Addison Wesley, 1988.

[136] Kit Ming Yeung, *On congruences for Binomial coefficients*, Journal of Number Theory **33** (1989), 1–17.

# Index

## A

*abc* conjecture, 62, 241, 277
Ackerman function, 11, 227, 232
  inverse of, 232
Adobe Illustrator, x
Alper, T., xii
Ambati, B., 20, 234, 269
Ambati, J., 20
André, D., 185
Applegate, D., 235
Apple Macintosh, x
Arrow notation, 11, 231
Atkin, A.O.L., xii, 14

## B

Ballot problem, 185
Beeler, M., vi, 269
Benes, J., xi, xii
Berlekamp, E.R., 269
Bernoulli numbers, 160, 173
BIGNUM multiple precision package, 245
Binomial coefficients, 63–73, 263
  evaluation of, 67, 242, 263, 265
  factorization of, 25–28, 67–70, 272, 277
  identities, 261

middle, 25–28, 67–73, 188, 241, 263
mod $p$, 70–71, 241–242, 263
mod $p^2$, 242–243, 279
Brent, R., 269
Bressoud, D., 270
Bump, D., xii

## C

Caesar, J., 44, 239
Calendar
  British regnal, 54
  French revolutionary, 46, 54–55, 239, 275
  Gregorian, 45, 50, 239
  Islamic, 45, 52
  Jewish, 54, 240
  Julian, 44, 48, 55, 239
Catalan's constant, 159
Catalan numbers, 187
Cejtin, H., xii
Chaitin, G., 233, 270
Chebyshev's estimate, 63, 70, 249–250
Chebyshev, P.L., 70, 244
Chinese remainder theorem, 93
Chowla, S., 242, 270
Chudnovsky, D.V., 159, 270
Chudnovsky, G.V., 159, 270